The Eagles
FAQ

The Eagles FAQ

All That's Left to Know About Classic Rock's Superstars

Andrew Vaughan

Backbeat
Books

An Imprint of Hal Leonard Corporation

Published in 2015 by Backbeat Books
An Imprint of Hal Leonard Corporation
7777 West Bluemound Road
Milwaukee, WI 53213

Trade Book Division Editorial Offices
33 Plymouth St., Montclair, NJ 07042

Except where otherwise noted, all images in this book are from the author's personal collection.

The FAQ series was conceived by Robert Rodriguez and developed with Stuart Shea.

Printed in the United States of America

Book design by Snow Creative Services

Library of Congress Cataloging-in-Publication Data

Vaughan, Andrew
    The Eagles FAQ : all that's left to know about classic rock's superstars / Andrew Vaughan.
    pages cm. — (FAQ)
    Includes bibliographical references and index.
    ISBN 978-1-4803-8541-2
1. Eagles (Musical group)—Miscellanea. I. Title.
    ML421.E14V39 2015
    782.42166092'2—dc23
                                                                    2014044253

www.backbeatbooks.com

To Michael, my son

Contents

Acknowledgments

Living as we do in the information age, research for this book has come from a variety of sources, from online blogs, Facebook pages, YouTube clips, and forums to newspapers, magazines, and, of course, books.

Marc Eliot's *To the Limit: The Untold Story of the Eagles* (Da Capo Press) remains the definitive work on the band's early years. *Rolling Stone* magazine legend Ben Fong-Torres' personal take on Henley & co., *Eagles: Taking It to the Limit* (Running Press), was illuminating, as were Barney Hoskyns' classic on California rock in the 1970s, *Hotel California* (Wiley), and Peter Doggett's *Are You Ready for the Country: Elvis, Dylan, Parsons, and the Roots of Country Rock.* I drew on my own book *The Eagles: An American Band* (Sterling) as well as Don Felder's *Heaven and Hell: My Life in the Eagles (1974–2001).* Also very useful were *Pete Frame's Complete Rock Family Trees* (Omnibus), John Einarson's *Desperados: The Roots of Country Rock* (Cooper Square), and Don Henley's *Heaven Is Under Our Feet: A Book for Walden Woods* (Longmeadow Press).

Thanks also go to Linda Ronstadt and her memoir, *Simple Dreams: A Musical Memoir* (Simon and Schuster), for painting such a vivid picture of 1960s Los Angeles. *History of the Eagles: The Story of an American Band* (Showtime, 2013) was a great source of background information, as was the BBC documentary *Hotel California: L.A. from the Byrds to the Eagles.*

Thanks to music critics and entertainment reporters from magazines and newspapers. Some publications are now gone, like *City Limits, International Musician Circus,* and *ZigZag;* those and others like *Rolling Stone,* the *Daily Mail,* the *New York Times,* the *Daily Telegraph,* the *Independent,* the *Tennessean,* the *Daily Mirror, Modern Drummer,* and numerous regional publications, were invaluable.

Online research reveals all kinds of valuable sources of information, from in-depth fan sites to casual bloggers and writers with captivating insights to industry movers and shakers like Bob Lefsetz. Thanks to Nancy and Lisa, who run two exemplary Eagles sites, EaglesFans.com and EaglesOnlineCentral.com. The information and passion they channel is simply awesome.

Special thanks to the University of Florida Archives, the Nebraska Rock and Roll Hall of Fame (facebook.com/NebraskaRocks), the Randy Meisner concerts page (angelfire.com/rock3/deliverin/MEISNER/randyconcerts.htm), and some excellent online music sites like UltimateClassicRock.com, Gibson.com, NME.com, and RollingStone.com.

As a music critic for over twenty years, I have had many conversations to draw on for this book, and I'd like to thank the many fascinating people who have regaled me with some of the stories that appear in this book or provide background for the tales it tells. They include John Tobler, Al Perkins, Shannon McCombs, James Stroud, Lee Williams, Ricky Skaggs, Shania Twain, Garth Brooks, Dwight Yoakam, Michael Nesmith, David Crosby, Jackson Browne, Bob Saporiti, Bernard Doherty, Richard Wootton, Timothy White, Tony Bywoth, Chris Charlesworth, Michael Snow, Stevie Nicks, Joni Mitchell, Paul McCartney, Byron Berline, Bernie Leadon, John Boylan, Jim Ed Norman, Don Felder, J. D. Souther, Jimmy Bowen, Mason Williams, Peter Rowan, Tanya Tucker, Clint Black, and many more.

I'd like to thank Robert Rodriguez for inviting me into the FAQ family and Bernadette Malavarca for being the most patient and understanding editor. Special thanks to super-diligent copyeditor Tom Seabrook, and to my project editor Jessica Burr, who brought to this process a terrific eye for detail and a genuine feel for the subject. Finally, I want to thank my son, Michael, for continually teaching me about courage and tenacity.

Introduction

The Eagles are the most popular American band in rock-and-roll history. No band before them had sold over ten million copies of two different albums, as the Eagles did with *Hotel California* and *The Eagles—Their Greatest Hits 1971–1975*. Indeed, the latter album is now certified twenty-nine-times platinum by the RIAA, which means twenty-nine million copies sold in the United States, a figure equaled only by Michael Jackson's *Thriller*.

The Eagles have scored twenty-one *Billboard* Hot 100 hits between 1972, when their debut cut "Take It Easy" climbed to #12, and 2003, when "Hole in the World" made the chart. Ten Eagles singles have made the Top 10, with five of those becoming #1 hits. On top of that, when it comes to their individual careers, the members of the Eagles have chalked up an impressive forty solo hits between them. Don Henley, not surprisingly, leads the pack with fifteen. The statistics go on and on. The Eagles have had seven #1 albums, and since their 1994 comeback, they have topped touring gross lists every year they've been on the road.

In 2008, they grossed over seventy million dollars in the U.S. alone, beaten only by Madonna and Celine Dion. Their most recent album, *Long Road Out of Eden*, sold exclusively through Walmart and went straight to #1 on its release in 2007. Looking at the Eagles' album sales in total, the band are in the Top 5 of the best-selling artists of all time in the U.S., right behind the Beatles, Elvis, Garth Brooks, and Led Zeppelin.

The Eagles surfaced from the folkie, hippie scene of the late '60s in L.A. and turned their mellow, country-rock sound into a worldwide brand, culminating in the international epic "Hotel California."

Don't be fooled by the outlaw/cowboy image. The Eagles, especially Don Henley and Glenn Frey, were part of a savvy new breed of rock-and-roller who understood the business side of music and demanded a fair share of the financial action. Teaming up with David Geffen, one of the toughest of all the '70s music execs, gave the band a degree of power and leverage unknown in popular music.

The story of the Eagles is also the story of most artists of their time. The drugs, the music, the excesses, the piles of cash—it affected them

Simply the most successful group in the history of American rock and roll, the Eagles are pictured here on the inside cover of their 2003 *Very Best Of* album.

all. But the Eagles took it to the limit. And in Henley and Frey, they had two songwriters who intuitively understood and accurately portrayed the changing America they were living in. They perfected the California sound, shifted the power from record company to artist, and pioneered the FM sound. Eagles songs of the period are incredibly memorable, while their most popular album, *Hotel California*, is a timeless record of the decadence of the '70s.

So popular were the Eagles in the '70s—and on their own terms, too—that many in the American music press and media gave them short shrift. Critics at the time failed to acknowledge Henley and Frey's social commentary, and they refused to give the band their due. Eventually, the sheer power of the music won out, and the Eagles were inducted into the Rock and Roll Hall of Fame in 1998.

Not that success didn't bring problems of its own. Eagles tours were outrageous fiestas of sex, drugs, and rock and matched only by the Who and Led Zeppelin for outrage and expense. Money and drugs, lawyers and accountants got in the way of the music, and some couldn't cope. Bernie Leadon and Randy Meisner called it quits early on, leaving Henley and Frey in charge of the beast. Things got so bad that individual Eagles stayed in separate hotels on tour. The Eagles became poster boys for bands that hated each other. Frey and Henley famously didn't speak near the end, and things got so bad that a longtime band member, guitarist Don Felder, was booted from the organization. As with all good rock-and-roll fables, an outside source—in this case a country-music tribute album—brought some harmony back to our divided band of brothers, and the Eagles had what Frey always refers to as a "resumption" (rather than a comeback) in their sometimes rocky career.

The country-music tribute album, *Common Thread*, catalyzed the reunion that produced the 1994 LP *Hell Freezes Over*, which sold more than ten million copies in a few months. But the old animosities resurfaced, and in 2001 Felder was fired, never to return.

The remaining members carried on, and in 2007 the Eagles released their first proper new album in almost thirty years, *Long Road Out of Eden*, which debuted at #1 on the *Billboard* chart and set the stage for more sellout world tours.

With their lasting success, the Eagles proved themselves to be one of the few early-'70s bands still current and relevant. Honoring the band's legacy, over forty years after the release of their first album, was the documentary movie *History of the Eagles*, which debuted at the Sundance Film Festival in 2013 and was screened by Showtime in two parts, and featured more than three cool hours of footage and interviews. The documentary has brought renewed interest in the group's incredible story.

Eagles albums still sell in platinum numbers, and Eagles tours out-gross those of most of their contemporaries. Their story is one of individuals, and of an era—an era that still fascinates and shapes the present day. This book looks at the whole career of the Eagles—their achievements and successes as well as their low points and disasters—and draws on interviews with fellow artists and contemporaries who watched the crazy tale unfold.

Coming to America

While the Eagles were largely responsible for exporting the "Southern California" rock sound around the globe in the 1970s, none of the four original Eagles were actually from California. All four were from different small towns in America, and were united by a love of music and a desire to be part of the blossoming social, political, and arts movement that was centered in Los Angeles.

A Bob Seger protégé called Glenn Frey (pronounced "fry") came to Hollywood from Detroit. The tough, streetwise Frey's roots were in rock and R&B, and he had played guitar and sung backup on Bob Seger's "Ramblin' Gamblin' Man" in 1968. Frey's rock and R&B roots would play a key role in moving the early Eagles country sound to FM rock.

Frey's future songwriting partner Don Henley was an educated young man and a gifted drummer, well established on the Texas bar-band circuit with his band Shiloh, when future country superstar Kenny Rogers advised him to try Los Angeles. Henley's friendship with Frey would form the cornerstone of the Eagles for the next four decades.

Every band needs a musical sorcerer, and Bernie Leadon brought the magic to the early Eagles albums. He started life in Minnesota but wound up in Florida, via San Diego, thanks to his father's career as an aerospace engineer. Inspired to play the banjo when he was very young, he learned that instrument, and guitar, well enough to join Don Felder (who would much later replace him in the Eagles) in Gainesville band the Continentals. He replaced another Felder bandmate, Stephen Stills, who had quit for Hollywood. When Leadon made his own trek west to California, he played with two of the most significant country-rock bands, the Flying Burrito Brothers and Dillard & Clark.

Bass player and high-harmony specialist Randy Meisner was raised on a farm in Nebraska. It was a tough upbringing, but his musical gifts gave him a way out and saw him playing in several local bands before he drove west to Los Angeles. He played with a prototype country-rock band called Poco that would be a major influence on the future Eagles band.

How these four separate characters came together as the Eagles is an exercise in synchronicity, a little puppeteering, and lots of luck. They all gravitated toward the Laurel Canyon/Troubadour scene that everyone on the streets knew about. Henley and Frey hung out with other like-minded writers and singers, like Jackson Browne and J. D. Souther. They wrote songs, recommended each other for gigs, and fell in love with the same girls. Browne lived in the same apartment complex as Frey and Henley, and Frey would often hear Browne working on a song that would become the Eagles' first big hit, "Take It Easy."

Like Frey, J. D. Souther came to Hollywood from Detroit, and they played in a band together in L.A. called Longbranch Pennywhistle. Souther wrote some of the Eagles' finest songs, including "Heartache Tonight," "Victim of Love," "New Kid in Town," and "Best of My Love." He released three critically acclaimed solo albums and two more as a member of the commercially unsuccessful but critically acclaimed Souther-Hillman-Furay Band, the supergroup that united Souther with '70s heavyweights Richie Furay (Poco) and Chris Hillman (the Byrds).

Fate, coincidence, ambition, and luck converged as various individuals played their part in the formation of America's most popular rock-and-roll band. Mid-to-late-'60s L.A. was the musical mecca for thousands of dream-fueled artists. It was an era of counterculture, "sit-ins," and "happenings." Students were marching, soldiers were dying, and musicians were upgrading from cannabis to acid and cocaine.

In the mid-to-late 1960s, the Troubadour nightclub was home to most of L.A.'s singer/songwriters and country folkies, from Bonnie Raitt and Neil Young to Linda Ronstadt and Stephen Stills—and, of course, the Eagles.

An East Coast record producer named John Boylan moved to California in 1969 to produce the Association and the Dillards. Immersed in the

Nobody captured the glamour and the underbelly of life in '70s Los Angeles better in song than the Eagles.   *Courtesy of Elisa Jordan, Lawomantours.com*

burgeoning Troubadour scene, he became Linda Ronstadt's boyfriend and producer, and recruited some players he knew—Randy Meisner, Don Henley, Glenn Frey, and Bernie Leadon—to be Linda's band.

It was at Disneyland in Anaheim, California, that the Eagles first performed together as backup for the country-rock queen in 1971. Ronstadt was about to hit the big time after one hit record with the Stone Poneys in 1967 (Michael Nesmith's "Different Drum"). Frey and Henley roomed together while touring with Ronstadt and found they had a mutual interest in starting a band. Linda blessed the idea, and now, with Bernie and Randy on board, they just needed some management. Fortunately, Jackson Browne had been working with a young hotshot agent-turned-manager who was hungry, passionate about music, and, most importantly, ruthless.

Working his way to the top after starting out in the William Morris Agency mailroom in 1964, David Geffen typified the new breed of record-company executive. Young, ambitious, and business savvy, the godfather of the California singer/songwriter scene would change the face of the record deal forever. Without Geffen behind the scenes, there may never have been an Eagles. But Geffen had a plan, and he picked a top rock-and-roll producer to launch his band on the world.

In the winter of 1972, the California boys headed to foggy England to work with famed Who producer Glyn Johns on their debut album. Excited about the idea of working in swinging London, the band were mostly miserable when it came to living and working there, but they did make a terrific debut LP.

Glyn Johns saw the Eagles as a country-influenced vocal group, and while the band didn't agree, he shaped them in that fashion, and the band's debut album, *Eagles*, launched them with three Top 40 singles. The first single, "Take It Easy," written by Frey and apartment neighbor Jackson Browne, went to #12. The Eagles had taken off.

Then they made a concept album. *Desperado* set up the Eagles as masters of mellow country-rock. It's a seminal album—as many of their peers discuss later—but it didn't sell well, and the winds of change were already blowing through Henley and Frey's heads.

Were the Eagles country or rock? The ongoing feeling in the Henley/Frey camp was that the band should abandon country and head rockward. Leadon suggested his old pal Don "Fingers" Felder might bring some weight to their sound. Felder had taught Tom Petty guitar back home in Florida, and his rocking, blistering slide-guitar work gave the band the cutting edge Henley and Frey had been searching for. They also fired Johns and switched to Bill Szymczyk, Joe Walsh's producer, who gave Henley and Frey more control in the studio.

Leadon, always the most country and folkie of the bunch, wasn't entirely happy at the new musical direction, and was also extremely tired of the excesses of life on the road. He asked the band to take a break to refresh themselves and pace their career. But Henley and Frey were hungry and ambitious, and they felt there was no time to waste on their way to the very top. Exhausted, Leadon threw a bottle of water over Frey's head and quit the band.

Sex and Drugs and Rock and Roll

The Eagles launched themselves full throttle into enjoying life on the road, 1970s-style. As the cash flowed in, so did the wine, women, and song.

Eagles tours became legendary, matched only by Led Zeppelin for their rock-and-roll outrage. Women on tour were given special "third encore" badges (an invitation to a post-gig orgy). They flew women in from L.A. on jets, which led them to coin the phrase "Love 'em and Lear 'em."

When Leadon walked away, a replacement had already been lined up: Joe Walsh. The ace guitarist came to the Eagles after a successful band and solo career. His previous band, the James Gang, had had hits with "Walk Away" and "Funk #49," and were greatly admired by Pete Townshend of the Who, who helped Walsh as much as he could.

The new lineup gelled for a while—long enough, at least, to make one of the greatest songs and albums of the '70s, and maybe the definitive Eagles work. *Hotel California* cemented the Eagles as a bona-fide rock band. There was a foreboding darkness and sense of conflict behind the music—a place where you could check out but "never leave." Henley and Frey were living life to excess yet warning against it on every cut.

With the Eagles now ensconced as America's Beatles, they enjoyed the same kind of lyrical analysis as the Fab Four. Some Christian groups decided that the song "Hotel California" referenced Anton LaVey of the Church of Satan, while hotel owners across California claimed the song was written about their establishments. Exhausted by the *Hotel California* tour, Meisner followed Leadon out of the band. He was replaced with Timothy B. Schmit—strangely, the man Meisner had replaced in Poco, all those years before.

Conceived as a double album, *The Long Run* was to be the band's mighty follow-up to *Hotel California*, but the group's internal struggles, lack of inspiration, and physical and mental weariness resulted in a single album instead. It would be their last studio album for almost thirty years, and while it had some decent material—and three hits, "Heartache Tonight," "The Long Run," and "I Can't Tell You Why"—the band were, to misquote Jackson Browne, "running on empty."

Everything came to an unpleasant end at a concert in Long Beach. Frey and Felder were at each other's throats the whole night. Initially, Frey blamed Felder for causing the antagonism, but in hindsight he recognized that the band had simply run its course. After the split, Henley said that the Eagles would only get back together again "when Hell freezes over."

With the Eagles over, the band members were free to pursue solo interests, to varying degrees of success. Frey released his first solo album, *No Fun Aloud*, in 1982. The song "Smuggler's Blues" appealed to the producers of the hit TV series *Miami Vice*, who used the track and gave Glenn a role in the show. He also had his own series, *South of Sunset*, but unfortunately for Frey, only the pilot episode aired. He did, however, appear in the TV series *Nash Bridges* and the movie *Jerry Maguire*.

Like Frey, Henley used the breakup of the Eagles to fuel a solo career. Henley's was the more successful, with a string of commercially successful and critically acclaimed albums and hit singles following throughout the decade, culminating in his best work, 1989's *The End of the Innocence*, which won rave reviews and a Grammy Award.

An English major at school, Henley had long been an admirer of Ralph Waldo Emerson, the nineteenth-century writer best known for his views on individualism, nonconformity, and respect for nature, and early environmentalist and writer Henry Thoreau. In 1989, while watching CNN, Henley discovered that developers were threatening the historic Walden Woods, the area that had inspired Thoreau. He got involved with a local group fighting the developers and soon founded the Walden Woods Project. Environmentalism and campaigning would become as big a part of Henley's life as music.

Meanwhile, Joe Walsh had an international hit single with "Life's Been Good," released several albums, and toured with Ringo Starr's All-Starr Band before publicly confessing his demons.

In the early '90s, the Garth Brooks–led country-music revolution saw country topping the charts in America. Drawing heavily on the Eagles sound, the new wave of Nashville acts put together *Common Thread: The Songs of the Eagles*, an all-star tribute. When Travis Tritt was asked to make a video for his track, "Take It Easy," he asked if he could get the Eagles in the video. Unbelievably, they agreed.

After the success of the *Common Thread* tribute album and the fact that they had enjoyed their day filming together, Henley, Frey, Walsh, and manager Irving Azoff met in Aspen, Colorado, to talk about a reunion. The result was an album and a tour, aptly entitled *Hell Freezes Over*.

With *Hell Freezes Over* going to #1 and selling over six million copies in the U.S., the band went back on the road, touring on and off until 1996. In 1998, they were inducted into the Rock and Roll Hall of Fame. Just for the occasion, all seven Eagles did two songs together, "Take It Easy" and "Hotel California."

Fired in 2001 over financial issues, Don Felder shot back with a lawsuit and wrote a tell-all autobiography, *Heaven and Hell.* "Unpleasant" hardly describes what followed, with Henley and Frey countersuing and stopping the publication of Felder's book for over six years.

In 2007, the Eagles released a single, "How Long," written by their old buddy J. D. Souther. It was a song they'd performed live for years but never recorded. They followed it with their first album of all-new material since 1979, *Long Road Out of Eden.* The album went straight to #1, and in 2008 the band grossed over seventy million dollars in the U.S. alone, surpassed only by Madonna and Celine Dion.

In 2013, the Eagles released a retrospective documentary and embarked on a tour with original guitarist Bernie Leadon, initially just in the United States but then later the rest of the world. That year, they played seventy-five shows in the United States, earning the band, according to *Billboard*, a cool $13,026,210.18 (for reference, Rihanna's earnings over the same period were $13,794,186.16), with an estimated $11 million in profit—proof that despite the long-term breakups, roster changes, infamous infighting, and too much living in rock-and-roll's fast lane, the Eagles remain both a major ticket draw and a huge cultural influence.

The Eagles
FAQ

No Fun Aloud

Glenn Frey, from Detroit to L.A.

n May 1982, Glenn Frey reminisced to Robert Hilburn of the *L.A. Times*, "We all watched the sunset in the West every night of adolescence and thought someday about coming out there. . . . It all seemed so romantic."

Not that Glenn Frey lived in the middle of nowhere. He was raised in the Detroit suburbs at a time when the city was on a rapid upswing. The automobile industry had never had it so good, and Frey's teen years coincided with Detroit's rise in the music landscape, with pop combos, vocal groups, soul singers, and garage bands popping up all over town. And as soul and R&B took hold of Motor City, a small indie start-up, Motown, not only revolutionized dance and pop music but changed the racial complexion of radio and TV with a stream of hit records and pop classics.

Motown

Berry Gordy Jr. was still an autoworker when he started a record label out of his house at 2648 West Grand Boulevard. Taking inspiration from the automobile production line he knew only too well, Gordy came up with a business model that operated very much like a car factory. First, songwriters and producers scrambled to attend the 9:00 a.m. meeting where songs to be cut were analyzed and chosen. Then, once the material was deemed good enough to record, the nine-to-five house band, the legendary Funk Brothers (who appear on more #1 hit records than the Beatles, Elvis, the Rolling Stones, and the Beach Boys put together) went to work with the singers.

The Motown label that emerged discovered and introduced a wealth of talent, notably the Supremes, Martha & the Vandellas, and the Temptations. As far as most of America (and certainly the rest of the world) was concerned, Detroit and Motown were synonymous. But while Motown had a huge cultural impact, within the city itself there was, naturally, a lot more to the pop story than the work of Berry Gordy, Diana Ross, and the rest of the Motown crew.

"Punk" Sound

At the same time Motown was putting Detroit firmly on the musical map, an underground, aggressive, and quite primitive strain of raw rock and roll

A very rare photo of young Glenn. He may have been picked on as a kid, but Frey became quite the athlete and self-styled rebel as he progressed through his teenage years, before he fell in love with rock and roll.
Courtesy of Muriel Versagi, Curator of the Royal Oak Historical Society

burst out of the city. A blue-collar riposte to the British sound emerged, as the prototype "punk" sound of the MC5 (who caused a major stir with tracks like the expletive-laden "Kick Out the Jams" in 1968) and their followers, the Stooges and the Up.

Frey failed to respond musically to the more spiteful punk sounds that spewed from his town, but he did relate to their maverick outlook, and the attitude that emanated from their take on the American rock-and-roll lifestyle. He was a natural-born rebel, mistrustful of authority and never afraid to rely his own instincts.

Dancing in the Streets

Besides its burgeoning identity as the home of a thriving and creative music scene, Detroit was yet another American city coming to terms with social change and political upheaval. The summer of 1967 (when Frey was just nineteen years old) saw the city in flames during five days of rioting that ended with over forty people dead, 7,200 arrested, and more than 2,000 of Detroit's buildings burned to the ground.

The unrest signaled the end of Detroit as a vital center of creativity and industry, as thousands chose to leave the city for the suburbs and far beyond. In the next twenty years, the city's population fell by more than 50 percent, leaving much of it barren and dangerous. It's no wonder, then, that Frey and those in his circle were driven to get away. His girlfriend, Joan Sliwin (also a singer), moved to California before Glenn and made that very point to Furious.com in March 2005: "You have to remember the summer of '67 was the riots. . . . We were in L.A. the two weeks that the riots occurred. The exact two weeks. My mom had tanks on the front lawn where we lived. It was a tense time, and we missed all that. Coming out to L.A., we thought we had died and went to heaven. Everything was fun, L.A. was less congested, and we were in a good place."

Frey would eventually find his way to the West, too. Detroit was danger-ous, tense, and lacking in hope or music for the future. The hippie ideals emanating from the left coast seemed all the more appealing—not that anyone who had been close enough to burning riots to smell the ugly odor of desperation and violence would ever be totally engulfed in the simplistic "love is all you need" philosophy that many of the young generation sub-scribed to in California.

Frey would be criticized in later years for displaying a hard-faced attitude to success, fame, and money amid a sea of kaftan-wearing non-materialistic musos. His formative years in Detroit undoubtedly played a significant part in the songwriter's more cynical approach to music and the music business, but at the time of the riots, he was hanging in bars, trying to master the art of underage drinking, and sports took up more of his time and enthusiasm than music.

Star Athlete Turned Musician

As with most teens, music was just one part of Glenn Frey's growing-up experience. It was something he enjoyed but it certainly wasn't a passion. It was always around, whether on the radio or on the TV, and Frey's parents had the family regularly sit down to watch *Hit Parade*, but initially it was sports that fired the young Glenn's passions.

The high-school athletics star from Motor City had a strict blue-collar upbringing. He went to school with the tough kids of car workers who thought nothing of giving the scrawny young Glenn a good beating. In April 1986, he told Jeff Yarbrough of *Interview* magazine, "I went to school with the sons and daughters of automobile factory workers—fathers who beat their wives and beat their kids. The kids would then go to school and beat on me! My father was a machinist in a shop that built the machines that build car parts. I had a pretty normal childhood. My parents weren't drinkers. I always had clothes. I always went to camp for a week in the summer. My parents didn't have enough money to buy me a car when I turned sixteen, but I had a great childhood."

Playing sports was an answer to bullying, and once he toughened up, Frey won a place on the school wrestling team and blossomed into a high school athletics star. He did dabble with formal music training, however. While at Dondero High School, he played trumpet with the school marching band and took piano and keyboard lessons from a concert pianist called John Harrison. (The Dondero High yearbook for 1966 sees Glenn Frey voted—quite prophetically, as it happens—"Most likely to inhale.")

The Beatles and Jelly Beans, Early Bands, and Bob Seger

On Sunday, September 6, 1964, sisters Lynn and Melissa Kaltenbach and their father drove to Detroit with Frey in the car. They were going to see the Beatles. Melissa recalled the day to Bill Castanier for the *Lansing Online News* in February 2014: "My dad drove us down and stayed with us. He was a bit eccentric and went around picking up fainting girls."

At first, Kaltenbach hadn't remembered who went to the concert with her and her sister Lynn, but later Melissa reminded her that Glenn Frey, founder of the Eagles, drove down to Detroit with them from their hometown of Birmingham. "I remember dad and Glenn arguing over a song," she told Castanier.

After short sets from the Bill Black Combo, the Exciters, Clarence "Frogman" Henry, and Jackie DeShannon, the Beatles took the stage. John, Paul, George, and Ringo played two shows that day, cranking out a mix of their own sublime pop hits like "All My Loving," "She Loves You," "If I Fell," "I Want to Hold Your Hand," and "Things We Said Today," as well as a couple of their staple rock-and-roll rants, "Roll Over Beethoven" and "Twist and Shout."

The original Britpop band delighted the 30,000-plus fans who showed up, but with Beatlemania and hysteria in overdrive, the Detroit concerts made the history books for a couple of non-musical reasons, as for the first time at a Beatles concert, security and police ejected several fans from the gig for throwing jelly beans at the Fab Four. The "candy tossing" trend had begun in England in 1963, when George Harrison let it slip in a jokey interview that Jelly Babies were his favorite candy, and that John Lennon had grabbed them from him. Big mistake, George. Initially, the British postal service delivered thousands of boxes of the squishy soft candy to the Beatles, care of EMI, their record company. Then, at the next Beatles concert, they were pelted with Jelly Babies. This was annoying to say the least, but nothing compared to what they'd find in the United States.

American fans, having read the press about the candy-throwing, decided that their beloved Beatles must like jelly beans (there being no such thing as Jelly Babies in America) and used these instead. Unfortunately, and unbeknown to the young fans, British Jelly Babies are soft, with no hard outer shell. Jelly beans, U.S. style, are small and hard and built like missiles.

The Beatles hated what was happening and were rightly concerned about injury. In a 1963 letter from Harrison to a fan sold at auction by Woolley & Wallis in England, the Beatles guitarist wrote, "P.S. We don't like jelly babies, or fruit gums for that matter, so think how we feel standing on stage trying to dodge the stuff, before you throw some more at us. Couldn't you eat them yourself, besides it is dangerous. I was hit in the eye once with a boiled sweet, and it's not funny!" At a press conference, Paul McCartney noted, "It has become a bit of a trademark with our shows, but we'd prefer they throw nothing at all."

Seeing, hearing, and feeling the Beatles changed everything in Frey's life that night. That was it for the boring piano lessons. Guitar was in, keyboards were out! Frey and some acoustic guitar–owning pals soon formed a group, the Disciples, but that was a fairly short-lived venture. At Dondero High School in Royal Oak, he teamed up with Doug Edwards, Bill Barns, Bob Wilson, and Doug Gunsch as the Hideouts, which were named for a popular nightclub, the Hideout.

"It was this really cool nightclub," '70s star Suzi Quatro, who grew up during the same era as Frey, told me in 1989. "Detroit was a 'buzzing' place, there was a huge teen scene with all these kids inspired by the Beatles wanting to get into music and do the band thing."

Young promoters Dave Leone and Ed "Punch" Andrews (today Kid Rock's manager) started their pop-music club in Harper Woods, Michigan, in 1963, and hosted pretty much every act of note that surfaced in Detroit in the mid-1960s. Suzi Quatro (then with the Pleasure Seekers), Bob Seger, the Fugitives, Ted Nugent, and many, many more were regulars. The club charged a one-dollar admission fee and became *the* place for Detroit pop fans to hang out, even spawning its own record label.

The Hideouts changed their name to the Subterraneans, but their music was all very light and poppy and Beatles-esque. After a while, Glenn fancied something a shade darker, and his next group, the Mushrooms, were definitely more rock than pop.

All the hopeful bands in Detroit looked up to Seger, who would go on to become a major global star himself in the 1970s. He was obviously the best local act in town, and the most likely to succeed, and all the start-up musical unions looked up to him and gravitated toward his orbit for advice and reflected glory. Seger's manager, Punch Andrews, also managed the Mushrooms—a happenstance that put Frey directly into the musical path of Detroit's best-known rockers.

The Detroit pop and rock scene was different from that of a lot of U.S. cities. Seger remembers that bands like Mitch Ryder & the Detroit Wheels, Ted Nugent & the Amboy Dukes, Terry Knight & the Pack, Suzi Quatro, and ? & the Mysterians (of "96 Tears" fame) played a very teen-oriented circuit in the region. "We didn't play bars," he told *Rolling Stone*'s Patrick Goldstein in July 1976. "There was no booze, just cokes, teenagers, and a couple dollars admission. There were probably thirty or forty of these joints around the state, places like the Mt. Holly Ski Lodge, the Riviera, clubs in Saginaw and Caseville, and we played 'em all. No one ever got paid more than a couple hundred bucks unless they were headliners; it was $500 tops."

While Frey may have learned some musical chops from Seger, it was Seger's understanding of the business part of the "music business" game that most affected the curious Frey. Frey explained the relationship to PBS' Tavis Smiley this way: "Bob Seger took a liking to me when he saw my band, and he kind of took me under his wing. He took me in the recording studio with him, he let me sing and play guitar on 'Ramblin' Gamblin' Man.' He showed me how to make records. He introduced me to Mickey Stevenson, who was a producer over at Motown."

Old-Time Rock and Roll

Bob "Night Moves" Seger made it big in 1976, but he'd been a mainstay of the Detroit rock-and-roll scene for over a decade before anyone outside of Michigan really knew who he was. The son of a Ford plant worker (and part-time musician, with his own big band, the thirteen-piece Stewart Seger Orchestra), Seger had never had a regular job. He'd started his first group, the Decibels, when he was just fifteen years old. They played hundreds of gigs, cut a few singles, and found a manager in Punch Andrews, who'd stay with Seger for years.

None of Seger's records were able to push him to recognition outside of the Detroit scene until he signed to Capitol in 1968 and put out "Ramblin' Gamblin' Man." The track reached #17 on the national charts and allowed Seger to tour a wider region, until he hit the big time with the global classic "Night Moves" in the mid-'70s. Seger was a genuine friend and mentor to Frey, and the two remained close over the years, later co-writing "Funky New Year" and "Heartache Tonight" together with the Eagles. He also made a few guest appearances on Frey's solo albums.

Frey reminisced about Seger in the *Detroit Free Press* in March 2004. "Punch put Bob and I together," he recalled. "He said, 'I'd like to record you, but you don't write any songs, so I'm going to have Seger write and produce for you.' The most important thing that happened to me in Detroit was meeting Bob and getting to know him. He took me under his wing. We'd drive around all night and smoke dope and listen to the radio. We'd drive to Ann Arbor and hang with (musician) Scott Richardson at his house, go to the Fifth Dimension club and see the Who and Jimi Hendrix there."

Seger's music-business savvy was taken to heart by quick-study Frey, who learned a few good lessons well, especially when it came to what makes an artist successful. Seger believed wholeheartedly that writing original material was the key ingredient in any success. "You're going to write some bad songs," Frey recalled Seger telling him, in an interview with Tavis Smiley, "but just keep writing, and eventually you'll write a good one."

Frey also joined a folksy band called the Four of Us, based in Birmingham, Michigan, who introduced him to the power and beauty of vocal harmonies. He told Smiley that they were doing "Beach Boy songs and Beatles songs and Buckinghams and songs with background vocals, so I really kind of got into the group singing thing and the melodic thing."

Frey's final Detroit musical adventure, during the latter part of 1967, was the formation of another rock band, this time the oddly named Heavy Metal Kids. Frey handled guitar and vocals, Lance Dickerson (who would go on to play with Commander Cody) was on drums, Paul Kelcouse played electric guitar, and old Mushrooms keys man Jeff Burrows completed the lineup. Nothing much happened for the Heavy Metal Kids, however, and Frey was ready to quit Detroit.

Frey recalled that feeling to Jeff Yarbrough in a piece for Andy Warhol's *Interview* magazine in April 1986. "It was 1967, and the hippie thing was happening. I got into experimenting with drugs while I was in college in Michigan. I didn't really try hard in college. I was much more interested in going to see the Grateful Dead at the Grandee Ballroom. I had been bitten by the rock 'n' roll bug, and I was sitting there in Detroit thinking, 'God, Buffalo Springfield is 2,000 miles to the west, and the Byrds, and the Beach Boys.' I read the *Life* magazine articles about free love and free dope in California. I said, 'That's the place for me,' and at age 20 I drove to Los Angeles."

First Days Out West

So, Glenn and his bandmates Jeff and Lance sold what they could—including Frey's '55 Chevy—for gas and supplies, and headed down Route 66 with a few other Detroit buddies. They stopped in Reno for some fun and rested in Oakland, California, where they crashed with a musician friend, Larry Welker, who was, at the time, bluesman Charlie Musselwhite's guitar player. They then cruised down the picturesque coast roads to Los Angeles to look up Frey's girlfriend, Joanie.

It was on this journey to the mythical City of Angels that Frey famously pulled in to the Laurel Canyon Country Store and spotted David Crosby, formerly of the Byrds, decked out in trademark attire, in a hat and a green leather cape. In September 1975 Frey told *Rolling Stone*'s Cameron Crowe that he took it as an omen.

Frey felt both daunted and excited to have landed in a town where you could rub shoulders with an ex-Byrd or two. As exciting as it was, as a genuine fan of the band's music and craft, he saw something quite daunting in pitting himself against the best in the business. Fortunately, soon after stumbling across one of the genuine leaders of the L.A. music scene, Frey ran into another hopeful young musician who would prove a valuable partner and great source of support over the next few years: J. D. Souther, an accomplished musician with no lack of confidence in his abilities. Their meeting and friendship arose from yet another strange but simple twist of fate.

Before Frey left Michigan for the sunshine, he had been dating Joan Sliwin, a singer in an all-white, all-female vocal group called the Mama Cats. They were based in downtown Detroit, and their concert repertoire was classic Motown. Frey's band the Mushrooms backed the Mama Cats at gigs, and when they got a chance to put out a single, it was written and produced for them by Bob Seger.

Like most acts with ambition, the Mama Cats understood that fame and fortune—and the experience of playing a part in the late-1960s music revolution that was happening on the streets and in the mainstream media—were not to be found in Detroit. At a time in history, long before society broke off into tiny subgroups and niches for its social and artistic entertainment, Americans enjoyed more shared, common experiences. With limited TV channels, a whole nation really could watch the Beatles play *The Ed Sullivan Show*—and all at the same time. When something, anything, stirred in San Francisco or Los Angeles, newsreel and television stations covered it. The young generation that the Beatles and Dylan represented was not just making its mark in pop and rock and roll: they were becoming journalists, writers, radio presenters, movie directors, and TV producers. Kids in Detroit, or Baltimore, or Memphis knew all about Dylan and the Byrds, and Laurel Canyon and the Troubadour. So, in 1968, it was the turn of the Mama Cats—Laura Polkinghome, Marsha Jo Temmer, and sisters Alexandra and Joan Sliwin—to quit Detroit for Los Angeles, hoping to find their own slice of success in Tinseltown.

They'd read all the stories of groups making it in Los Angeles after being spotted in the right place at the right time. Fantasy, perhaps? Perhaps not. Remarkably, the Mama Cats got lucky with their very first meeting after impressing record-biz icon and impresario Lee Hazlewood. Hazlewood gave them a record deal with his own LHI label, changed their name to Honey Ltd., and put them in the studio.

Things didn't work with regards to breaking into the big time, but the Mama Cats had a fun run in the California sun. And, through Joan, the group played a significant part in the Glenn Frey Hollywood story, too. When Glenn decided to follow Joan to California, he found himself a new musical soul mate. His girlfriend's sister was dating John David Souther. "So I started hanging out with him," Frey told Tavis Smiley. "He was into a lot of music that I wasn't familiar with—jazz, R&B. We had a lot of time to burn, so we listened to a lot of records the first couple years I was out here."

The relationship was intertwined with music, but Frey and Souther would have become friends regardless of their chosen professions. Both were handsome, athletic young men with an eye for the ladies, and they had no trouble finding female companionship. They were popular and cool, even if Frey's motormouth upset a few along the way.

It made sense to try a music project together, so Frey and Souther formed a folk-rock duo with the odd name Longbranch Pennywhistle. They practiced, wrote songs, and played the folk circuit as often as they could get a booking or an open-mic slot, depending on the venue. And they became pretty good very quickly.

A few degrees of Texas separation later, Longbranch Pennywhistle landed a deal with Jimmy Bowen's Amos Records. They recorded one self-titled album in 1969, but the label was going nowhere, sales were small, and the arrangement subsided. Frey and Souther were so filled with ambition and talent, though, that they saw these setbacks as mere bumps on the road to musical success.

One of their fellow strugglers was a young songwriter called Jackson Browne, with whom they shared an Echo Park apartment complex. Frey explained the setup in his notes for *The Very Best of the Eagles* in August 2003. "Jackson Browne, J. D. Souther, and I all lived at 1020 Laguna in Echo Park. J. D. and I shared a $60-a-month, one-room apartment, a couch, and kind of a bed with a curtain in front of it. Right underneath us in an even smaller studio apartment was Jackson. He had his piano and guitars down there. I didn't really know how to sit down and work on a song until I heard him playing underneath us in the basement."

One of the songs Frey heard over and over from Browne's room was a lilting rock song with a country twist. That song was "Take It Easy," a tune that Frey would tweak after Browne offered it to him for his new project, the Eagles.

2

Long Way Home

When Kenny Rogers Calls

For years, fans and critics alike have debated the country-music credentials of the Eagles. The band started off with a healthy dose of twang but definitely moved toward rock and roll later, especially with the addition of heavy-rock guitarist Joe Walsh. But later, when Nashville—America's mecca for all things country—embraced the Eagles in the '90s with an all-star tribute album, Don Henley returned the favor by duetting with country starlet Trisha Yearwood (also the wife of Garth Brooks), and the "country or rock" debate fired up all over again.

Make no mistake: Nashville and its inner circle of writers and artists are typically reluctant to allow rockers into their Music City midst. Outsiders are treated with skepticism and disdain (ask Shania Twain!), unless, of course, they really do have some serious country credibility.

That Henley was the Eagle who scored a hit with a bona-fide country star should be no surprise, though, to anyone familiar with the singing drummer's geographical and musical background.

Deep in the Heart of Texas

He may have composed some of the greatest lyrics about the West Coast for "Hotel California," but Henley was no Angeleno. He was born and raised Southern, in Linden, in the Piney Woods of deepest Northeast Texas. Not that being raised in Texas necessarily ensures a country music sensibility, but Henley's musical influences, from a very young age, must surely have played some part in his chord and harmony sense, as well as his method of storytelling. In July 2013, Henley told Chuck Yarborough of the *Cleveland Plain Dealer*, "My native Northeast Texas was a musical, cultural crossroads— a sort of twilight zone where the Old South meets the West. As a kid, I was exposed to a great variety of musical styles: There was bluegrass from the

Ozarks, blues from Texas and Louisiana, gospel, country & western, western swing; there was the music of New Orleans coming up over the airwaves."

Radio Days

Henley grew up in a fairly modest house in small-town Linden, a place with a fine musical heritage that includes Scott Joplin, country crooner par excellence George Jones, and blues heavyweight T-Bone Walker.

Henley's father had amassed a large collection of big-band records, featuring the likes of Glenn Miller and Tommy Dorsey, from his time with the U.S. Army. Henley's grandma on his mother's side lived with the family and liked nothing better than sitting on the porch singing hymns and old-time classic pop songs of the day.

Henley's father was a huge country-music fan and an avid listener to the legendary *Louisiana Hayride*, one of the most influential broadcast machines in country-music and rock-and-roll history. The *Hayride* was broadcast across twenty-eight states from KWKH in Shreveport, Louisiana, throughout the

Don Henley (top right) on the back cover of the *Shiloh* album.

1950s. Henley and family listened religiously to the country notables of the 1950s—artists at the top of the charts like George Jones, Kitty Wells, Hank Williams, Slim Whitman, Faron Young, and Patsy Cline.

Influences

It was on the *Louisiana Hayride* that a young Memphis singer named Elvis Presley made his radio performance debut in 1954. Presley's own fusion of country music, the blues, and the new sound of rock and roll would have a dramatic effect on popular music. Like the Beatles, Elvis made a deep impression on Henley; later on, it was Henley's ability to reimagine such childhood musical voices that would help give the Eagles their genre-busting and hard-to-categorize sound.

Henley was also influenced by African American church music. A local Baptist church held baptisms in a pond in the woods close to Henley's childhood home. As Henley later stated in a Warner Bros. biography, "They would wade out into that muddy water with their arms stretched toward the sky. I remember the women being all dressed in white. The singing was unforgettable. At first, the whole thing was a little frightening, but the longer I watched the more I started to get into it. Underneath the fervor, there was a sincerity and openness about it—an expression of faith and longing like I had never heard before. That experience stays with me, not necessarily in terms of its religious connotations, but in terms of its humanity."

As Don got older, his transistor-radio listening habits shifted more toward rock-and-roll stations. In his teens, he listened far into the night to the powerful KOMA, which broadcast from Oklahoma City, and the compelling tones of the iconic Wolfman Jack (a looming figure in almost every article or book on the early days of rock and roll and the British Invasion of the United States), whose station carried across most of the country from its headquarters in Mexico.

Band of Brothers

Aside from passively listening to gospel, country, and rock and roll, Henley became an active musician, playing first the trombone—which didn't last too long—and then the drums.

Henley's close friend growing up was Richard Bowden. Bowden lived nearby and had his own band. When their drummer left, Henley—who'd shown an aptitude for rhythm while tapping away on school books in class and had utilized his newfound talents drumming in the school jazz band—got the gig. (In fact, Henley's aptitude for the drums helped the school band win a state contest in 1964.)

Bowden's band called themselves the Four Speeds, and they were quite a talented bunch. Jerry Surratt played above-average trumpet; Freddie Neese was a more-than-capable guitarist; Henley could play rock, country, blues, pop, and jazz, if needed; and bass player Richard Bowden oozed personality and exhibited a raw sense of stagecraft. But they didn't really have a designated singer, which caused some debate among the group; no one wanted to volunteer, so Bowden's father arranged an audition between the band members. Henley took his turn with single-minded aplomb. They all agreed that he was a natural and would sing and play drums.

High school rock-and-roll bands have a tendency to break up as players come and go, but the Four Speeds were more consistent than most. Bowden left town first, traveling to Stephen F. Austin University in Nacogdoches after graduating high school in 1964. Henley followed a year later, but the band kept going. He and Bowden both moved to North Texas State University in Denton, and the Four Speeds changed their name to Felicity. (Later on, the band would change its name again, to Shiloh.) Henley's college pal, keyboard player Jim Ed Norman, and Richard Bowden's cousin Mike also joined the group.

Initially influenced by the Ventures—the 1950s instrumental combo so often referred to in rock-and-roll histories and encyclopedias as "the band that launched a thousand bands"—Felicity came to rely more and more on the Beatles for inspiration. Rock and roll was one thing, but the Beatles were quite another.

According to Henley, nothing could compare to the impact made on music by the Liverpool four-piece in their U.S. explosion of 1964. As he explained to Blair Jackson for *BAM* magazine in November 1982, "When the Beatles came along in the 1960s, it completely changed my life, and I knew I wanted to be involved in music. I said, 'This is it.'" He told *Modern Drummer*'s Robert Santelli, "I don't care what anybody says about Ringo. I cut my rock -n- roll teeth listening to him."

Unlike Henley, who was his group's main vocalist, Ringo only got to sing occasionally, but the simplicity of his approach was perfect for the role. Emulating Starr's left-handed technique forced Henley to keep things simple. Talking to *Modern Drummer*, Henley explained, "The simple drummers were always my favorite kind of drummers."

Bowden and Henley were friends first and bandmates second, and so it was with Norman (who would become a major music-biz figure in his own right in the 1970s and 1980s, working on several Eagles albums and running Warner Bros. Records in Nashville for many years in the 1980s). Henley and Norman shared a common passion for live music, notably the hard-driving bluegrass outfit the Dillards, who were one of Henley's all-time favorite bands. The two friends made many a trip from college on weekends to see the Dillards' blistering stage show. Norman, a skilled keyboard player, recalled to me in 2009 that his audition was more social than musical when he ventured back to Linden with Henley.

Years later, Norman talked to me about the musical value of the early Henley music. "I hadn't listened to the Shiloh album in at least twenty years but I was recently transferring it to my iPod, and it's an interesting record. Generally it was a mishmash of different kinds of material and there's a lack of consistency, which would make it difficult on a marketing level. But I was also reminded about the songwriting talent of Don. I was an instrumentalist; I grew up with classical music so it took me a while to understand the role of the lyrics in music. Don was the one who understood. He got the importance of lyrics. We never really talked about it but it was obvious that Don, with his English major background, understood the value of the lyric."

Felicity picked up a healthy following in the Texas, Arkansas, and Louisiana area, playing a wide range of Top 40 material as well as some originals. The band pulled in decent money (up to $800 per show), bought a van, and booked even more gigs. Henley was also the band's primary songwriter, and one of his compositions—a tune called "Hurtin'"—was even produced and recorded by a local record company, Wilson Records, which released it in 1965. *Billboard* called the single "teen-oriented rhythm-ballad material featuring an emotional performance backed by a Bo Diddley beat," and went on to suggest that it "could prove a blockbuster."

Mr. Rogers

It was the spring of 1969 when Felicity got their chance at the big time. It all started when they ran into Kenny Rogers, then touring with his band the First Edition, in a clothes store in Dallas. Rogers had been signed by Jimmy Bowen to Amos Productions and was recording for Reprise at the time. He wasn't a big star yet—that would follow in the 1970s—but he was a dozen rungs higher up the music-biz ladder than either Henley or Shiloh.

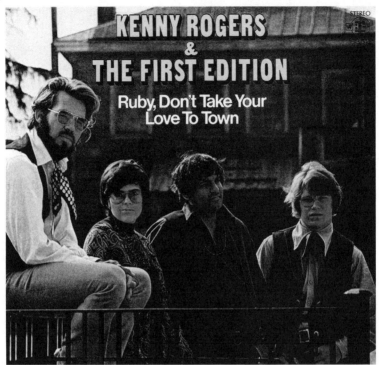

Kenny Rogers, country star of the '70s, had some early success in the '60s with the hard-to-label First Edition. Originally known as *the* First Edition and looking like a typical folk act, they became much more than that, dabbling with pop and rock and even touching on psychedelia. Rogers was the first pop "name" to back the young Don Henley and his musical ensemble.

Country Music Hall of Famer Kenny Rogers was born in Houston and was in a fairly successful high-school rockabilly band (the Scholars was the name, and they got as far as appearing on the TV show *American Bandstand*). After that early flush of pop fame, Rogers veered away from rockabilly toward jazz and played stand-up bass for the Bobby Doyle Trio jazz ensemble. He later became a member of the popular folk group, the New Christy Minstrels.

Formed by Randy Sparks in 1961, the Minstrels were a middle-of-the-road-pop-meets-folk act with a revolving door of members. As folk became more politicized on both the East Coast and the West in the middle of the decade, so the New Christy Minstrels became marginalized from the youth movement. Kenny Rogers and Kim Carnes (another performer set to be a star of the 1970s) joined for a while near the end of 1966; Mike Settle and Rogers left the group in 1967, looking to get a little closer to the bubbling-under counterculture style that was grasping at the reins of folk music and the folk lifestyle, and formed a far hipper group together, the First Edition. They went for a poppy, psychedelic sound and had themselves a #5 hit with the quirky tune "I Just Dropped In (To See What Condition My Condition Was In)." They repeated that chart success in 1969 with a song that would become part of Rogers' identity over the rest of his career: "Ruby, Don't Take Your Love to Town," a dark but melodic song about a wounded and paralyzed Vietnam veteran begging his wife not to leave him stuck at home and go into town to look for love by herself.

Rogers was a star on tour, as far as Henley was concerned—a connection with the "scene" in Los Angeles that they heard tales and read articles about in the music press. They started talking and traded phone numbers. Rogers recalled the Henley meeting to *Billboard*'s Chuck Dauphin in October 2013, noting that Henley "stayed at my house with the rest of his group (Shiloh) for about four or five months. I produced an album on them. I had all of his publishing, and when he went with the Eagles, he said he couldn't really do it if he didn't have his publishing rights. So, I gave him his publishing back, and said 'good luck,' and look what's happened to him!"

Rogers remembered the band when he was offered the opportunity to produce an album for Jimmy Bowen at Amos Records and decided to bring the kids with an interesting sound and a terrific lead singer (now calling themselves Shiloh) to California to record a single, "Jennifer."

Steel

Back in Texas one night, Shiloh were gathered together rehearsing in an old church building when several of the group got the urge to ride trail bikes. Tragically, Jerry Surratt rode his bike head-on into the path of a car and was killed.

Shiloh regrouped, however, and decided to add a keyboard player and a steel guitarist. The steel player, Al Perkins, was a Texas prodigy who every band on the scene knew about. A gifted guitarist, he excelled on the steel and played country-music exhibitions around Texas.

Perkins' music career playing with some of country and folk music's all-time greats—the Flying Burrito Brothers, Stephen Stills, Bob Dylan, Emmylou Harris, Mike Nesmith, Chris Hillman, and Dolly Parton—began when he was very young. Back then, a representative of a music school in Texas came knocking on Perkins' door offering steel-guitar lessons. Hawaiian music was popular at the time, thanks to the success of a prime-time radio show that featured Hawaiian tunes, so Perkins' parents agreed to pay for some lessons. The teacher recognized that Perkins played naturally by ear and offered to give Al private tuition. Perkins quickly became the company's star pupil and began playing talent shows as a music-school student rep. Delighted with their son's progress, Perkins' parents somehow came up with $1,000 (a huge amount of money for the time) for one of the first Fender 1000 pedal-steel guitars.

Pedal steel is an extremely complex instrument to learn and master, but it was a key component in Texas-style country music, and an essential part of the L.A. country-rock sound of the late '60s. The pedal-steel guitar comes on a stand with legs that hold a series of foot pedals that are used to adjust the strings and hence the sound of the instrument. Good pedal-steel players are few and far between; great ones are a very rare find. Perkins was gifted with the pedals, too, and got as much work as he needed from country-music groups in the local area.

A little later, Perkins' appetite for electric guitar was whetted by the instrumental band the Ventures, and with a new Gibson Les Paul Jr. in hand he dropped the steel for a while and perfected his electric lead skills. "I just loved learning new things," he told me in 2009. "Steel was my passion, and then I found I could play pretty good lead electric guitar, well that took my interest for a while. I figured it could only be a good thing to be proficient on electric guitar as well as pedal steel, if I was going to be a serious professional musician." The army interrupted Perkins' musical progress for a year or two, but after that he'd been playing in a Texas band called Foxx when Henley's boys came knocking.

Shiloh

"I liked the guys in Shiloh but I wasn't sure about their music style," Perkins told me in a 2010 conversation. "You know, this was the time of heavy blues, Clapton and Cream and these guys were doing Poco, Burrito Brothers country stuff. It was the Eagles sound really, if you think about it. And none of those L.A. country and rock and roll bands had been too successful. They are probably better known now than they were back then, you know, like Gram Parsons is revered now but pretty much ignored back in the day. And I'd been out to California before. I went with another musician, and we were part of a band called Sparkles. But the whole thing was very Hollywood. We had this kind of showbiz manager, and he changed the band's name to Pearly Gates, and well, it just wasn't right for me."

This self-titled album by Shiloh—formerly Felicity, and before that the Four Speeds—remains a stellar example of the pioneer days of country-rock, laced with some very 1960s psychedelia. Don Henley (seated, left) surfaced from this band, of course, and so did several others, including Jim Ed Norman, who became head of Warner Bros. in Nashville, and Al Perkins, who joined the Flying Burrito Brothers.

But Perkins recognized quality where he saw it, and Shiloh were a better-than-average young band. Everyone could play, and they appeared serious and professional—far more so than most of the bands he encountered on the circuit. "There was a good feeling about the band, so I did indeed agree to join them full time. Some artists you meet and work with just have that seriousness and such dedication and professionalism that you know they will do well. Don had that, I remember clearly, he had a great rock-and-roll voice, but he had this mentality you need in the music business."

Even more so than his passion for music, Henley's personality and character were ready for both success and a geographical move. He was too intellectual, too liberal, and too curious about the world and its new thinking to not leap at the chance to try a new landscape, especially California, where so much change was happening. He certainly didn't fit in in his hometown.

"If you didn't play football, you were nothing, zero," he told Robert Hilburn in an *L.A. Times* article in May 1982. "One of the only things that kept me going was music, especially the Beatles. I would go in and listen to the Beatles records every morning just to get me through the day. I kept waiting until the day I could get out of school and out of town on to someplace where I would fit in better."

Music and some good experiences at college gave Henley the inner belief to take the risk to leave the familiar and pursue his dreams. His parents scrimped and saved to send him to college. His father worked in an auto-parts store and was not a wealthy man, but he saved as much as he could for Don's education.

Aside from the friends and colleagues Don gathered through his college experiences, it was a teacher who really fired the desire in him. As he recalled to Cameron Crowe in a *Rolling Stone* interview in September 1975, said English teacher had a profound effect on him as an eager young man. Henley was struck by the man's uniqueness—he was the first bohemian Henley had ever encountered—particularly his wild clothing and the way he would teach seated on his desk with his legs crossed. He gave one piece of wisdom that Henley would always remember: "Frankly, if it takes you your whole fucking life to find out what it is you want to do, you should take it. It's the journey that counts, not the end of it. That's when it's all over."

3

Journey of the Sorcerer

Bernie Leadon's Country-Rock Foundations

T he first Eagle to fly the nest, after he quit in 1975, Bernie Leadon was the ensemble's senior figure in their fledgling Los Angeles days. At the time of the band's creation, he was, by several degrees, the best known and most experienced musician of them all. Indeed, it was Leadon who acted as unofficial spokesman for the band when securing their original contract with manager and youthful rock-biz guru David Geffen in 1971.

Leadon's first love—bluegrass and folk music—would bring him into conflict with the rest of the band as they sought a more pop/rock sound in later years. But as the instigator of the original country-rock blueprint, Leadon was a major architect of the classic Eagles sound.

Leadon's musical bent might suggest a rural, "country" upbringing, but he only really lived in the country until he was ten. His family then moved from just outside of Minneapolis, Minnesota, to San Diego for his father's career, and then to Gainesville, Florida. Both moves came about as a result of Bernie being the son of a very prominent aerospace engineer who was deeply involved with the United States space program in the 1960s. He taught at the University of San Diego before heading to Gainesville to teach aerospace engineering at the University of Florida.

Seeing Stars

Leadon's father would prove to be Leadon's most significant influence—character-wise, at least. "He was a really solid guy, a real man," Leadon told *Hit Channel* in 2012. "He was an aerospace engineer and worked on aspects of the 1960s space program. But his father was a railroad engineer, and that was a difficult working class job, although a prestigious one. So my dad was the first in his family to go to college, and he helped his brother and sisters to go to college."

But while Bernie's work ethic, analytical mind, and independence of thought may have come from his father, the music bug started with Mrs. Leadon. In a 2007 interview with Barry Baumstein of Gainesville's Matheson Museum, Leadon recalls his mother's piano playing. "I was born July 19, 1947. Classic Boomer, born right after the war. Mom played really great piano. She played piano in a local department store. She demonstrated sheet music for people. I got programmed with a lot of great music. Mom played organ in church, too. I would sit inside the choir when I was little and started playing piano when I was six. Started trombone when I was eleven, guitar when I was thirteen."

Music first became a genuine interest when Bernie was in California and the Kingston Trio struck it big with songs like "Tom Dooley," and "Where Have All the Flowers Gone?" The group popularized folk music nationally, and local folk combos began to pop up across America. Leadon first came across a young San Diego folk combo, the Scottsville Squirrel Barkers, at a church concert near his house, and was immediately inspired by their banjo player, Kenny Wortz. The group also included a young mandolin player who would go on to play a vital role with '60s rock-and-roll icons the Byrds and their early development of folk and country-rock in Los Angeles: Chris Hillman.

Blue Guitar

Word of mouth among musicians led Bernie to the Blue Guitar, a music store on Midway Drive that had become the epicenter for all aspiring folk-music enthusiasts.

Steve Neal, who has been involved in the running of the Blue Guitar since the folk boom of the mid-'60s, told the *San Diego Reader* in 1999, "In the 1960s, guitars were sold, repaired, and restored at the Blue Guitar. You could take lessons there, you could even see shows. We had Mason Williams and Hoyt Axton perform there, all friends of the shop. Chris Hillman was an old friend of ours, from a group called the Scottsville Squirrel Barkers—and that was the Blue Guitar bluegrass band. That was the house band. All the guys in it owned the shop, worked here, or hung out here."

Leadon learned as much banjo as he could until he was able to pick up gigs at coffeehouses around the San Diego area like the Upper Cellar, Circe's Cup, the End, the Pour House, and the Mantiki. He eventually replaced Kenny Wortz in the Scottsville Squirrel Barkers when the inspirational banjo player was drafted into the U.S. Air Force. But Leadon's musical journey in California was to be interrupted when his father again took a job in another state, this time farther south in Florida.

Florida, the Allmans, and Tom Petty

When his father took a job at the University of Florida, Bernie settled in the cool college town of Gainesville and immediately checked out the local music scene. "We moved here in August of '64," he told Barry Baumstein. "I started senior year of high school in Gainesville, and started working in a local music store in Lipham's Music, which was off of Main Street, at that time."

One of the musicians he rubbed shoulders with was guitarist Don Felder. "Yeah, well Bernie and I were in a band in high school," Felder told me in 2010. "Bernie moved to Gainesville, Florida, from San Diego. His father was actually hired by the University of Florida to found the nuclear-research division of the university. He was a nuclear physicist. Bernie moved there and the first thing he did was going to the music store and ask, 'Who's the best guitar player around here?' And they said me. And so he picked me up at the bus station on my way back from doing a gig by myself. Bernie did not own an electric guitar at the time, and I didn't own an acoustic because I wanted to play electric."

The talent in North Florida at the time was quite remarkable, as Leadon recalled to Michael Buffalo Smith. "I got to know the Allman Brothers when they were the Allman Joys. . . . Don Felder ended up in my high school band and I met him in high school . . . Tom Petty was from around the block, and he was in a band at the same time with my brother Tom, and they were the junior high band, and we were the high school band. Tom Petty would be in my brother's bedroom jamming when they were thirteen. That was a cool scene."

Covered Up

By the mid-'60s, Leadon was playing in a Top 40 covers band, the Maundy Quintet. "This is around '65–67, and I started playing in a Top 40 band that played at the local fraternity center around North Florida," he told Barry Baumstein of the Matheson Museum. The Maundy Quintet was the band in question, with the unusual name coming from Bernie, or so fellow band member Tom Laughon recalled.

New York folk and jazz artist, guitarist, and producer David Bromberg, pictured here on the album cover for *Out of the Blues: The Best of David Bromberg*, brought his not-inconsiderable fiddle skills to the recording of Bernie Leadon's "Journey of the Sorcerer."

"We were trying to think of something that wasn't a standard name," Laughon told GainesvilleRockHistory.com, "so Bernie says: 'how about something with Maundy in it?' And we're thinking, 'wow that sounds kind of British, that sounds cool, what does it mean?' Bernie, being Catholic, said Maundy Thursday is the day before Good Friday. We knew we couldn't just be Maundy, and we wanted it to sound British, so we thought Quintet; there's the Sir Douglas Quintet, we could be the Maundy Quintet; but to show how stupid we were, all of us figured the Sir Douglas Quintet was English. . . ." (Actually, they were from San Antonio, Texas.)

Significantly, since Top 40 cover songs would not figure too prominently in Leadon's career, it was his involvement with the more academic folksy crowd that provided him with the musical tools necessary to make such a country and folk impact when he did head west to California. "I also had bluegrass folkie buddies. So I had these two different strains of musical activity," he explained to Baumstein.

First Cut Is the Deepest

Before Leadon could even contemplate pursuing a professional music career, the United States Army needed him for its own purposes for a while. Fortunately, some inside information helped keep him in the U.S. for the two-year duration of his service. Then, with his army duties taken care of, Leadon was free to think for himself once again, and he decided the time was right to get out of Florida and find fame and fortune. Los Angeles seemed the most likely destination, since some of his old San Diego music buddies had gone there and found some success—notably Chris Hillman, who was enjoying Beatles-type fame with the Byrds.

Larry Murray, another musician friend from the San Diego days, was in a band called Hearts & Flowers, who had been signed by Capitol Records. They were ready to cut their second album but had recently lost a guitar player, so Bernie Leadon was invited to join. Leadon made the journey out to Los Angeles and slept on Murray's couch for a while before moving in with banjo pioneer Doug Dillard. Dillard was an incredibly gifted banjo player, revered and admired by his peers, and had been playing the instrument ever since first hearing the great Earl Scruggs play that fast, rolling bluegrass style as a kid in Missouri. Dillard's open-mindedness about music meant he led the way in the folk world in blending different styles. He saw no reason not to fuse traditional acoustic music with loud electric playing. Given that Leadon had for some time been playing Top 40 covers as well as hardcore unplugged folk music, it was natural for the two musicians to find plenty of common ground.

Bernie only played on one Hearts & Flowers album, *Of Horses, Kids, and Forgotten Women*, a solid record but one that couldn't break out of local radio into the mainstream. But Leadon was already in demand. The band's producer, Nick Venet, also worked with the Stone Poneys, featuring Linda Ronstadt on vocals. So quick and note-perfect was Leadon's playing that Venet found plenty of session work for him. When the Stone Poneys collapsed, Leadon played on and off with Ronstadt for some years before eventually lining up behind her with Glenn Frey, Randy Meisner, and Don Henley in the most famous backing band of all time.

Before that, though, Leadon fell into another project via Doug Dillard. Staying with Doug led to many impromptu jam sessions, with ex-Byrd Gene Clark even sometimes coming around. This provided the blueprint for another significant country-rock outfit: Dillard & Clark. Leadon played a key role in their first album, the seminal *The Fantastic Expedition of Dillard & Clark*. His guitar work blended superbly with Dillard's banjo, and the record even featured a future Leadon Eagles song, "Train Leaves Here This Mornin'."

From there, Leadon moved on to the Flying Burrito Brothers, which Hillman had formed a year earlier with Gram Parsons (now considered the tragic father of country-rock, having died young after some very fast living). When the band's bass player quit, Chris Hillman switched over to bass and Leadon came in on guitar. Leadon made two records as a Burrito, one with Parsons (*Burrito Deluxe*) and one without (*The Flying Burrito Brothers*).

Parsons was a very troubled artist. When he befriended rock-and-roll wild man Keith Richards, becoming all-consumed with the Rolling Stones, his drug usage spiraled out of control. A country-music aficionado determined to marry country with rock, he turned the Stones—and Richards in particular—on to country music, but addiction hindered his progress as a writer and an artist.

"Gram was gifted, but very erratic," Leadon told the Rock of Ages website. "It's common knowledge now about his drug and alcohol use and abuse. He managed to actually die of an overdose at age twenty-six. That takes focus and concentration, but he was only focused on his career in a haphazard way. He got kicked out of his own band, the Burritos, for not showing up, and not being professional."

Despite the distractions and dramas, Gram was always the soul of the Flying Burrito Brothers, and when the post-Parsons lineup failed to make any commercial inroads, Leadon decided it was time to find another gig. As fate would have it, he'd been rooming on the last Burritos tour with their new pedal-steel player, Al Perkins. Perkins had come to L.A from Texas with a band called Shiloh. And it was Perkins who first told Leadon about a talented singing drummer out of Texas.

Leadon already knew Glenn Frey and J. D. Souther from the Troubadour. John Boylan set about assembling the musicians into a backing band for his new charge, Linda Ronstadt. Linda was always going to ask for Boylan to get Bernie, if he was available. They had history, and Leadon was her favorite guitar player in Los Angeles. And once Frey, Leadon, and Henley worked together, it was clear to Leadon that Henley and Frey had the talent and ambition to do more with country-rock than the other bands he had been involved with or watched from a distance.

In a music scene that was attracting literally thousands of young wannabe artists every day, from all over America, it became increasingly difficult to sort the serious from the fun-loving kids intent on having a good time playing the part but never really having the drive to make it in rock and roll. Musicians like Leadon had seen so many of them come and go, and he knew that anyone who exhibited musical talent as well as a genuine sense of commitment, drive, and professionalism was a rare find. Frey and Henley—for all the criticisms they might receive in later years for perfectionism, for taking too much control, and for focusing more on business than rock-and-rollers should—were young musicians who had exactly the sense of dedication needed to have a chance of making it through the increasingly tough and unforgiving music industry.

Once they did get together, it was Leadon's experience with Hearts & Flowers, with Gene Clark, with Doug Dillard, and most importantly with Gram Parsons and the Burritos that ensured that he would be the initial band spokesman and business advisor. "We made a lot of great decisions in the beginning," Leadon told Barry Baumstein, "because I'd learned what decisions were good and what were bad. What didn't really work. And so we went to find the best manager and best record company we could and we hooked our wagon to David Geffen when he was twenty-six and on his way up."

Indeed, Leadon was the natural leader of the Eagles in the early days. Henley and Frey were the instigators, the creators, and the band's heart and soul, but before those two songwriters took ultimate control of the group, Leadon was the obvious spokesman and father figure. He had, after all, been around the record-biz block a few times, and he knew how it all worked. He also exhibited the confidence of a musician who knew that his reputation as a player kept him in heavy demand around town. Leadon's attitude and charisma, especially in the beginning, are too often overlooked in histories of the Eagles. But make no mistake: Bernie was key to the band jumping from Poco wannabes to major-league and major-label stars.

4

Pickin' Up the Pieces

Country Boy Randy Meisner

When Randy Meisner got tired of life in the fast lane with the Eagles, he went back to his country roots in Nebraska and bought a farm. It was a little bigger than the one he was raised on, but it was a return to nature nonetheless.

Born March 8, 1946, Randy Meisner grew up in a middle-of-nowhere farming community in Scottsbluff. As he told *People* magazine's David Sheff in January 1981, "Farms and corn were just about it."

Music and cars were a teenage obsession. The music came from his grandfather, a classical violin player, and like his Eagles cohorts, Meisner was initially drawn to rock and roll, especially Elvis Presley. First he played guitar, then picked up the bass in a local band called the Dynamics (after 1962, the Driving Dynamics), alongside Larry Soto, Richard Rhone, and John Ankeny. The band played shows at various dancehalls and even made an EP, with Meisner singing Sam Cooke's "You Send Me."

A few personnel changes and several gigs later, the Dynamics styled their looks on the über-popular Beatles and picked up a decent following, recording a single for Sully Records in 1965.

Battle of the Bands

Things were looking up for the group, and their audience was growing. That same year, the Dynamics drove to Denver for a Battle of the Bands contest. They didn't win; a band called the Soul Survivors did. They also stole Meisner away and took him to Los Angeles to make their name. "They'd lost their bass player . . . he'd joined the army or something like that," Meisner told KKTV in 1995. "And so they saw us play and heard me sing and I had you know a real high voice . . . and so they asked me if I wanted to come to Colorado and Denver. And I played about five or six gigs there and then they wanted to go to California. And so we all moved out there to California."

Discovering that there was already a band called the Soul Survivors in California, Meisner & co. became the North Serrano Blues Band for a few months in 1966 before taking on a new and none-too-imaginative name reflecting their own lack of success and financial status: the Poor.

Poor Boys

So poor were the Poor, in fact, that the whole band shared a one-bedroom apartment at a cost of $80 a month. They did make a self-titled album for Revola, plus a handful of singles, and played some opening slots for Buffalo Springfield, but nothing was happening in terms of profile or radio play.

By the end of 1968, the Poor were no more. Randy Meisner picked up sessions on the country, folk, and rock circuit, and was tipped off by a road manager Miles Thomas, who had trekked to L.A. with him, that Buffalo Springfield were calling it a day, and that Richie Furay and Jim Messina were audition bass players for a new band. Two future Eagles bassists, Meisner and Timothy B. Schmit, tried out, but Meisner got the gig. The new band—naively, perhaps, as they'd soon find out—chose to name themselves after a comic book character, Pogo.

Pogo were Meisner (bass and vocals), Furay (guitar and vocals), Messina (guitar and vocals), George Grantham (drums and vocals), and Rusty Young (pedal steel guitar, guitar, and banjo). Musically, the band worked, especially Meisner and Furay's vocals. *Where* they worked, however, was another matter. Pogo rehearsed at Richie Furay's hippie home in Laurel Canyon—at least until the neighbors called the police. Next they tried San Fernando Valley, but again the band was too loud for the neighbors.

Timeless Flyte

If necessity really is the mother of invention, then that plus some luck and shrewd thinking combined perfectly in one of rock and roll's oddest stories.

Neil Young was never the most reliable band member, and more often than not didn't use the airline ticket that the roadie bought for him. The unused tickets were stashed away in the glove box of manager Miles Thomas' Volkswagen. The tickets were in the name of one N. Young, which is where the story takes an odd turn, since steel player Rusty Young's real name was Norman. "He went out to his car one day and

Crazy Eyes was Poco's sixth album, and probably their best known. (It features future Eagle Timothy B. Schmit, who had replaced Randy Meisner in the band years before.) The title song refers to Gram Parsons, and the record, uncannily, came out just a few days before Parsons died on September 19, 1973.

opened up the glove compartment and out fell all these airline tickets," Rusty told the *Houston Chronicle*'s Rick Campbell in November 2008. "We took all of Neil's tickets down to the airline counter and cashed them in. It amounted to like $4–5,000." The money paid for rehearsal space at SIR studios in Los Angeles.

By the fall of 1968, Pogo were ready to play live. They auditioned for Doug Weston, owner of the prestigious Troubadour club on Santa Monica Boulevard, and were offered a slot opening for the Nitty Gritty Dirt Band. A month later, they were rewarded with their own headlining gigs—two weeks of them, in November 1968. The band played several shows in Los Angeles before the owners of the comic strip character forced them into a name change.

Comic Strip

"Pogo" was the name of a critically acclaimed cartoon strip that had been created and drawn by Walt Kelly. It was a light, good-natured satirical cartoon, created in 1948, that gently mocked stories in the news. The cartoon takes place in Georgia, in a swamp, and features a cast of animal characters who make fun of human silliness. The main character is an effervescent, cup-is-always-half-full possum named Pogo, the complete diametric opposite of the pessimistic Albert the Alligator.

Pogo became Poco on December 31st when cartoonist Kelly, who was not too keen on sharing the name of his comic-strip possum with a rock-and-roll band, hit them with a cease-and-desist order before a big concert at the Shrine Hall in Los Angeles. The band replaced the "g" with a "c" in a name that is still used today.

Poco then got a record deal and put out a highly regarded album, *Pickin' Up the Pieces*, in 1969. The record would neatly bridge the gap between the folk-rock of Buffalo Springfield and the Byrds and the country stylings of the Flying Burrito Brothers, and in many ways can be viewed as a musical blueprint for the Eagles' first recordings.

For What It's Worth

The folk and rock boom, which attempted to blend the Beatle beat with Dylan's earthy folk, was a catalyst for a series of musical combinations and unions. Some, like the Turtles, achieved some fame and chart success; others, like Buffalo Springfield, burned out fast but played a hugely significant role.

Stephen Stills, who'd been in the local band scene in Florida with Don Felder, wanted to break away from the folk music he'd been playing and get into a sound with more rock-and-roll energy. Having been turned down for the *Monkees* TV show in 1965, he was now playing sessions around Los Angeles. A producer told him to form a rock-and-roll band, so he bugged Richie Furay to start a group with him.

Meanwhile, Neil Young had also come to California to make his name, along with bass player Bruce Palmer. Legend has it that their destiny was set on one fateful day in an all-too-familiar L.A. traffic jam. Stills, Furay, and Young had met previously, and now Stills was shocked to see Young and Palmer in the traffic. The Canadians were on their way out of L.A, but Stills and Furay knew it was them because Young drove around in an unmistakable black hearse. The stars were in alignment, as Furay recalled to *Uncut* magazine. "What an historic moment, we were all pretty amazed. It was nothing short of fate and destiny."

With the addition of another Canadian, drummer Dewey Martin, the musicians had the right ingredients for a band. With two songwriting and guitar-playing talents like Stills and Young in tandem, it was no surprise that once they started playing, word in the street was that there was a new band to see. Stills witnessed a minor riot on Sunset Strip and wrote "For What It's Worth." The resulting song, as played by Buffalo Springfield, was sparse and direct, and found a new sonic home, somewhere between folk and rock, that no other band had yet discovered.

Personality clashes, drug busts, and personal ambition meant the band changed lineups too often to maintain the momentum, and they finally broke down in 1968. But by then, a legend was born, and the influence of Springfield only grew as the band's members went on to more success. Neil became a solo superstar. Stills did much the same, but with Crosby and Nash (and Young, too, at times), and Furay and latter-day member Jim Messina started Poco.

If any one band was a blueprint for the Eagles, it was Poco. Richie Furay worked with guitar player and steel-guitar specialist Rusty Young on some of Buffalo Springfield's final sessions, and he and Jim Messina sounded pretty good together. With George Grantham and Randy Meisner on board, Poco—or Pogo, as they still were at that point—had the nucleus of a great band.

Word got out in L.A. that there was something cool going down with Furay's new band, and as Rusty Young told ClassicBands.com, "Everybody wanted to come see us. Richie had really come up with the concept of the country/rock thing that wasn't being done. Everybody was ready to jump on the bandwagon. In the Troubadour, there'd be a booth, and there would be Ricky Nelson and Ozzie and Harriet. The whole gang would be there in their booth. The Smothers Brothers came down. George Harrison and John Lennon came down because they tried to sign us to Apple at one point. Pretty much all the L.A. people you can imagine would be in the audience on any given night."

Poco's first album, *Pickin' Up the Pieces*, was an upbeat, shimmering experiment of a group—this, remember, was four years before Henley, Frey, Meisner, and Leadon debuted their take on country mixed with rock and roll. Of all the Eagles, Frey was probably the most greatly influenced by the music of Poco, having watched them every opportunity he got.

Country-rock aficionados have long pondered the dilemma of how a band so important and so good failed to find real commercial success.

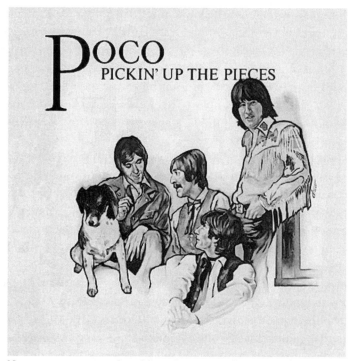

Not everyone gets replaced by a dog on an album cover, but Randy Meisner did.

Perhaps, with a couple of hit tunes and some more business-savvy management, Poco might have given the Eagles a run for their money. Unfortunately, Meisner had already quit the band when the album appeared on the streets. Furay and Messina exerted a little too much control in the band, refusing Meisner the opportunity, for example, to listen to the mixes of the recordings they had made. Meisner wanted to be a full and respected member of a democratic group. If he'd wanted to be a sideman, there was plenty of work in L.A. Being in a band was paramount, as far as Randy was concerned, and if Poco were not going to be that band, he would move quietly on.

To rub salt in his wounds, Meisner was removed from the album cover artwork and replaced with a dog. "They went ahead and took my voice off of one of the songs on the album that I'd already sang and took my picture out of the original one," he told KKTV. "I think there's a dog in there now. The dog might have been there anyway but I always say they replaced me with a dog . . . [and] I love dogs, so I like it."

Dismayed by the music scene, Meisner returned to the tranquility of the country for a while. "I went back to Nebraska and worked with a friend of mine who owned a John Deere dealership," he told *Smooth Jazz Now*. "I was like a parts man for eight months, and then Ricky Nelson called me and I played with him for a while."

Full Nelson

Fifties teen star Ricky Nelson was all grown up by 1969 and looking to relaunch a career that had been derailed by the Beatles and the so-called British Invasion of the mid-'60s. New York–raised record producer John Boylan went to see Poco's first gig on November 19, 1968, and took Nelson with him. Nelson and Boylan were plotting Rick's return to music, and the *Ozzie and Harriet* star was deeply into Dylan, Buck Owens, and Harry Nilsson. He had seen Poco play live in Los Angeles and liked what he heard, so asked Meisner to help him put together a backing band. Meisner, ever the team player, went back to his Poor days and recruited Allen Kemp and Patrick Shanahan. The group quickly became the Stone Canyon Band, and would play a major part in Nelson shrugging off his teen-heartthrob image and being hailed, finally, as a genuine musical artist.

Early in 1970, Rick Nelson and the Stone Canyon Band toured Europe. After the tour, Meisner decided to leave the group. He was disappointed by the bad conditions on the road and wanted to concentrate on session work in order to have a regular income. Fortunately, Hollywood was a close-knit community with a small-town vibe, and producer John Boylan, who was a major Meisner admirer, had a new project Randy might be interested in.

5

The Pretender

Given the "family" nature of the singer/songwriter scene in Hollywood in the late '60s and early '70s, it's hardly surprising, and actually rather fitting, that the Eagles story should include a couple of songwriter characters who would play the role of brothers in arms, or maybe musical cousins, as the four Eagles found their feet.

Indeed, over the years, J. D. Souther and Jackson Browne have both been labeled the "fifth Eagle," as critics attempt to give credit to a pair of artists who did in all actuality play significant roles in the band's early history.

Jackson Browne

In 2014, a group of rock and roll's finest singers and songwriters assembled for a tribute album to honor the life and work of one of their own: *Looking Into You: A Tribute to Jackson Browne.* The list of contributors included Lyle Lovett, Keb' Mo', Bonnie Raitt, Bruce Springsteen and Patti Scialfa, Lucinda Williams, J. D. Souther, and of course Don Henley, who writes in the liner notes, "It is astounding to think that Jackson wrote 'These Days' when he was only sixteen years old. But then, he was always a step ahead of the rest of us."

Unlike Souther and the original Eagles, Browne did actually grow up in Southern California. A precocious talent with a gift for wise lyrics that disguised his youth and a sense melody that was just right for blending folk with rock and roll, Browne started younger than most and was playing in folk clubs in Orange County as a teen. The coolest of these was a club called the Paradox, where the likes of Tim Buckley, Steve Noonan, Hoyt Axton, and blues legends Sonny Terry and Brownie McGhee plied their craft. Browne sang his introspective songs as a solo act and fell in with a jaunty jug band, the Nitty Gritty Dirt Band, singing lead with them for a few months in 1966.

Saturate Before Using

JACKSON BROWNE

LOS ANGELES, CALIFORNIA

Browne was still only twenty-three years old when he released this, his debut album, which showcases a sophisticated songsmith—probably the most technically gifted of his West Coast compadres. The picture features Browne's face on a water bag, hence the "Saturate" warning. This eponymous album has, incorrectly, been known as *Saturate Before Using* for years.

The folksy group based themselves around McCabe's Guitar Shop in Long Beach, from which they planned their own individual take on the folk-rock movement. Image-wise, they were initially known for wearing 1920s-style suits with cowboy boots. It was a different look, and one that got the band noticed on a busy folk circuit.

Dirt Band original Jeff Hanna remembered Browne's early days with his group in 1966, when talking to Pete Cooper of the *Tennessean* newspaper in July 2012. "I met him when he was fifteen, and he was already writing songs. And they were really, really good songs. I remember him playing one called 'These Days' in the alley behind the Paradox, and we were all just stunned.

I was so intimidated by his writing that for years I was like, 'Why bother being a songwriter?'"

New York, New York

Jackson Browne's first official music contract was with Elektra, signed in 1966 while he was still in high school. He learned a lot early on, especially on trips to New York, where he hung out with both Andy Warhol and Lou Reed. He played in Tim Buckley's band for a while and then played electric guitar for Nico, appearing on her *Chelsea Girl* album.

When that deal ran down, the label came up with the notion of the Elektra "farm," whereby a group of young songwriters could just hang out and create at a physical location, owned and operated by the company. The idea was cool but the execution less so. To finance the project, Elektra wanted an album of material from the writers at the camp, which meant they were immediately under pressure to create to deadline and write commercial records.

The dream was over, and Browne, without even a publishing deal, headed back to Los Angeles. But he had learned a great lesson, as he admitted to *Rolling Stone* in March 1974. "You had to be serious about what you were doing, and that it took a lot to make a record, and you couldn't just float into the studio. Maybe Bob Dylan did, from all accounts, and maybe I had to cope with the fact that I wasn't Bob Dylan. And I suddenly realized that I wasn't gonna get to be Bob Dylan."

Browne became a regular at the Troubadour, where his youthful striking look and magnetic presence were only magnified by his making it very clear to everyone that despite his handsome good looks, he was unavailable for romantic commitments, such was his single-minded desire to take his writing seriously and become an accomplished artist.

Byrds of a Feather

Browne knew Glenn Frey and J. D. Souther from the Troubadour scene, having seen them both play on several occasions, and he liked what they did. He asked them to check out a new song he'd recently finished, "Jamaica Say You Will." Frey and Souther were amazed at his talent.

Any curiosity they might have had as to how one so young could come up with such beautifully crafted material was answered when Frey moved into an apartment in Echo Park. Below him lived Browne, and so began Frey's crash course in songwriting as a profession. "I heard these songs start from just a verse and a chorus," Frey told the *L.A. Times* in January 1993. "And I couldn't believe how religiously he worked on these songs and got up every morning and played through the three or four songs he was working on for three or four hours. Then he'd break and go to lunch, have a meeting, and then come back and be working on them again and again. I began to see there was a lot of perspiration involved, and it didn't just come out of him instantly."

Many of L.A.'s music elite championed Jackson Browne, so obvious was it that the singer they called "the kid" at the Troubadour had more talent than most. David Crosby was a huge fan. "Man there was some amazing talent drifting through the scene back then," he told me in 1988, while promoting his autobiography. "I cannot think of a time in rock and roll, before then or since, when so many incredible artist and songwriters arrived in one place at one time. Jackson was this kid who saw the world so differently. He had this wisdom and compassion. Only a fool couldn't see that he was destined for great things."

Browne himself recalled those early days when we talked in his London hotel suite during his World in Motion tour in 1989, and had nothing but kind words for the songwriting community he'd sprung from in the 1960s. "It was an amazing time and there were some wonderful people. There was a definite community feel about what we were doing. We helped each other, recommended friends for gigs, helped each other out, and learned from each other. Crosby helped me and I championed the Eagles with David Geffen. Geffen was this guy who was one of us; he wasn't the old school record business guy. It was a cool time."

David Crosby suggested that Browne get in touch with the hotshot management guy currently ruffling a few Hollywood feathers: David Geffen. Browne had signed a publishing deal with Criterion Music and called on Frey and Souther to help him record demos of some of his songs. (Writers signed to publishing companies are paid a "draw," or weekly advance, on future royalties. They are also given a budget to record their new material by the publishing company. These recordings are then used to showcase the material to artists looking for tracks for their new projects.)

Browne sent David Geffen his demo of "Jamaica Say You Will" from the recording session at Criterion Studios, along with a photograph. Geffen initially ignored him, but fortunately his secretary liked the photo enough to give the music a listen. Naturally, once Geffen actually listened to Browne, he fell in love with his songs. Geffen snapped Browne up to a representation deal and set about finding a record company that would be the best fit for this remarkable—and very marketable—young talent.

One of the people Geffen spoke to was Ahmet Ertegün of Atlantic Records. Shocked at Ertegün's rejection of his new protégé, Geffen ended up signing Browne himself after Ertegün encouraged him to start his own company, Asylum Records. *Jackson Browne* came out in 1972. According to *Rolling Stone* magazine's original review of the album, "Jackson Browne's sensibility is romantic in the best sense of the term: his songs are capable of generating a highly charged, compelling atmosphere throughout, and—just as important—of sustaining that pitch in the listener's mind long after they've ended."

J. D. Souther

He may be best known these days as Watty White, the fictional record producer on the hit ABC TV series *Nashville*, but J. D. Souther has a legacy and pedigree to rival most in contemporary rock-and-roll history.

An integral player in the L.A. singer/songwriter world in the early '70s, Souther, like Browne, was practically an unofficial member of the Eagles—a friend, a confidante, and the writer of many of their biggest and most instantly recognizable hits, including "New Kid in Town," "Best of My Love," and "Heartache Tonight." In fact, all the songs Souther wrote with the Eagles are major songs: "Doolin-Dalton," "Funky New Year," "How Long," "James Dean," "Last Good Time in Town," "The Sad Café," "Teenage Jail," "Victim of Love," and "You Never Cry Like a Lover." And yet he never joined the band!

Amarillo by Morning

Like Glenn Frey, John David Souther started life in Detroit, Michigan, but he spent much of his early childhood in Amarillo, Texas. There was little doubt that he would become a musician. His father ran a musical instruments store, and J. D. soon became more than proficient on several instruments.

As a teen, ready to play music live, Souther focused on the drums, but he could chip in with violin, saxophone, and clarinet if needed.

His influences ranged from R&B great Ray Charles to Miles Davis, Ella Fitzgerald, and Mose Allison from the jazz world. Despite living in Texas, Souther's parents despised country music, so his only real exposure to it was through the jazz-oriented western swing that was heard all around the Amarillo region.

Souther played drums and sang for an Amarillo college band, J. D. & the Senders, who played a hybrid of country and R&B. He recognized that Los Angeles was where he needed to be, musically, but he was the only Sender who was serious about trekking west. Fortunately, another Amarillo band, the Kitchen Cinq, were ready to make the commitment, and J. D. traveled with them to California in search of the big time—or at least a good time.

The big time, for a while at least, revolved around house painting, roofing, and other construction work to pay the bills. But Souther's instrumental skills and versatility brought him some stage and session work, notably with a Norman Greenbaum band, Natty Bump, plus the Icehouse Blues Band and Bobby Doyle. Those jobs, while not significant in themselves, connected him to several small music-publishing companies. Souther was a novice songwriter, but with his trusted Gibson Dove acoustic guitar in hand, he was good enough to pick up a few small contracts.

When Souther hooked up with Frey in 1969, his jazzy Texas leanings, laced with some Tim Hardin and Bob Dylan, blended nicely with Frey's raw and rockier sound. Souther was a musical sponge, taking in everything he came across, open to any new kind of music that could add to his repertoire and help him creatively in his writing. He lived with Linda Ronstadt for a while, and she introduced him to the bluegrass side of country music. His writing skills gradually grew to match his instrumental virtuosity. "I kept trying," he told *Interrobang*'s Ray Bennington in June 2013, "and was hanging around with some really great songwriters, like Lowell George and Joni Mitchell, and eventually I got to be fairly decent at it. When it comes down to it, writing a song is easy to do. But writing a great song—and writing more than one—is almost impossible to do."

With Souther passing on what he had learned about the beauty of bluegrass and folk music to Frey—who was already enamored with the floating country-meets-rock sound of Poco—the duo found more common ground in the Flying Burrito Brothers' brand of hippie-fied country-rock. It was the music of the time and the place. Souther and Frey joined forces as Longbranch Pennywhistle and immersed themselves in the singer/songwriter world of Los Angeles. When they weren't playing, they were watching

The 1969 debut album of the duo Longbranch Pennywhistle featured some of rock's finest players, notably James Burton, Larry Knechtel, and Ry Cooder.

others, learning and observing. They fit well with the Troubadour crowd and mixed easily with the likes of Warren Zevon, Doug Dillard, Ned Doheny, Neil Young, John Hartford, and Jackson Browne.

Crazy Horses

"It was a great time, 1969 in L.A.," Souther told me in 2009. "There was just an explosion of talent, some amazing singers and writers that all seemed to be in the same place at the same time. Seemed like everyone knew everyone. Glenn and I got a record deal, and we really didn't have a clue what we were doing."

Amos Records didn't skimp on the budget for Frey and Souther's debut album, with musicians of the caliber of James Burton (Elvis' guitarist of choice) and fiddle supremo Doug Kershaw brought into the studio. The

John David Souther keeps his boots firmly on the ground in this back-cover photo from Longbranch Pennywhistle's debut album.

artwork for the album was lavish, too, with a double foldout and some top-dollar artistic photography.

Souther enjoyed the freewheeling lifestyle that Hollywood offered and encouraged, but his work ethic drove him to continually aspire to professionalism, especially when he discovered that he had a knack for writing songs that other people liked.

Ironically, it was the songwriting that ended his and Frey's short career with Amos Records. Having made a promising self-titled debut record (albeit one that lacked cohesion or direction), they wanted to take more control. They knew their songs better than any producer, they reasoned, so it would be best if they were allowed total control in the studio. The duo approached a new producer, David Briggs, who was fresh from working with Neil Young and Crazy Horse, and recorded several tracks at his studio. They did it their way, and they were delighted with the results.

Henley

While Frey and Souther had decided that they needed more musical control, their record label felt that what was actually needed was more outside songs by hit writers, and more guidance for the newcomers in the studio. When Souther and Frey submitted the Briggs-produced tapes, Amos was unimpressed. The duo's days on the label were almost over.

Also unhappy and frustrated with Amos was a country-rock group from Texas, produced by Kenny Rogers and led by a drummer named Don Henley. That group, Shiloh, had also put out an album, which featured three Henley songs. The album showcased a mix of country-blues and rock and roll, but it was Henley's "I'm Gone" and "Same Old Story" that stood out from a mix of good and bad but always beautifully executed songs.

Fired up by the apparent refection, Frey was determined to continue—to prove the naysayers wrong and surface with a band. Souther, a more introspective character, opted to satisfy his musical muse by writing. Ironically, David Geffen, who had met Souther and Frey through Jackson Browne and Linda Ronstadt, now wanted to sign Souther for his songs but felt that Frey was better suited to being part of a group.

It didn't take long for Frey's band to come to fruition, and Souther even sat in on a few rehearsals. He could have joined, such was the esteem he was held in by all, especially Henley. "There was no point, though," Souther explained to me. "They were just so good as a four-piece. It was obvious right from the start that they had that magic. They didn't need me. And for my part, a solo career was always more fitting to my character. And the kind of touring commitments they had would not have appealed to me."

Frey and Henley, however, had found common ground in their frustrations at Amos—and their holding-pattern music careers in general—and connected personally and professionally. John David Souther, along with Jackson Browne, would be an essential member of the gang, floating in and out as time and career permitted. But now the core of a new band was firmly in place. It was simply a matter of finding the right opportunity.

6

Hollywood Waltz

The Musical Mecca of Los Angeles, and the "Peace and Love" Generation

The relationship between the 1970s and the 1960s is still being analyzed and dissected by academics and social scholars around the globe. Suffice it to say, in the worlds of popular culture and rock and roll, the differences would not become truly apparent until the 1980s.

As the '60s turned into the '70s, the world was changing fast. The idealism and community spirit of the optimistic, pot-driven '60s was to slide into a "me, me, me" ethos of a cocaine-fueled decade of indulgence and cynicism. Like blues pioneer Robert Johnson in 1930s Mississippi, Los Angeles in 1970 was at a crossroads.

Drop Out

Sure, a few would later sell their souls to the devil in return for fame and fortune, but in 1970, L.A. was still all about the myth of freedom—at least in the minds of the stream of America's youth, who headed west in search of peace, love, and understanding. Future Eagle Glenn Frey read magazine articles that talked about the free love and plenty of dope to be found in California, and he wanted a bite of this new Eden's apple. Los Angeles was rife with invention, creativity, and art. The man who put the Eagles together, record producer John Boylan, compares L.A. in the 1960s to Paris in the 1930s or New York in the 1950s. It was a time of "happenings," psychedelia, artistic and lifestyle experimentation, dramatic political change, and the peak of the American counterculture that had been brewing since the 1930s. Stars of the fine arts like David Hockney and Ed Ruscha innovated and created, giving Los Angeles a thriving and significant art scene for the first time in its history.

Turn On

The pill had changed everything, giving women power and choice they'd never enjoyed before. And the contradictions followed. "Wimmin" talked about feminism, but "chicks" still followed bands, lived the free love life, and took pride in being groupies. *The Electric Kool-Aid Acid Test* opened minds to the wonders of the universe at the same time as TV viewers faced the horrible reality of war, with the conflict in Vietnam becoming compulsive viewing on the America's TV sets.

Tune In

Television had muscled movies out of the way to become the most powerful medium of the decade. Almost every home had a set by 1970, and TV itself was in a rate of rapid change. Shows like *The Smothers Brothers Comedy Hour* brought the counterculture to a national audience, and such was the importance of music to the pop culture of the day, the biting satire of the show was backed with appearances from the biggest, most significant music acts of the period, from Buffalo Springfield to the Doors and the Who.

Musician Mason Williams headed to L.A. from Oklahoma to be part of "the scene," winding up playing folk gigs and making records before being hired by alternative comedian Tommy Smothers as head writer for his game-changing *Smothers Brothers Show*. "It was a very exciting period," Mason told me in 2013. "There hasn't been one quite like it. It was a revolution across the board. It was music, it was art, it was lifestyle, it was clothes, and in our case television."

Race, age, sex—everything was up for grabs as the youth of America found unity in rebellion and rock and roll. *The Smothers Brothers Comedy Hour*, like so much youth TV ever since, was driven by comedy and music. It just so happens that the artists involved are still revered as some of the most significant musical talents of the pop music era. L.A. in the late '60s was bursting with rock-and-roll talent, from Neil Young and Joni Mitchell to the Doors, Carole King, Love, and James Taylor.

Most of those involved in the California music scene had been inspired by the cultural whirlwind that arrived in America from Liverpool in 1964: the Beatles. The Monkees' Mike Nesmith, whose own rocket ride to fame was in a TV series about a Beatle-esque rock-and-roll band trying to make it in Hollywood, told me that in his view almost everything back then was defined by John, Paul, George, and Ringo. "It was the single most significant cultural element of the time. I was a fan; everyone was a fan. They were just so good that America fell in love."

Stills and Nash, Buffalo Springfield, Neil Young, the Doors, Love—and later, of course, the Eagles—all came into existence on the West Coast. Many formed as a direct result of the tremendous visual and musical impact that the Beatles had made in 1964.

Just like the thousands of kids who joined bands in 1977, inspired by the Ramones, the Sex Pistols, and the Clash, so in 1964 kids in America tried desperately to emulate the Fab Four. Most failed, many gave up, and none managed to truly match or even come close to the magic of Lennon and McCartney, but mid-'60s California did rock with the sound of several bands that may have copied the Beatles stylistically in the beginning but quickly developed their own musical stance and style. Sure, Beatles-influenced groups (and they were called "groups" in the mid-'60s; "bands" came later) such as the Turtles and the Leaves surfaced from the thousands of Fab Four impersonators in American garages and bedrooms, but the most significant, in terms of musical impact and style, was a group who managed to seamlessly blend folk and pop and rock: the Byrds.

Dressed like the Beatles, the Byrds combined folk and rock and roll like nobody had ever imagined, thereby uniting two sectors of music fans: the Dylan-leaning cool folkies, and the pure pop lovers who preferred the Liverpool boys.

Strip Club

In the mid-'60s, the L.A music scene was focused on the Sunset Strip, a one-and-a-half-mile section of Sunset Boulevard in West Hollywood. Michael Nesmith recalls that there seemed to be music coming from every building. It took hours to navigate the few thousand yards of the "scene," so heavy was the traffic headed out to see a selection of new music artists (Cher, the Byrds, the Turtles, and the Doors) that would forever change the shape and history of rock and roll.

David Crosby described the mid-'60s Sunset Strip to me as "the center of the music universe—it was pretty incredible. And one of the coolest things is that we kids in America were experimenting with communes and being free spirits and we weren't just preaching these idea we read or picked up somewhere, we were actually living these lives ourselves. Community was important, which is why there are so many musical connections when you

COS-103 STEREO

THE MONKEES HEADQUARTERS

COLGEMS

Michael Nesmith, pictured here (left, rear) as a member of TV pop group the Monkees, played a vital role in blending rock and roll and country music.

look back. If it looks to you that we all knew each other, it's because we probably did."

The Byrds were a significant influence on the Eagles, and indeed on all bands that arose from the Hollywood streets after the arrival of the Beatles and Dylan. Indeed, the Byrds' great success was in combining the Beatles' pop sensibilities and image with Dylan-style folk. They heralded a new kind of American rock and roll, Beatles-influenced but with a bedrock of American folk and country music that gave it a very different sound. Buffalo Springfield—the band that gave rock and roll Neil Young and Stephen Stills—took much from the Byrds and pushed the rock edge a little further. Poco, Linda Ronstadt, and the Burrito Brothers brought country music to the forefront, and up from the streets. But it wasn't their look that appealed to Henley or Frey—it was their sound.

Los Angeles was rock and roll's most exciting city, and hopefuls arrived every day from all across America wanting to play their part in the music revolution. Anything was possible, it seemed—at least for a while. They called it the Summer of Love in 1967, but before long even the ultra-positive and optimistic West Coast vibe was rocked backward by events that were the very antithesis of the hippie generation.

Manson

L.A.'s artistic community, whether rock-and-rollers or movie stars, had gravitated to the Hollywood Hills, and to Laurel Canyon in particular. It was a beautiful place: rural but still close to Hollywood. The ambience was peace and love, kaftans and sandals, sharing and caring, and making the world a better place. Singers showed up at each other's houses, passed the guitars and joints, and plotted to change the world through personal analysis and introspection.

Then, in the summer of 1969, the shocking Manson murders woke the Laurel Canyon crowd from their dream. Cult leader Manson sent a team of followers to commit multiple murders. This was shocking enough, but what was most unsettling was the fact that Manson was, ostensibly, one of them. He looked like a hippie, acted like a hippie, and was even part of the singer/songwriter rock-and-roll community. He was a friend of Terry Melcher (son of Doris Day), producer of the Byrds, the band that launched David Crosby, who would play a key role in the development of the 1970s Southern California sound, and Chris Hillman, a former friend and bandmate of Leadon's. These weren't random people from the newspaper but people from the seemingly safe and cozy community that so many embraced when they arrived in Hollywood.

Altamont

Then there was Altamont. The tragedy at the Altamont Speedway, close to San Francisco, was a significant rebuttal to the belief that rock and roll represented anything more than a celebration of youthful abandon and indulgence.

The Rolling Stones had put on a free concert, fitting with the anti-materialist vibe of the era, and a repeat of their successful show at London's Hyde Park. Some 300,000 showed up for the party, which turned into a logistical disaster. Hundreds overdosed on drugs, one kid jumped from a bridge onto a freeway after a bad acid trip, and the ultimate tragedy occurred when Hells Angels (ironically hired for security) killed an eighteen-year-old

Canyon Country Store, 2108 Laurel Canyon Boulevard. This was *the* place to hang, *the* place to be seen. Hollywood's hippie elite congregated at the Country Store, picking up supplies and catching up with rock-and-roll gossip. Regular visitors included Frank Zappa, Mama Cass, Joni Mitchell, and Jim Morrison.   *Courtesy of Elisa Jordan, Lawomantours.com*

African American from Berkeley. Check out the documentary movie of the festival, and you'll see a confused and concerned Flying Burrito Brothers, with recent hire Bernie Leadon on guitar, onstage when a series of fights erupt in the crowd below.

Altamont was not just a disastrous music event. For many, it was a very real, somewhat frightening, firsthand glimpse at a side of human nature that had been avoided or at least glossed over, during the heady days of flower power.

Bill Thompson, manager of the Jefferson Airplane, was at the festival, and believed it symbolized the end of an era. "Altamont in December 1969 seemed to signify the end of the sixties," he told Pat Thomas of Roomonetwofour.com, "symbolically as well as literally."

Kent State

Just to make sure that the '70s would indeed be defined rather differently than its predecessor, May 1970 saw one of the most unsettling events in America's youth movement. Early that month, students took to the streets at Kent State University in Ohio in response to the news that President Nixon had sent troops into Cambodia. The response from authorities was swift and forceful, with some 900 heavily armed soldiers sent to quell the rioters. Four students were killed when troops opened fire, setting off a series of campus rebellions across the nation.

Joe Walsh, who had taken time off from his studies at Kent State to tour Europe with the James Gang at the invitation of Pete Townshend and the Who, was back on campus when the shootings happened. Once again, this wasn't just social upheaval to be read about or watched on TV. Like Leadon at Altamont, future Eagle and rock-and-roll wild man Walsh was right there on the scene. He quit school for good and set about pursuing a career in rock and roll with dedication and gusto.

It's All About Me

A new psychology began to develop, in America first and around the rest of the world later. If the dream of a new cooperative, peaceful world was over, then maybe we'd better take care of ourselves in the face of violence at home and abroad. At the same time, the American economy began to suffer, with unemployment increasing and warnings of recession becoming all too common. The loud, cutting-edge Hendrix style of rock began to soften, as music became more of a "comfort food" than a tool of social change. Artists went back to nature, recalling a mythical bygone age when life was less complicated, freedom was tangible, and authority less corrupt and violent.

Aside from looking to escape the turbulence of the decade, however, Americans looked inward and become more self-centered. "It's a very selfish decade. It's all me," California politician Tom Hayden told *Newsweek*. Writer Tom Wolfe called the 1970s "The Me Decade," as he, like Hayden, noticed a shift from community to self. People needed therapists and counselors, self-help books became a boom industry, and America's youth worked on changing themselves rather than changing the world. Despite temporary economic downturns, most Americans had more cash in their pockets, real disposable income rose almost 30 percent during the decade, and the baby boomers had money to burn, or smoke and snort. Drugs became part of the consumer society.

Rock and roll came of age financially in the Eagles decade, the 1970s. In 1973, the record business was controlled by seven major corporations: CBS, Capitol PolyGram, MCA, RCA, A&M, and the top two, CBS and Warner-Elektra-Asylum-Atlantic, who between them sold over 38 percent of the music consumed in America. The record industry was now a billion-dollar business, and artists, wary of the horror stories of their predecessors winding up broke and down and out, were determined to set themselves up as very rich individuals through rock and roll.

Henley and Frey's approach to rock and roll, as they explained it to *Rolling Stone*, was more matter of fact—some may say cynical—than that of many bands in the 1960s. Henley and Frey had learned from watching peers like Poco and the Burrito Brothers fail to make the leap to the big time. The Eagles wanted critical acclaim, the respect of their fellow musicians, hit songs and albums, and fame and fortune. Frey told *Rolling Stone*'s Cameron Crowe in September 1975 that it was all about "oohs for bucks."

Won't Get Fooled Again

In exactly the same way that the Beatles were a product of their generation, with an uncanny ability to document their era, so the Eagles were a product of the period they had come of age in. Their world was part hippie, peace-and-love '60s, and part cynical '70s, where self-preservation was seen as more acceptable and certainly more important than community. They were no different from the rest of the nation's young Americans, who had felt their hopes dashed by reality checks like Altamont, Kent State, Vietnam, assassinations of leaders who promised change, a tokenistic end to racism, and serial-killer nightmares inside their own worlds.

From a music-business standpoint, Henley, Frey, Meisner, and Leadon (and later Walsh) had one very powerful element in common: they all understood the rock-and-roll *business*. They'd seen their bands break up amid acrimony and envy. Friendships they built had been busted by ego and ambition. They'd seen colleagues and peers make bad business decisions and be chewed up and spat out by the recording machine. Most of all, they recognized that in the big machinery of rock-and-roll commerce, the artists—the creators of content—were the smallest, least significant cog in the wheel. At least as far as the major corporations were concerned.

These were educated, literate rock-and-rollers, brought up as part of a generation encouraged to be self-reliant and independent. They knew all the stories of great and revered artists who found themselves homeless after making millions of dollars for agents, bookers, managers, and record companies. The Beatles' breakup played out in the newspapers and on TV. The idealistic songwriters were suddenly knee deep in litigation, sometimes fighting against themselves and dealing with management takeover bids from tough-guy negotiators like Allen Klein.

Henley, Frey, Meisner, and Leadon had read stories in the music press about Led Zeppelin's notorious manager Peter Grant battling the "suit" for his boys. They knew, as Bob Seger had explained to Glenn Frey many years before, that the real money was in songwriting and its vast publishing rewards.

One very real reason for bands' infighting is always the number of songs on an album by each writer. The main writers don't want filler material, of course, but at the same time the other guys feel they deserve a piece of the songwriting pie. It's an issue that would impact even the business-savvy Eagles nearer the end of their "original" career.

Henley, Frey, Leadon, and Meisner weren't just the topic of articles in *Billboard* and *Rolling Stone*—they were also the readers, the consumers of information about an industry that would make more money in the 1970s than any of the great acts of the '50s and '60s, including the Beatles and Elvis, could have ever imagined. It's why the Eagles' management, first David Geffen and later Irving Azoff, created an artist-comes-first, screw-the-record-company mentality. They realized that their artists knew where the power lay in the music business. Nobody would take care of the writers and singers unless they looked after themselves.

In some ways, the Eagles were no different from millions of other young Americans living through the early 1970s. They, like the rest, were products of their times; the difference was that the Eagles instinctively understood their era better than most, and had the talent, and the vehicle, to express and vocalize the very nature of the world.

7

The Sad Café

Tales from the Troubadour

The history of rock and roll is littered with eccentric characters whose actions, which usually stemmed from a deep-seated passion for music, would up playing significant parts in the story of rock and roll and popular culture. Think of the outrageous and colorful king of self-promotion, Malcolm McLaren, and his SEX shop, which gave us the Sex Pistols. How about the troubled gay son of a department-store owner in England who had failed in several businesses and was finally allowed to tend the family store's small record department? He discovered the Beatles and guided them to the very top of the pops. Or maybe the reserved and unassuming Michael Eaves, a British farmer who gave over some land for a hippie arts festival near Glastonbury in the early 1970s and found himself creating the biggest rock-and-roll event in the world.

Then there's Doug Weston, a tall, wild-haired, music-loving man, often seen in his favored green corduroy suit, hence the nickname of the Jolly Green Giant. Weston opened the Troubadour coffeehouse on La Cienega Boulevard in 1959 before quickly moving it to its current location at 9081 Santa Monica Boulevard, past North Doheny Drive and the border of Beverly Hills. He started the establishment because he'd heard there was a nice profit to be had from selling coffee to students and hipsters, and named it after the famed London folk venue the Troubadour. A few years later, Weston was running one of the most significant and influential music venues and talent-breeding grounds in the world.

Songwriter, musician, and television comedy man Mason Williams recalled how the "Troub," as the insiders called it, developed and grew into a rock-and-roll institution. Initially, it was more than just a folk club. "In 1961, when I played there, they had plays up until midnight," Williams told me. "They didn't have any folk acts until after midnight." By the time he moved to Los Angeles in 1964, it was a full-blown folk club, and had

The Troubadour was the hippest club in town for any young musician with aspirations of the singer/songwriter variety. Eccentric club owner Doug Weston ran the show, practically inventing open-mic nights, and the names of many of those who were regulars have become legendary: Neil Young, Jackson Browne, Joni Mitchell, Bonnie Raitt, Linda Ronstadt, the Eagles . . .

Courtesy of Elisa Jordan, Lawomantours.com

become a very influential place—soon to be one of the most significant music venues in California.

Pandora's Box

The rock-and-roll scene in L.A. centered on Sunset Strip, a hive of musical activity every night of the week. It was much quieter a mile south at the Troubadour. When the police tired of dealing with the teenage crowds that massed everywhere they looked, they brought in curfews and reportedly began to harass the kids and treat them way too roughly. Eventually, in the December of 1966, there was a protest at a coffee shop called Pandora's Box that turned into an unpleasant riot.

As a result of the riots, several nightclubs closed down as business waned. But when one club's doors closed, another's opened. Weston, aware that the Troubadour was located in a different police jurisdiction, with no curfews and little police harassment of young people, encouraged bands to play at his club rather than deal with Sunset Strip. That's not to say that the Strip died, but the move to Santa Monica Boulevard appealed to a certain crowd of folk-meets-singer/songwriter types who made the Troub their home.

Weston was a smart owner. The nightclub held around 300 in its main stage area, for which he booked acts and charged a cover. But at the front of the faux-Elizabethan building was a bar, with no entrance fee, that was always packed with stars and wannabes. As the Troubadour picked up through the late 1960s and into the 1970s, it was absolutely the place to go—the place to be seen and to build a career in. Musicians, groupies, photographers, and eventually forward-thinking record executives like David Geffen and Elliot Roberts spent hours drinking, chatting, and connecting at the Troubadour. At different levels of fame among the clientele were Bonnie Raitt, Joni Mitchell, Linda Ronstadt, Stephen Stills, Harry Nilsson, Mickey Dolenz, Alice Cooper, Neil Young, Carole King, James Taylor, and on and on.

The venue was even the subject of a PBS documentary in 2011, *Troubadours: Carole King / James Taylor & The Rise of the Singer-Songwriter*. In the film, King says that the country's social upheavals caused a hunger for intimacy and a demand for the kind for introspective material she and her colleagues were writing. Certainly the music industry had changed in the wake of Dylan and the Beatles. It was now presumed that artists wrote their own material; Tin Pan Alley was in decline, and singer/songwriters were all the rage. As Jackson Browne notes in the documentary, "Maybe what it was is that people who wrote their own songs were in ascendance. The authenticity of somebody telling their own story was what people were interested in."

Hootenanny

Another of Weston's bright ideas was to turn an otherwise quiet Monday night into one of the most popular evenings of the week when he started the hootenanny open-mic nights.

Before he was signed up to play a musician on a TV show, Michael Nesmith was just another out-of-town folkie who gravitated to the Troubadour and got a gig in 1965 hosting the "hoot" nights. "It was the center of the folk-music community; Linda was there, Roger McGuinn and Crosby, Neil Young, Stills," Nesmith remembered, when we talked about the impact of new music in Los Angeles back in the 1960s. "I ran the hoots for a while on Monday nights, got to play a few songs. It was coming from a folk music frame of mind. Songs were passed around; ideas were exchanged. It was very fluid and informal, and for a while it was extremely productive."

Bonnie Raitt, reminiscing with me in a London hotel suite in the late 1980s, compared the Troubadour/Laurel Canyon experience to being in college for music. "It was a very cool period of learning and creating and experimenting and meeting different kinds of people with different outlooks and different way of expressing themselves. It was remarkable, and the number of talented people who were hanging around the Troubadour is mind-blowing. It really is."

But the Troubadour did more than just provide a home for California's sensitive singer/songwriters. From the mid-1960s through to the formation of the Eagles, it played an integral role in the development of country-rock as a genre.

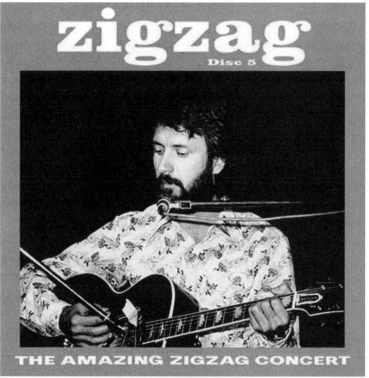

Disc 5 of *The Amazing Zigzag Concert* (a 2010 album of a 1974 performance) features a Michael Nesmith set, including "Different Drum." It was a recording of this song, which Nesmith wrote while hosting the hootenanny nights at the Troubadour, that gave Linda Ronstadt her first taste of success in 1967. Nesmith's post-Monkees country-rock records pointed the way, stylistically, for the Eagles.

Country Roads

Many of the artists who frequented the Troubadour lived in the hippie community of Laurel Canyon. It was L.A.'s rustic alternative, a maze of winding, tree-lined lanes with quaint A-frame houses. It was a center of community activities, jam sessions, poetry, art, and politics.

Perhaps the desire for natural living, and the "back to the land" trend, were a reaction to the Vietnam War and the civil rights protests of the era, a sanctuary from the conflicts and ugliness now in everyone's homes thanks to the widespread appeal of television. The fact is that rock and roll on America's West Coast went, to use a phrase from a different era, unplugged.

Graham Nash recalls that it was in Joni's house that he, David Crosby, and Stephen Stills first tried out their harmonies. Fiddles, banjos, and acoustic guitars were commonplace in Laurel Canyon. Initially, the Byrds had driven the folk-rock movement, before turning their not inconsiderable genre-bending talents to country music. With David Crosby leaving the band to work with new musical friends Nash and Stills, the Byrds invited Gram Parsons into the fold. With country-music ally Chris Hillman, who had played bluegrass with Bernie Leadon in San Diego, Parsons was able to steer the Byrds to a different sound. They didn't have much success commercially, however, as what they did was too country for rock radio and way too weird for Nashville (where they were booed at the Grand Ole Opry). But they did record a classic album, now regarded as the blueprint for all things country-rock: *Sweetheart of the Rodeo*.

Parsons was deeply passionate about country music and championed it everywhere he went. Indeed, it was Parsons who exposed Keith Richards and Mick Jagger to country music. The Byrds' album was one of those influential rather than popular records and now features in numerous artists' lists of albums that that changed their lives.

Parsons quit the Byrds after refusing to tour South Africa, and he and Hillman then formed another iconic country-rock group, the Flying Burrito Brothers, whose 1969 album *Gilded Palace of Sin* was a delightful fusion of traditional country, psychedelia, and rock and roll. Musicians loved it, and Bernie Leadon joined the band after their debut record. Sadly, it appears that Parsons' need for heroin was greater than his love of country music, and he was eventually kicked out of his own band by Hillman. Parsons lived way too fast and died way too young. He was gone at twenty-six, dead following a drug overdose in small hotel room in the desert at Joshua Tree—where, a few years later, the Eagles would shoot the artwork for their debut album.

It was then that country music began to infiltrate the mainstream. Bob Dylan changed his voice, and his music style, in 1968, when he emerged from hiding after his motorcycle accident and recorded in Nashville. The resulting *Nashville Skyline* was as shocking to rock fans as Dylan's move to electric had been to the traditional folk fans at the Newport Folk Festival back in the summer of 1965, when the young darling of the trad-folk scene brought out an electric band and proceeded to burn the hell out of his catalogue while many in the audience sighed, booed, and even called him a traitor.

Speaking of the mainstream, no group sold more records in 1967 than the Monkees—not even the Beatles or the Stones. The pop/television phenomenon's lineup contained a former Troubadour songwriter, Michael Nesmith, and slowly but surely he ushered his Texas twang into the musical mix of the show. Millions of kids across America (and the world) heard banjo and steel guitar for the first time courtesy of a Monkees episode or record.

The Troubadour played a vital role in connecting all these singers, songwriters, and country-rock dots, creating an environment that would allow first Poco and then the Eagles to really develop the genre and establish it as a genuine American art form.

8

My Man, John Boylan

Pulling the Strings

n the 1960s, rock and roll was still in its infancy. For a young record producer named John Boylan to land out west, fresh from a more constrained, stifled, and old-fashioned New York scene, it was like seeing the world in color for the very first time. The pop world had witnessed the rebellion of early rock-and-rollers like Jerry Lee Lewis, Chuck Berry, and Little Richard; it had seen Elvis take a mass-market version of music to the silver screen and fallen in love with the Beatles, who quite simply wrote the score and sang the soundtrack of the youth movement, and the new phenomenon of a generation gap, with musical originality, sheer will power, and a seemingly unconscious ability to tap into the popular consciousness.

But the music scene was still young, fresh, and idealistic, and when the word had it that L.A. was the place to be in the late 1960s, suddenly it was, and thousands of America's finest artistic talents descended on Hollywood. But that in itself did not make a movement. It was the connection of smart, savvy artists with the sense of community that pervaded the Los Angeles youth scene in the mid-1960s that gave, folk, country, and rock and roll the chance to truly breathe, grow, and create.

The tragic and ugly events that followed might have soured the optimism of the "hippie" mentality but they failed to ruin the homely, commune flavor of the singer/songwriter and folk and country scenes that spawned so many superstars, from Joni Mitchell to Neil Young, from the Byrds to Buffalo Springfield, from Linda Ronstadt and Crosby, Stills & Nash to, of course, the Eagles.

This was a musical family, with in-laws, brothers, sisters, and cousins united on some mystical and magical musical path. Some were naïve but most were not, and while the first blossom of folk and country performers may well have been too trusting, too honest, and too idealistic to really tackle the commercial machine that was the record business (even in the low-key 1960s), the second wave of talent—the Mitchells, the Ronstadts, the

Jackson Brownes, the Eagles—laced their back-to-nature, caring and sharing ideals with some financial nous and reality that would allow them to become global in scope and build lasting and solid musical legacies.

East West

It was this ambitious, self-aware world of hope that welcomed record producer John Boylan when he arrived in L.A. from New York in 1968. A novice producer, he was there to record the Association. It was just another job for Boylan, who was forging a career as an engineer and producer after the "artist" path took too many wayward zigzags.

Boylan and his brother Terry opened for hip Greenwich Village acts like the Lovin' Spoonful and James Taylor, while John's music-business career kicked off with a stint working entry-level jobs for a publisher in Tin Pan Alley, Koppelman/Rubin. One of his college pals on the music scene also made comedy videos—Chevy Chase was his name. The Boylans and Chase played in a local band that also featured a couple of musos who'd find superstar fame in the following decade: Walter Becker and Donald Fagen, or Steely Dan, as they became known around the globe.

Bard College, where Boylan and his brother went to school, was a ridiculously hip place in the late 1960s. Various Rolling Stones dropped by every now and then, while Bob Dylan often bunked in Terry Boylan's room.

From one center of cool, to another, the Boylans found themselves working with some of the most credible young musical talent in rock and roll and folk music, notably the Lovin' Spoonful and Tim Hardin. And when one of John's songs, "Suzanne on a Sunday Morning," was cut by Rick Nelson in 1967, he stepped into another blossoming and creative talent pool that would lead to his leaving New York for California and playing a vital role in the formation on the Eagles.

Catalyst

Boylan produced two Nelson albums, *Another Side of Rick* in 1967 and *Perspective* the following year. Nelson was saddled with a dated image and a TV-pretty-boy past and dearly wanted to be taken seriously as a current act. Only Elvis outsold and out-trended Ricky Nelson in the late 1950s and early 1960s. Before that, he had been a child star on the popular radio show *The Adventures of Ozzie and Harriet* from 1949. The show transferred to the powerful new medium of television in October 1952, and Nelson was

A child TV star and adolescent pop and movie star (he even appeared alongside John Wayne in one of the greatest westerns ever made, *Rio Bravo*), Ricky Nelson reinvented himself, with John Boylan's help, as a folk-meets-country stylist in the mid-'60s. Country-rock genre pioneer Michael Nesmith himself cites Nelson's version of "Hello Mary Lou," from 1961 (and featuring some killer James Burton twang guitar), as a forerunner to Los Angeles' country-rock movement of the late 1960s and early '70s.   *Photofest*

adored by the nation. He then made the crossover to pop, recording Fats Domino's "I'm Walkin'" in 1957 and becoming what would today be called a "triple threat" star.

Teen stars—especially those launched via TV—rarely have genuine musical talent. Ricky Nelson did. He played several instruments and was a keen student of pop and rock and roll—factors that would prove significant in terms of him being taken seriously when he reinvented himself in the late 1960s as a country-rock act.

Boylan's sense of the contemporary scene and Nelson's own desire to make his mark as an artist led to them ditching studio players and cherry-picking an actual backing band that would be a perfect musical fit for the hipper, more street-level Dylan-influenced sound that Nelson was dabbling with.

Soon after that, tired of pushing catalogue material for a publishing company, Boylan went independent and got a job producing an album for the Association. It was a job that would require relocating to the West Coast and a very different music scene. Boylan next worked with hip country-rock pioneers the Dillards, and it was this that cemented the New Yorker's country and folk cred around the Troubadour and Laurel Canyon scene.

Once Boylan was firmly ensconced within the L.A. scene, he discovered that the Troubadour was the "in" place to be. "There was a good music community then in Los Angeles in the late 1960s," he recalls. "Everyone used to hang around the Troubadour." Boylan and Ronstadt hit it off in the Troubadour and ended up moving in together. This precipitated a short but intense relationship, with the sophisticated and urbane Boylan becoming Ronstadt's boyfriend, manager, and record producer. The relationship soon imploded, but not before John and Linda had actively helped put the individuals who would become the Eagles together as a band.

Boylan offered to set Ronstadt up with an accomplished band of musicians for her next tour and album. He was a Randy Meisner fan, having worked with the mild-mannered singer and bass player on his Rick Nelson projects. One night, Boylan and Ronstadt were witness to a stunning rendition of a country song that Linda had made her own, "Silver Threads and Golden Needles," at the Troubadour. It was by the singer/drummer with a group called Shiloh. Ronstadt jokingly remarked to Boylan that they should get the drummer, since he already knew her material so well. The well-connected Boylan was already aware of Shiloh and Henley, who had previously passed Boylan a tape of Shiloh songs, hoping that Ronstadt might be interested in some of their original material.

Ronstadt had some gigs coming up soon, and Boylan asked Henley if he'd like to play them with her. Henley declined. He was already playing on one of the nights in question—or at least he thought he was. But Boylan knew that the gig Don was referring to had been canceled, so he continued in his attempts to persuade Henley to play with Linda. Bernie Leadon, Linda's favored guitar-picker was busy, so Boylan offered $250 a week to Glenn Frey to take the job.

Along with Ken Bloom (formerly of Lewis & Clark) on pedal steel and guitar, Casey Van Beek on drums, and Boylan himself adding some guitar, Henley and Frey headed to Washington D.C.'s Cellar Door club for the first date of the run. Henley and Frey knew each other from the Troubadour, but traveling together allowed both men to find the common ground in both music and drive to succeed that would set the pair up as the engine room of the Eagles. When Bloom left the band, one of Henley's old Shiloh pals, Michael Bowden, joined as replacement guitarist. Van Beek's replacement was the now-available Randy Meisner, whom Boylan knew and trusted from Poco and the Stone Canyon band. Three quarters of the Eagles were now playing together regularly, smoothing out the rough edges and honing an identifiable sound that would explode across America in the next couple of years.

Aside from putting together personnel for the tour, Boylan was contracted to produce Ronstadt's next album. At her instigation, he planned to go more country on the next project, and chose to record some the sessions in Muscle Shoals, Alabama. "I was producing Odetta at the time for Polydor," Boylan told me, "and I thought it would be cool to record a great roots singer at the same place that Aretha Franklin and Wilson Pickett recorded. Linda liked the sound of what Odetta and I did, and we decided to try a couple of cuts there with her."

Henley, Frey, Meisner, and Leadon all played on various sessions for Ronstadt's album, but never with all four at the same time. "All the albums I've done with Linda were recorded in different places at different times, with varying lineups," Boylan confirms. "The Eagles all played on the Capitol album [*Linda Ronstadt*], but not at the same time."

Linda Ronstadt was recorded in Hollywood and Alabama and included several live tracks. Despite the record featuring some sterling material from new writers like Jackson Browne and Eric Anderson, however, Ronstadt herself sounded too traditional—too country & western, perhaps—for mainstream radio, and the album sold poorly. But the live cuts recorded at the Troubadour give a fascinating glimpse into the state of country-rock, as it was in the safe in the hands of Linda Ronstadt and the future Eagles circa 1971–1972. "It was a remarkable series of events," Boylan told me in 2009. "They all played at Disneyland for the first time, and that gig was the first of a number of shows. After that they did at least one other gig [in Chicago] that I remember—maybe more. It's been a while!"

9

Eagles

Getting Mystical, Naming Rites, and the Beginnings of the Band

Glenn Frey and Don Henley roomed together on the D.C. trip with Linda Ronstadt in spring 1971. It was the start of the partnership that would drive them to achieve the kind of success and acceptance that both had been aching for since leaving their hometowns. They had both felt like big fish in small ponds, and they shared a thirst for discovering new kinds of music, as well as for learning the business skills necessary to survive in what they recognized was an uncompromising industry.

They were complete opposites in character—Henley intense and serious, Frey more affable and outgoing—but they shared an inner toughness and worldview. Many who hung around the Troubadour loved the vibe, but Henley and Frey both picked up on a dark desperation—a tangible melancholy that Henley would express most poetically years later in the song "Sad Café."

Jackson Browne had touted his buddy Glenn to manager David Geffen. Just to get an audience with Geffen was a big deal, so busy was he with his superstar acts. But however business-focused Geffen was, he never lost his core-level love of music. It's the indefinable, intangible that made Geffen's management different. Sure, he was tough, but was more than just an end-justifies-the-means operator. Geffen had an artist's soul—an instinctive ability to "get it." He liked Frey and admired his ambition but didn't think he had the necessary personality or skills to be a solo act. Geffen told him he needed to be in a band.

This was insightful advice indeed for a headstrong young Detroit transplant who lived his life like he was on a sports team, with pep talks, meetings, and lots of practice sessions. Frey was a natural team player, and Geffen knew it. Somewhat dejected by the advice at first, having taken it as a slight, Frey nonetheless determined to take Geffen up on his recommendation and build himself a band.

Money Talks

Don Henley had seen Al Perkins give up on Shiloh and go up a division by joining the Flying Burrito Brothers, and was himself ready for a change and a challenge. The more Henley and Frey shared their frustrations and discussed their hopes and dreams, the more they realized that despite the external differences, they were indeed very similar people.

Neither wanted to lose. They couldn't understand the mentality of rock-and-roll failure, of the glory of being a neglected and ignored cult act. Like the Beatles before them, they aimed high, determined to show the world that a country-influenced rock-and-roll band could be commercially successful as well as critically cool.

The Ronstadt tour brought the idea of a band to reality. On July 12, 1971, Frey and Henley were joined onstage behind Linda Ronstadt by Randy Meisner and Bernie Leadon. Here was the dream team. Two hungry kids—determined, ambitious, and talented—who had moved to L.A. to make their mark joined by country-rock royalty in the shape of the ex-Poco and Stone Canyon Band bass player who sweated cool and the master guitarist who by 1971 was an intrinsic part of the authentic country-rock, folk, and bluegrass community in California.

The four men began to rehearse at Studio Instrument Rentals, and everything clicked nicely into place. Linda Ronstadt let them rehearse vocal parts one afternoon in her house on Camrose Place while she was out. When she came back she saw the four musicians sitting with acoustic guitars working on the harmonies that would become their trademark. The song was "Witchy Woman," and Ronstadt knew they had everything they needed. She wished them well. John David Souther sat in on a few jam sessions and realized that the four original Eagles had a country-rock blend that was as authentic as anything Gram Parsons or Poco had done.

This new four-piece was unusually melodic, with a built-in, almost organic sense of commercialism. They had all the ingredients necessary to succeed. On top of that, they had Geffen, who Frey figured would be impressed by this lineup. Geffen had told him to find a band, and find a band he had.

Of course, when the four musicians did meet with Geffen in his fancy offices, all three future Eagles deferred to the experienced and somewhat "direct" Leadon, allowing him to make the pitch. Leadon was clearly as confident as Frey, asking Geffen straight out whether he wanted to manage the band or not. He did.

Name Game

Every band needs a name. Teen King & the Emergencies—an early suggestion based around a name Frey called himself back in Detroit—was never
going to fly. Nor was the Saltines, or the Small Frey Dance Band. At the time,
Carlos Castaneda–style mysticism was all the rage, and Leadon and Henley
fancied some kind of mystic connotation. Frey also wanted something direct
and sporty for his "street-fighting man" personality. Eagles fitted the bill.
Short, sharp, and filled with mysticism.

Henley felt the name should be very American but also go against the
trend of weird and wacky names. He told the BBC's John Tobler in 1977 that
they wanted "something American and we wanted something that was easy
to remember and something with a little spiritual value. Somebody—I think
Glenn—was reading some book about Hopi mythology. Also it sounded very
American, football teams and street gangs."

Initially, they were simply *Eagles*, not *the* Eagles. It was Frey's idea. In a
feature about the new band in September 1973, for *Zoo World* magazine,
journalist Cameron Crowe began a question by referring to the band, as
Frey preferred, as just Eagles—"Eagles played a lot or new material . . ."—but
then Frey, the man whose idea it was to drop the "the," replied, "I guess
you'd say the Eagles were the ones."

Actor, comedian, and bluegrass banjo player Steve Martin was a
Troubadour cohort of Frey and Henley, and recalls Frey taking about his new
band's name one night in the club in his autobiography, *Born Standing Up*.
"One night I was lingering at the bar and talking to Glenn Frey. . . . He said
he was considering a name for his new five-man group. 'What is it?' I said.
He said, 'Eagles.' I said, 'You mean, the Eagles?' and he said, 'No, Eagles.'"

The official name of the group remains, of course, Eagles. As the always-
eloquent Martin implies, Eagles without the definite article does sound a
little odd. They have retained that name, officially, but despite what it says
on various album covers and posters and the like, the band members do
typically say "*the* Eagles." Even in the *Zoo World* article, Frey stated, "I'm not
gonna do a solo album, just play with the Eagles and look for people to write
songs with." Steve Martin would like that.

Eagles Take Flight

Geffen put the Eagles on a $200-a-week salary each and sent them off to
Colorado to rehearse. Away from the pressures of Hollywood and the distractions of friends and lovers, the four Eagles could work up material,

The cover of the 2003 greatest-hits collection *The Very Best Of* gives the band's original name "Eagles" and not the more familiar "The Eagles." The album includes a fascinating Cameron Crowe interview with Henley and Frey in the accompanying booklet.

develop an understanding, and prepare for the big time. They were all young enough to have the necessary drive to climb to the top but they had also seen enough of the ugly side of the business to be nothing but professional and workmanlike. As Bernie Leadon told *Uncut* magazine in April 2013, "When we got together we defined our business plan: we wanted to be successful, world famous, acclaimed and rich. One of the first things (Glenn) Frey said was, 'OK, let's keep this simple, No Christmas cards.' Did we go on holiday and call each other? No."

10

Born to Boogie

Linda Ronstadt Launches the Band to Stardom

W hen Linda Ronstadt was inducted into the Rock and Roll Hall of Fame in 2014, she was too sick from Parkinson's disease to attend. But her old friend Glenn Frey was on hand to accept the honor on her behalf and give the induction speech, in which he said, "I first met Linda in 1970 at the Troubadour bar. For my part, it was love at first sight. There was just one problem: a guitar-slinging, love-rustler from Amarillo, Texas, named John David Souther. He beat me to the punch, which would become a pattern throughout our careers—thank God he never met my wife."

Father of Chicano

Alongside the Eagles, Linda Ronstadt owned the country-rock airwaves throughout the 1970s and into the 1980s. Later, she would move into theater and Mexican music, rediscovering the musical culture of her childhood.

Tucson, Arizona, is a Southwest town where America's western style blends so colorfully with Native American and Mexican culture and heritage. The Ronstadt family had played a significant role in its industrial and musical development. Linda's father, Gilbert, ran a local hardware store that had been started by her grandfather. Gilbert, like his own father, was a singer, and Gil Ronstadt & His Star-Spangled Megaphone often played the Fox Tucson Theater. He was well connected in the music scene, and even managed one year to wake Linda for her birthday song with his good friend Lalo Guerrero, one of the great Latin singers of all time, and a man often called the Father of Chicano.

Artist bios are filled with stories of people growing up around music and singing as soon as they could walk. Often this is gentle exaggeration, sometimes just rose-tinted nostalgia, but in Linda Ronstadt's case she really

LINDA RONSTADT

Producer John Boylan assembled a stellar crew to play on Linda Ronstadt's self-titled release in 1972. All the future Eagles played on the album, either live or in the studio. The album was a commercial disaster, reaching a sad #163 on the *Billboard* chart, and its failure led to Ronstadt moving from Capitol Records to David Geffen's new Asylum army.

was born to sing. He older brother Pete sang folk music in Tucson's coffee-houses, and Linda followed suit as soon as she could. Initially she just sang harmony, but as her confidence grew she found her own voice, discovered a love of both music and performing, and chose to take it very seriously.

Linda sang all the time at home, raised as she was in a house that had no television until she was eleven years old. She found school too formal and strict and preferred instead to self-educate by reading the books she loved rather than those imposed by authoritarian teachers. No wonder, then, that she quit the University of Arizona after a couple of months, grabbed the 1898 Martin acoustic guitar that had belonged to her grandfather, and headed to the West Coast, eventually hooking up with some musician friends who'd already made the move to California.

Ronstadt already knew singer Bobby Kimmel, who was working with Kenny Edwards in L.A. They formed what was essentially a classic folk trio with Kenny on a mandolin, Bobby on guitar, and Linda on harmonies. They

The front cover of Linda Ronstadt's 1973 career-making album, *Don't Cry Now*. Not only did the part–John Boylan, part–Pete Asher production give her a hit record with her take on the country classic "Silver Threads and Golden Needles," it also led to her being picked as the opening act for Neil Young's *Time Fades Away* tour. She'd never look back.

called themselves the Stone Poneys, after bluesman Charley Patton's "Stone Poney Blues."

In the days before sexual liberation, Ronstadt at first took a back seat to her male bandmates, but she slowly became confident enough to seek out material with which to convince others. The group became a very popular live act, with Linda, in mini-skirts and bare feet, getting more than her fair share of record-company attention. Some tried to turn her into a solo act, but Ronstadt stayed loyal to her group. Capitol Records took advantage of the group's local popularity and made a couple of very folky and folk-meets-pop albums, the second of which included a song that would launch the group to stardom but also kill them off.

Monkee Business

That song came from the imagination of Michael Nesmith (in the days before both the Monkees and his pioneering country-rock combo the First National Band), who was embarking on his own Los Angeles adventure, having moved out to California from Texas with his wife and baby son in 1965. Before Nesmith donned a green woolen hat and acted goofy for twenty-seven or so minutes every week as one of television's Monkees, he was a folk singer with a country-music twang who found composing easier than most did and made his initial foray into the serious biz at the Troubadour.

"I hosted the Monday night hoots for a while, before the TV show," he recalled. "It was this incredible talent pool with some highly creative and highly evolved artists in their formative years. I was just one of many trying their luck. Back then, in the folk world you traded songs. I'd play a new song to somebody and they'd play one of theirs. If you liked a song you'd probably learn it. That's just how it worked in the folk scene."

One of those songs was "Different Drum." Nesmith played it fast and direct—very different from the Ronstadt and Stone Poneys version that would eventually make it to the radio. John Herald of the Greenbrier Boys, a bluegrass band, loved the song, too, and recorded a bluegrass-style version of it.

It was this version that Ronstadt had in mind when the Stone Poneys recorded their take on Nesmith's ode to leaving with producer Nick Venet. Surprisingly—at least for the band—Venet completely changed the bluegrass arrangement, adding a harpsichord part and using top L.A. session players. Of the Stone Poneys trio, only Linda appeared on the finished single. Nonetheless, the band's version of "Different Drum" hit the *Billboard* Pop chart on November 11, 1967, and stayed there for a long seventeen weeks, climbing as high as #13.

Flying Solo

The single's success spelled the beginning of the end. Capitol was determined to market the group as Linda plus backing band, and while work continued on a follow-up album, Edwards decided he'd had enough and left for India. Kimmel and Ronstadt kept the Stone Poneys name going, even touring with the Doors, but a solo career was too obvious to put off, and *Hand Sown, Home Grown*, Ronstadt's first solo LP, appeared in 1969. The record didn't make too much noise in the charts but did boost Linda's national profile. Touring and TV appearances clearly helped, too, but finding the right musicians was always a challenge.

Ronstadt knew plenty of musicians, and many were thrilled to work for her, even if they did find it tough taking direction from a "chick." Chris Darrow and Jeff Hanna had quit the Nitty Gritty Dirt Band for a while in 1969 and formed their own outfit, the Corvettes. Mike Nesmith was under contact with Screen Gems as an artist at the time but was free to work as a record producer. He recorded a couple of singles for the Corvettes that came out on Dot Records. The Corvettes played beautifully, and Ronstadt brought them in as her backing band on several tours. She gave them the utmost respect and allowed them their own slot as the Corvettes on every show.

Eventually, Jeff Hanna returned to the Dirt Band, and was replaced for a few shows by Ronstadt's old friend and favorite twangy guitarist, Bernie Leadon. Keeping bands together was extremely difficult in the very fluid live scene in Hollywood. Leadon left to play with the Flying Burrito Brothers, while bass player John London and drummer John Ware became integral parts of Nesmith's groundbreaking First National Band.

It was the never-ending search for great band members that led Linda Ronstadt to Don Henley and Glenn Frey. She saw Henley singing one of her favorite songs, "Silver Threads and Golden Needles," at the Troubadour one night with Shiloh, and was immediately struck by how good they were.

Frey was already part of Ronstadt's inner circle, as Ronstadt told *Goldmine* in February 2014. "Glenn was my friend. He was the singing partner of J. D. Souther, who was my boyfriend at the time, and I was living with J. D. So I introduced Glenn to Don, and they started working together."

King of Hollywood

Meet the Shark

I t wasn't just hopeful singer/songwriters, bluegrass pickers, Beatles obsessives, poets, and vocalists who descended on the Troubadour scene. The small but hugely influential club also attracted another brand of young, hip music fan looking for a career in the business, inspired by the voice of creativity and change that was so tangible in Hollywood as the 1960s became the 1970s.

David Geffen would grow into one of the most powerful and feared entertainment executives in the modern showbiz era, but in Los Angeles in the early '60s he was another Beatle-struck fan looking for an angle, searching for a way to join the rock-and-roll revolution that was bubbling under on the West Coast.

There was a power shift on the horizon when the New York–raised Geffen first came to California. New York was traditionally the home of the record industry, its publishing companies, and their famed Tin Pan Alley. L.A. was a slightly wacky showbiz cousin, as far as New York was concerned, with more emphasis on movies than music. It had its uses, naturally, but it was hardly a vital sector of the business.

This would change, of course, when bands like Crosby, Stills, Nash & Young and the Eagles became artistic and economic powerhouses from a home base in Hollywood. Geffen didn't cause the change, but he recognized the signs, saw the opportunity to impact the business, and acted always with a ruthlessness and speed that would prove the secret weapon in the hands of the "change the world" musicians who preached hippie values while banking millions of dollars.

King David

Raised for greatness in Brooklyn by a mother who called him "King David," Geffen was scrawny and, in noughties parlance, a bit nerdy. He was never going to be the quarterback or the lead singer. What Geffen had was determination and a set of street smarts that saw him rise rapidly through the entertainment agency business, understanding very well that sometimes corners need to be cut and stories might be somewhat embellished for the common good—initially his own.

Geffen's first dealing with the Ashley–Famous Agency taught him well. He told David A. Kaplan of *Fortune* magazine in July 2013 that he had learned to be dishonest from the very beginning, when agency owner Al Ashley mocked him for not embellishing his resume and turned him down for a job. Geffen remembered that and was determined not to be embarrassed again. When "King David" applied for a job at William Morris, he took Ashley's advice and told them he had graduated from UCLA. Panicked when he heard that a colleague at William Morris was let go for resume fabrication, Geffen took action with a move that would provide a blueprint for his business dealing over the next several decades.

"I came in early every day for six months till I intercepted the letter from UCLA saying they'd never heard of me," he told *Fortune*. "I replaced it with a letter that said I'd graduated. . . . Did I have a problem with lying to get the job? None whatsoever."

It was a practical solution—a deviously simple solution—and one that took a good deal of graft and bloody-minded nerve to pull off. And it worked. Geffen rose through the ranks, forged a partnership with another young agent, Elliot Roberts, and figured that rather than muscling in on established, older acts, he and Roberts should go with what they knew. And young, hungry, talented rock-and-rollers fit the bill perfectly.

Laura Nyro

Starting with oddball singer/songwriter Laura Nyro, Geffen and Roberts set up shop on Sunset Boulevard in Los Angeles, convinced that they could do as well as anyone else—probably better—on promoting the new talent they'd sensed was flowering on the streets of Hollywood. After all, he'd learned another significant lesson at William Morris. "The epiphany for me at William Morris was realizing, 'They bullshit on the phone! I can bullshit on the phone too!'" he told *Fortune*.

Instinctively, Geffen understood the artistic mind-set. Some agents and managers operate as field generals, dictating the artistic journey, zigzagging the minefields of the entertainment business but with a didactic voice. Some artists respond well to being treated like kids, groomed and directed at every

Gonna take a miracle
Laura nyro and Labelle

Geffen launched his music biz career with singer/songwriter Laura Nyro. He signed her after she played Monterey Pop in '67, made millions from her song publishing, and planned on making her his first signing to his own Asylum Records. She chose another company instead and, tough guy that he was, according to his memoirs Geffen was heartbroken.

step. Others—especially the younger element, smoking weed, watching the Beatles' revolution, and dropping out of conventional America—needed a different approach. When David Geffen saw Nyro struggle for acceptance at the Monterey Pop festival in 1967, he took her aside, bonded with her fragile, artistic self, and became her partner in the journey, rather than her "boss."

Crosby, Stills, Nash & Young

Elliot Roberts, meanwhile, had been close to David Crosby for a while when the Byrds started to implode. He offered to manage Crosby—already one of the more flamboyant and magnetic characters in the Hollywood music world. Geffen and Roberts hatched a plan to bring Crosby and some

David Geffen, seen here in 1972, not only played a huge role in launching the Eagles; his approach to the music business also changed rock and roll forever.   *Photo by Michael Putland/Getty Images*

key members of the Troubadour scene into their new family operating at 9126 Sunset.

Geffen and Roberts targeted Stephen Stills and Graham Nash (from British band the Hollies) and Neil Young. They got them all. From 1969 to 1971, CSN ruled the folk roost with the supergroup template working on debut album *Crosby, Stills & Nash* and even more so when they added Stills' old Buffalo Springfield colleague Neil Young for *Déjà Vu*. The group(s) epitomized the free-flowing flower-power era and offered the perfect American response to *Sgt. Pepper* and "All You Need Is Love" as the kaftan-and-sandals crowd spread and grew by millions, first in the U.S. and then around the world.

Geffen and Roberts had taken a disparate group of musical talents, all well known in their various circles, and melded them into a genuine rock-and-roll powerhouse. The only thing messing with the formula was the explosive personal dynamic between the band members. But what Geffen brought to the table—aside from doing outrageous business deals in his artists' favor with record companies and booking agents—was a management model that combined the "us against the world" siege mentality with a ruthless good cop/bad cop negotiation style that allowed the artistic souls the freedom to espouse, evoke, and express the beauty of communal living and loving and the need for peace and love in the world, all while bulldog Geffen made them financially secure for life. It was the perfect music-biz storm—at least for a while.

Crosby would later refer to Geffen as a shark, but he told me in 1989 that the man was a genius when it came to protecting the artists. "He was on our side, he made that clear from the start and the other thing that endeared him to us back then was that he really, truly loved music. He was one of us, in many ways, but with the tough business skills that none of the musicians wanted to deal with or even cared about."

Crosby had a feeling that a young writer he'd heard might just have what it would take to make it to the very top. Crosby told Jackson Browne that Geffen was the kind of manager he needed to succeed and the young writer sent a demo tape and a black-and-white photo to Geffen's office. It was probably the striking photo that persuaded Geffen's secretary to give the songs a listen. When she did, it was an easy decision. The songs were wonderful: different but definitely of their time.

Granted Asylum

Geffen went to Atlantic Records and urged Ahmet Ertegün to sign Browne. Unconvinced, Ertegün declined. When Geffen pushed harder, Ertegün protested. He suggested Geffen start his own label and sign Jackson himself. Geffen decided he would do just that, if only to prove how shortsighted his mentor had been in turning down Browne. But Ertegün did more than encourage his disciple. He offered to go in 50/50 with Geffen in the label—for now to be called either Benchmark or Phoenix—with Atlantic handling distribution and covering all expenses.

Essentially, Geffen received a brand new record label without spending a penny. "It was an astonishing deal that would not cost Geffen a cent," his biographer, Tom King, later wrote. The label would be called Asylum Records, the name reflecting the artist oasis philosophy of Geffen's business style that would warm those talents he signed and nurtured.

Working with a fresh, eager artist with serious talent would probably be more rewarding than dealing with the internal personality clashes within CSNY, Geffen reasoned, so he set about launching Browne on the world. Browne's debut album was *Jackson Browne* (often erroneously called *Saturate Before Using*, thanks to that phrase appearing on the cover) and included some of his best songs, like "Doctor My Eyes" (which went Top 10), "Rock Me on the Water," and "Jamaica Say You Will." The press heralded the album; *Rolling Stone* loved it, while *Circus*' Ed Kelleher stated, "Browne is his own best interpreter. He just eases back and lets the song come. He has the soul of a poet and the stance of a troubadour. Unlike many of his contemporaries, he has not fallen victim to the trap of overproduction—the record has been crafted with care and purity."

In early 1972, Geffen sent Browne on the road with Joni Mitchell. A star was born—a star who used his status to help further the careers of his Troubadour friends, especially Glenn Frey and Don Henley.

12

London Calling

Foggy England, Shepherd's Pie, and the Who's Producer, Glyn Johns

Who'd have imagined that a band that—more than anyone bar the Beach Boys—came to represent the ethos and lifestyle of sunny California actually cut their breakthrough tracks not in Hollywood but in London, England? It wasn't the strawberries-and-cream London of Wimbledon in June, either, but a damp gray stay in the middle of winter 1972.

The reason was simple. David Geffen's belief in his Eagles was such that he offered them the best and, being David Geffen, usually made the impossible happen. He needed an experienced record producer used to working with top musicians, and in the early '70s, British engineer and producer Glyn Johns was rightly regarded as one of the very best record-makers in the business.

Who's Next, Glyn Johns

Johns hailed from the same town as Jimmy Page in leafy Surrey in southern England (later claiming to have been in a local band with Page for all of five minutes). He was initially mentored by Kinks producer Shel Talmy (engineering the hits "You Really Got Me" and "All Day and All of the Night," among others), before working his way up from freelance engineer to producer through the 1960s. He worked on some very significant records, engineering the Small Faces' *Ogdens' Nut Gone Flake* and doing the same for the Rolling Stones' *Beggars Banquet* while also working with the Yardbirds on the tracks that eventually became Led Zeppelin's debut earth-shatterer. He recorded rock and roll's royalty, doing the live tracks for the Beatles' *Let It Be* sessions (later finished by Phil Spector) and eventually finding his production peak with the Who's *Who's Next* in 1971.

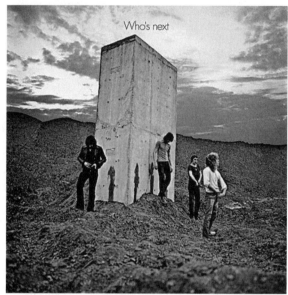

Who's next

Determined to rock out with the best, the Eagles were delighted to work with Glyn Johns, a man who had played a key role in producing the Who's loud and punchy *Who's Next*.

Henley was excited that Geffen intended to set the band up with a producer the drummer regarded as the best in the world. Leadon, who had more studio and recording experience that any of his bandmates, was delighted, and expressed his enthusiasm to U.K. music bible the *New Musical Express*: "We all wanted to record in London ever since we heard those early Beatles and Stones records—the mystique of British rock!"

Way Out West

Geffen was astute enough to realize that Glyn Johns could be key to making the Eagles project work. He also knew that Johns was much in demand. Geffen coughed up the cash to bring the British producer over to Colorado from England to see the fledgling Eagles in action.

Geffen had spent well over $10,000 on sound equipment for the Eagles and told them to become a bona-fide musical unit, sending Meisner, Frey, Henley, and Leadon to Aspen, Colorado, where they worked out their initial musical kinks by playing for several weeks in a little club called the Gallery.

David Geffen planned on charming his chosen A-list producer and genuinely believed that having Johns see the band in their own musical comfort zone would be best for Henley & co., such was their natural ease and musical chemistry onstage. The idea backfired, however, and Johns—who had no reason to lie, since he hardly needed the gig—told Geffen that he was wasn't especially moved by the new band's live performances and headed back to the U.K. unconvinced.

As ever, Geffen refused to give up, and next time around he invited Johns to see the band in an L.A. rehearsal studio. This time Johns got it, as he witnessed the close harmonies, the natural blend of voices and styles, and the pure musicality of the individual Eagles.

"They were trying to be a rock 'n' roll band but they couldn't play it to save their lives," Johns told *Uncut* in 2011, describing his first impressions of the band. "Their set was OK, but as we were about to take a break somebody said, 'Hold on, why don't we play that ballad Randy has written?' They picked up acoustic guitars, stood around the piano, and played 'Take the Devil,' with the four of them singing. And that was it. Astonishing."

Geffen got his man, but with the stipulation that they record in Johns' hometown, London.

London Town

The Eagles' initial excitement about working in London was short-lived once the band, used to the sunny California lifestyle, touched down in a freezing February 1972. Cold, gloomy London wasn't exactly what the California boys had in mind, but it was what the producer had ordered. "He pretty much insisted," Henley told John Tobler in 1977, "because he wanted to use the studio over here [London] because of the equipment. We thought well, we'll get to see London and get away from Los Angeles and all its distractions, with the phone ringing and people coming in to the studio and bothering us and stuff. And we were left alone because we didn't know anybody and it was miserable."

Not only was England in February cold and dreary, foggy and wet, but the nation was in serious conflict in several key economic and political areas. Britain was in the midst of conflict with the Irish Republican Army in Northern Ireland—a conflict that had spread over to British soil when an IRA bomb killed five women and a priest at the 16th Parachute army barracks in Aldershot, Hampshire. More despair followed that winter, with a miner's strike.

As the Americans settled in to life in London, Marc Bolan's T.Rex went to #1 on the pop singles chart in Britain, Paul McCartney initiated a very low-key college tour with his new band Wings, and the country was plunged into darkness with regular power outages that lasted up to nine hours at a time—and which event affected the studios where Johns plied his trade. To deal with the crisis, the U.K. government tried to keep the country running by instituting a three-day business week in an attempt to conserve precious energy.

Olympic Medals

Frey, Henley, Meisner, and Leadon recognized that Britain was undergoing a temporary economic and social crisis, but what they found more irksome and somewhat frustrating was the confining and limiting nature of England's many antiquated customs and laws. While they delighted in joining the exalted company of so many rock legends who had used Olympic Studios' state-of-the-art facilities—the Rolling Stones, the Faces, the Beatles, and even Jimi Hendrix among them—the location was less than ideal. Olympic was in the 'burbs. Barnes was, and is, a leafy, well-to-do suburb some six miles west of London's cultural heartbeat, the West End.

Frey did take a shine to Guinness ale and British food staples like shepherd's pie, but the rigid pub hours, extraordinarily limited TV channels (only three at the time, all of which went off the air before midnight), and overall staid and old-fashioned vibe proved a terrible culture shock for four hip dudes from the sun-drenched entertainment center of America.

The foursome lived in a rented flat (or apartment, as they might have called it) where they did little but drink tequila to pass the time between being driven to and from recording sessions. No wonder tensions began to surface, especially when the initially starstruck musicians discovered that the man who produced the Who, the Kinks, the Beatles, the Stones, and Zeppelin was himself not very "rock and roll." Johns took his job extremely seriously, exerting total control over the recordings, and laid down the law about musicians' behavior in his studio.

Henley felt that Johns was unnecessarily dictatorial, later telling *Musician* magazine, "He was a complete tyrant. I'm still friends with him, but we were really young and green, and he just lorded over us, man." According to Henley, Johns would give the group three shots at laying down a track or vocal, and no more.

"Peaceful Easy Feeling"

And if that wasn't enough for the tequila- and dope-loving Eagles, Johns operated a strict no drugs policy and became increasingly irritated by the band's frequent "smoke" breaks. "I remember Johns didn't like dope, so we'd have to sneak off to the bathroom to do dope," Henley told *Musician* magazine's Mitchell Glazer.

Most frustrating for Henley & co., however, was the dawning realization that their top-drawer producer—a man with more heavy-rock credibility than anyone in the recording biz in 1972—didn't see the Eagles as a rock-and-roll band at all. For a man raised on loud, raw British rock, à la Zeppelin and the Who, the Eagles were lightweight soft rock at best.

As Henley told *Musician*, "Glyn had an image of us as a ballad group; he didn't want us to be rock 'n' roll and he didn't think we could play rock 'n' roll, and he'd engineered the Stones on LPs like *Exile on Main Street*, so who the hell were we to be wanting to play rock 'n' roll?"

But what they did have was an uncanny ability to sing harmonies and play some of the best country-meets-rock Johns had ever heard. "I tried to introduce more of that acoustic sound and concentrate on vocal blend and arrangements," Johns told *Uncut* in 2011, citing Bernie Leadon's double-time banjo on "Take It Easy" as an example.

Despite the martinet approach and Johns' failure to recognize the Eagles as a rock-and-roll band, Henley had, by 1975, begun to appreciate some of the legendary producer's vision and direction for the group. "Glyn made us very aware of all the little personal trips within the band," he told Cameron Crowe, for *Rolling Stone*. "He'd just stare at you with his big, strong, burning blue eyes and confront you with the man-to-man talk. You couldn't help but get emotional. We even cried a couple times."

The Eagles' first recording sojourn in Britain was brief. But since there was little to do besides rehearse and record, the two weeks they spent living and working near England's capital city were enough to complete the quite remarkable tracks that would become their groundbreaking self-titled debut album.

The album's first single, "Take It Easy," with its snappy country guitar licks and lilting harmonies, conjures up delightful images of a sun drenched, laid-back Hollywood lifestyle. Few could have imagined that the song was recorded in cold, gloomy London, and in circumstances far removed from the easy-going California vibe the band were singing about.

13

Take It Easy

Eagles Take Off

If Henley and Frey had intended to take the best of Poco and the Flying Burrito Brothers and blend it into a new, dynamic sound for the 1970s, they achieved their goals with the Eagles' terrific self-titled debut album in 1972.

Despite their rapid formation and the quick recording of this debut, it is amazingly polished and has a remarkable level of pop sensibility. *Eagles* spawned three Top 40 hit singles, all which remain very popular to this day, while much of the rest of the album contains well-constructed songs with incredible vocal harmonies by all four band members.

Eagles kicks off the with new group's first single, "Take It Easy," a simple and infectious medium-paced country-rocker written in the main by band pal Jackson Browne with help from Glenn Frey and released on May 1, a month ahead of the album. Bud Scoppa, writing for *Rolling Stone*, called it "simply the best sounding rock single to come out so far this year."

In August 2010, Browne told *Uncut* magazine that the song came to him during a studio break from the sessions for his own album. "I took a road trip in this old beat-up Willis Jeep and I went to Utah and Arizona. On that trip I started to write 'Take It Easy,' and when I came back, I played it for Glenn Frey, and he asked if the Eagles could cut it when it was done. So I said, 'Just finish it,' and he wrote the last verse and turned it into a real song. It was their first single, and what those guys did with it was incredible."

The single set the tone for the rest of the album—and, indeed, for the rest of the Eagles' 1970s output. It's well crafted and immaculately produced, with plenty of instrumental dexterity (in this case Leadon's effortless lead guitar twangery and banjo master class) dovetailing with a blend of vocal harmonies of the quality not heard since the golden age of the Beach Boys and the Hollies, or maybe early CSNY.

The Eagles' debut album appeared in 1972 and contained three Top 40 singles: "Take It Easy," "Witchy Woman," and "Peaceful Easy Feeling." This laid-back, mellow fusion of all the best parts of Los Angeles' country-rock scene launched the Eagles with two key elements that would remain constant over the decades: superb musicianship and radio-friendly hit songs.

Leadon's Wizardry

The second single, "Witchy Woman," follows "Take It Easy" in the album's running order, and while not quite as catchy as Browne's lilting classic, Leadon's finest writing moment—one that dates back to his days with the Flying Burrito Brothers—is a solid track that has grown into one of the group's most popular and beloved songs over the years. It's a magnificent slice of Americana mysticism wrapped around an insistent Leadon guitar riff that's as heavy as the Eagles get.

With Leadon's instinctive melodic sense in full flow, balancing melodic guitar lines spin around in the mix, giving the track an immediate identity. Henley's lyrics significantly show the seeds of the deft wordplay and intelligent comment that would eventually make him one of American pop music's finest social observers. His words came to him in the midst of a fever, as he would later reveal in the liner notes to the band's 2001 compilation *The Very Best of the Eagles*. Don Henley remembered being somewhat delirious at the time. He was reading a book about Zelda Fitzgerald while he was in his sickbed, and that book, combined with his own memories of days at the clubs in L.A., were fired by the fever into some quite remarkable lyrics. And if Frey's vocals were infectious and disarming on "Take It Easy," Henley's are moody and magnificent on Leadon's offbeat tune.

The next single, "Peaceful Easy Feeling," wasn't penned by an Eagle at all. Jack Tempchin, an old pal of Frey's, wrote it. It's very much in the "Take It Easy" groove, with plenty of country-flavor vocals, country lyrics, and a solid rock-and-roll beat that drives it on to becoming the perfect summer song. It was the band's third Top 40 smash, reaching as high as the #22 spot.

The rest of the album is strong, too, with blistering guitar from Leadon on Frey's "Chug All Night," typically lonesome Meisner vocals on "Most of Us Are Sad," and more of Jackson Browne's optimistic whimsy on "Nightingale," while Leadon shows more of his beloved folky, country, Byrds-meets-Burritos style on a mellow but hypnotic ballad co-written with ex-Byrd Gene Clark, "Train Leaves Here This Morning."

Bud Scoppa of *Rolling Stone* magazine was impressed, recommending readers snap up a copy and placing it "right behind Jackson Browne's record as the best first album this year. And I could be persuaded to remove the word 'first' from that statement."

Branded

The album hit the stores in the summer of 1972 (June 1 in the United States) on the back of some tried and tested record-business promotion and marketing. Geffen and the band wanted to market the Eagles correctly. Just like the Beatles and the Stones in the '60s, a good band needed an image, a brand to set them apart from the competition. Drawing on the American feel of the band's name and interest in the Wild West (*Desperado*'s outlaw theme was gestating long before they recorded the album), Geffen hired top album designer Gary Burden and his photographer of choice Henry Diltz to set the visual tone.

For Burden, the desert was a magical place. In August 2011, he described his love of the desert to NationalParksTraveler.com: "It was so powerful and beautiful I wanted to immerse myself in it. I was intrigued by the stories of Cabeza de Vaca, the sixteenth century Spanish conquistador who got separated from his troops and wandered across the desert alone for six years. He made it out and was a hero."

Diltz and Burden had been responsible for the striking artwork for Jackson Browne's debut album, plus LP covers for Crosby, Stills & Nash, Neil Young, the Mamas & the Papas, and the Doors' *Morrison Hotel*. Diltz told RockCellarMagazine.com in February 2012 that they did almost all the art work for David Geffen and Elliot Roberts' artists. "We were like the in-house team. Plus we knew all these guys, we hung out with them at the Troubadour and all over. And I was a musician so we were all friends. So we did [the Eagles'] first album cover out in the desert, in Joshua Tree. We just drove out there in the middle of the night, climbed a mountain, ate peyote buttons, and spent the day laughing and taking photos. So that was the first cover, which was really just cactuses and the sky."

Opening Up

David Geffen had the band start a summer tour in support of the record. The newbies opened shows for a select bunch of rock acts, including Jethro Tull, Procol Harum, Humble Pie, Edgar Winter, and Yes. Touring on a national level was new and fun. Arriving in different cities, they'd meet new friends, spend time with musicians they'd only previously read about, and generally enjoy the novelty of being part of a band.

Dan Fogelberg, who would play several shows with the Eagles during the 1970s, recalled meeting the group back in 1972. "We finally met in Nashville when I was making *Home Free*," he told RATW.com. "I was in the hotel room at the Holiday Inn for months on end, and the Eagles came in and it was their first tour. They were opening for Procol Harum. We went next door and they said, 'Hi, man, we're the Eagles from Los Angeles,' which they're still saying. And I remember meeting Bernie and Glenn and Don, I think. They were in there and they were out of marijuana. So I gave them a lid [*about an ounce —Ed.*] and we were fast friends ever since . . . a little Tennessee green, you know? It was really funny."

Opening acts always face a tough baptism, especially on their first tours. Headliners don't always treat their support artists with respect, and often there's no real time to soundcheck. Most importantly, the audience is there to see the main act, not the band trying to launch a career. Teaming up with the right headlining act, then, is incredibly important. Unfortunately, the laid-back, denim-and-cowboy-boots mellow California boys looked wildly out of place at many shows, notably those where they opened for Jethro Tull and Yes, image-conscious and performance-driven British pomp-rockers who looked and sounded a million miles from the downbeat Eagles.

The biggest contrast between the Eagles and the majority of the headliners they supported was in stagecraft. Most bands—especially the more dramatic prog-rockers—preferred to make the rock-and-roll stage into their theater. The Eagles, confident that their musicianship, songs, and vocal mix were all they needed to deliver a song, kept things simple. When Cameron Crowe asked the band about stage theatrics for *San Diego Door* magazine in November 1972, Henley said, "American groups just like to stand up there and play the songs. Try to get by on just the music. It really depends on the age your audience is. Younger kids dig to see all that shit, but older kids just come to listen more or less."

Mostly, the musicians kept their heads down, played the music, and moved along. But one night at New York's Madison Square Gardens, a tetchy Frey had had enough of feeling ignored and disrespected, and made a dig at what he perceived to be New York's uppity attitude. He slammed the city's darling New York Dolls and left the gig broody and unhappy. It wasn't much of an incident in itself, but Frey's comments were picked up by the East Coast press and would come back to haunt the Eagles time and again as the 1970s progressed and their influence grew.

Still, by playing constant shows across America, and with radio embracing the band, the Eagles made decent inroads into the music world of 1972. Pretty quickly, their debut album went gold (which at the time meant 500,000 copies sold). The Eagles had landed.

14

Desperado

Wild, Wild West

The Eagles' debut album dramatically changed the lives of the individual musicians. To start with, there would be no more tiny apartments in Echo Park. Money was flowing in, and Frey and Henley moved to houses in Hollywood. Henley went high into the hills, to a small wooden house on stilts previously owned by Byrds leader Roger McGuinn. Frey got a place nearer to the action, on Ridpath and Kirkwood, that would quickly be dubbed the Kirkwood Casino & Country Club and become known as a late-night adult-entertainment rendezvous for the Troubadour crowd.

Asylum's radio promotions guy, Paul Ahern, worked tirelessly to push the band, visiting DJs and station managers in an attempt to establish them across America. With three radio hits, sales continued to grow, and Geffen was more than happy to allow the record to breathe. There was no need to follow up with another album while the debut was still hot. When they weren't on the road, the Eagles were encouraged to keep busy and maintain their inner-circle connections by guesting on outside projects. Glenn Frey was delighted to help out on his old partner J. D. Souther's debut album, while Leadon added some his unmistakable guitar licks to Rita Coolidge's *The Lady's Not for Sale*.

Cowboy Junkies

After a few months of this laid-back musical lifestyle, Geffen figured that the time was right for his fledglings to get serious and record a second album. And serious they got, recording what was tantamount to a concept album—something most bands and artists leave until they at least have a sizable body of work under their belts.

On the surface, *Desperado*'s outlaw theme can be taken as a continuation of the dusty desert and western imagery captured by the Eagles name and the visual imagery created around their debut album. But in fact, the idea for the record came long before the Eagles existed as a band. Jackson Browne and another member of the band's songwriter circle, Ned Doheny, gave Frey a Wild West photo book as a gift. The book featured stories of the great outlaws, including one about Bill Dalton and Bill Doolin that especially struck a chord with Frey. Frey saw a connection between his life as a struggling singer and songwriter and the young kid featured in the story. He told *Circus* magazine in 1973: "When a kid sees a guitar in a shop window today, he sees it in the same way as the kid on the old west saw the gun. It's the mark of a new kind of man the way he can make a fortune and a name for himself while thumbing his nose at the things society wants him to be."

Browne, Souther, and Frey worked on turning the Old West concept into an album's worth of songs. The idea of a western-themed album struck a chord with all the Eagles, as Leadon remembered when interviewed by *Uncut* magazine in April 2013: "All of us went out west. People would go to L.A. and fail and the responsible one would move back home and start a family, while the malcontent never-say-die type personalities said, 'No. I'm staying.' That was our story."

Coincidentally, Don Henley had been tinkering with a song he'd had lying around since 1968. Frey first heard the half-finished song shortly after the band returned to sunny California after their short recording vacation in cold, damp England. In the *Very Best Of* liner notes, Frey remembers hearing Henley's soon-to-be-classic song—"Desperado"—for the first time: "Originally, it was written for a friend of his whose name was Leo. And so the song started out 'Leo, my God, why don't you come to your senses. You've been out ridin' fences for so long now.'"

Writing Wrongs

Remarkably, the songs that were surfacing all fit with the theme they'd been tossing around, and Frey added his own input and *Desperado* (whose title track is perhaps the band's best known song after "Hotel California") was born. That moment of Henley and Frey collaboration also marked the beginning of the Henley and Frey writing partnership, which would prove to be one of the most successful of the 1970s.

Since their debut album had proven more successful than anyone at Asylum could have hoped for, the Eagles' suggestion of a cowboy and gunfighter concept album was not greeted the chorus of derision that might have been expected. As Frey and Henley presented the concept, it became clear that this was far more than an intellectual dalliance with history, or just a bunch of overgrown boys wanting to play cowboys and Indians. Frey and Henley genuinely believed that there was something tangible to their connection between the outlaw gunslingers of the 1870s and 1880s and their own position in society as musician, writers, and, most recently, rock stars. They, too, were outlaws—in their minds at least. They had avoided nine-to-five drudgery, lived on their wits and hard work, and had continually taken risks that others wouldn't countenance.

Gun Fight

David Geffen, recognizing wisely that talent has to be given a free rein sometimes, agreed to the risky project and bankrolled some even more expensive artwork than the band had used on the first record. He hired the art team of Diltz and Burden once again, which made sense since the first

The Eagles followed up on the sound and style of their debut with *Desperado* in 1973, but it couldn't quite break into the *Billboard* Top 40. The overall western/outlaw theme holds up well, largely because the band themselves genuinely believed in a tangible connection between the gunslingers of the Old West and their own adventures in the record business.

album had received good reviews for its style, and the imagery had made sense with the look of the individual Eagles amid the subtext of Wild West mysticism they all enjoyed playing with.

The initial concept was for a gatefold double album, with the band dressed as outlaws. The front cover would show the gang in all their maverick glory, while the back cover would show them after being killed in a shootout. In between would be assorted images of gunfights and the Wild West.

Diltz and Burden drove the Eagles gang—as well as some "extras," in the form of producer Glyn Johns and songwriters and friends, J. D. Souther and Jackson Browne—up to the Paramount ranch, an old movie western set in Malibu Canyon. On the way they stopped at a rental store, Western Costumes, for authentic costumes and thousands of rounds of blank ammunition. The outlaws especially enjoyed the costumes, as Diltz recalled to *Uncut* in 2007: "The gear they got really could have been worn by John Wayne, because it came from the same rental place that supplied all the big movies. The band loved those clothes so much, they refused to return some of them, which must have cost David Geffen . . ."

The band also reveled in the mock gunfight, and the pictures Diltz captured managed to bring authenticity to what was essentially a bunch of rock stars playing at being cowboys and movie stars for a couple of days. They spent two days at the ranch and got so deep into character that one intense mock gunfight caused so much smoke to hang over the Wild West movie set that their neighbors called the fire service. Several fire trucks quickly arrived on the scene, expecting to put out a major fire.

New Music Express

With the artwork under their belts, it was time, Geffen decided, to record the music for the new Eagles album. Despite some friction in London the year before between no-nonsense producer Glyn Johns and the increasingly control-focused Henley and Frey, Geffen returned them to Johns' more-than-capable hands. But the old musical tensions were to arise again.

Johns was delighted with the country-heavy sound of the first album, some of the Eagles less so. Leadon and Meisner witnessed the growing partnership of Henley and Frey, whose songwriting relationship was beginning to flower. Instead of focusing on their own material, however, Frey and Henley began to critique and tweak material brought to the party by the other two musicians and writers. Henley felt justified in doing so, as he told *Rolling Stone* in September 1975: "We didn't want any filler. No stinkers."

The album appeared on shelves in April 1973. In May, the album was received well by *Rolling Stone*, with the magazine's reviewer Paul Gambaccini concluding that it "won't cure your hangover or revalue the dollar, but it will give you many good times. With their second consecutive job well done, the Eagles are on a winning streak."

If *Eagles* was an upbeat and commercially minded introduction to a band, then *Desperado* was a more genuine and authentic glimpse into the musical minds and hearts of Henley, Meisner, Frey, and Leadon. Country-rock had been bubbling under since the mid-1960s, when Gram Parsons attempted to give traditional country a rock-and-roll beat. Poco were good at blending the two formats but somewhat lightweight, and Michael Nesmith's groundbreaking work with the First National band just after quitting the Monkees was never going to get radio play, such was the negativity he faced from the "legitimate" Los Angeles industry for being a Monkee.

So it was down to the Eagles to truly create an organic, holistic brand of country-rock that was both true to its musical heritage and also offered enough commercial appeal to make it more than a niche genre. Much of this was down to the synergy of the Frey/Henley partnership, the quality of the material, and the instinctive musicality of the unit that had surfaced initially as Linda Ronstadt's backing band. With Henley finding his voice—literally—and blossoming as a writer, and before internal politics and rock-and-roll excesses began to damage the musical muse, the Eagles were country-rock's flagship act.

The guitar-and-harmonica simplicity of the opening bars of "Doolin-Dalton" are so evocative at transporting the listener back a century to a time of lawless outlaws settling the American west that the rest of the album neatly slips into place with the right atmosphere and ambience. This isn't a fully blown Yes, Pink Floyd, or Pete Townshend–style concept album but more a moody recreation of a bygone era that expertly brings past and present into contrast and connection. Henley's and Frey vocals are nicely matched while Leadon and Meisner's backing vocals lift the song to a harmony perfection that very few singers could even strive for, let alone achieve with this kind of aplomb. The story they all tell—of a disastrous bank robbery in Coffeyville, Kansas, in 1892, whereby the Dalton gang was violently decimated—is itself intriguing and compelling. In the hands of the Eagles, who are obviously very passionate themselves about telling the story with authenticity and care, it becomes a masterpiece.

The Eagles didn't release the title track as a single. Indeed, it was Linda Ronstadt's version that became a radio smash around the world, but Henley's vocals are so incredibly good on this original take that his is still the definitive vocal performance of a truly classic song. The haunting strings were arranged by Henley's old college friend and Shiloh bandmate Jim Ed Norman, who told me in 2009: "It was the quality of that song. That's what the Eagles had over everyone else—great songs. And Don, well he had this incredible attitude. He's a perfectionist. He'd work on a song until it was right. That's dedication to your craft and it's a key part of what made *Desperado* a classic album."

Like "Desperado," Bernie Leadon's "Twenty-One" was written long before the Wild West theme existed, but his tale of a young outlaw desperate to prove himself in the world fits the overall conceit perfectly. On top of that, Leadon's musicianship on this track, on which he shines on banjo, is exemplary. Meanwhile, "Out of Control," from the new writing partnership of Henley and Glenn Frey, suggests that the Eagles did get their way at times in the ongoing battle for a dirtier sound with producer Glyn Johns.

The magic of the album is the way the material does indeed connect the lives of twenty-something rock-and-roll outlaws with the criminal gunslingers of a century before. The debauchery and abandon detailed in "Out of Control" could have occurred just as easily in some lawless Western saloon as in Frey's own den of fun and frolics on Laurel Canyon. The same can be said of the more lilting "Tequila Sunrise," a whimsical song that uses alcohol beautifully as a coming of age metaphor. The authenticity of the album as a whole is remarkable. Leadon's haunting guitar work on "Bitter Creek" is oddly prophetic, given Eagles events that would take place in the following couple of years. The song talks about hitting the road one last time, suggesting an acceptance that their lives are soon to change forever. The peyote references and overall sense of stoned freedom make the song an artifact of an era that would burn bright but fast.

Speaking to *Zoo World* in May 1973, Glenn Frey explicitly connected the album with the Eagles' experience as musicians: "It has its moments where it definitely draws some parallels between rock 'n' roll and being an outlaw. Outside the laws of normality, I guess. I mean, I feel like I'm breaking a law all the time. What we live and what we do is kind of a fantasy."

The finished album would receive mixed critical acclaim at the time but become a classic in retrospect. Not everyone felt the Eagles had played the rock and roll game long for enough and hadn't paid their artist dues to even be contemplating let alone already making grandiose and pretentious concept albums. As Robert Christgau wrote (courtesy of RobertChristgau. com): "With its barstool-macho equation of gunslinger and guitarschlonger, its on-the-road misogyny, its playing-card metaphors, and its paucity of decent songs, this soundtrack to an imaginary Sam Peckinpah movie is 'concept' at its most mindless. I don't know, fellas, how do ya 'tell the dancer from the dance'? Have to get people off their asses first. C."

How dare they? This was the privilege of the elite rock-and-roller. The Who and the Beatles, the Kinks and the Rolling Stones could play around with the rock-and-roll and pop music form and express themselves in conceptual and theatrical ways, but clearly a regular old country-rock band from Los Angeles should stick to sing songs about feeling peaceful and taking it easy. For others, the western motifs were too limiting, the record not universal enough. Certainly, many at Asylum were confused by the tracks Henley & co. gave them.

Record promotions departments have to deal with radio stations and retailers, and albums and singles that don't fit neatly into a box are much harder to build a campaign around. Without the record company being passionate about it, there's not much chance of an unusual album achieving commercial success. *Desperado* would have needed marketing and advertising that was as creative, evocative, and beautifully formulated as the album itself. Asylum didn't have any such campaign.

Good Reviews, Poor Sales

Desperado made it only to #41 on the *Billboard* album chart and didn't contain a single hit single. Producer Glyn Johns blamed Asylum for not getting properly behind the album with a concerted marketing and promotions push, believing that David Geffen was too distracted with his campaigning to sign Bob Dylan (a massive coup at the time) to Asylum Records. In Johns' view, Geffen just didn't have the energy, vision, or focus to put his personal stamp on selling *Desperado*.

It could simply be that, as with many pioneering pieces of art, the album was ahead of its time. The songs grew and grew on FM radio—not just in America but around the world—and, unusually for a 1973 release, the album never stopped selling. In fact, in 2001 the 1973 album went double platinum, having sold two million copies.

The finished album would receive mixed critical acclaim at the time but become a classic in retrospect. Looking back on it now, *Desperado* is one of country-rock's finest moments, and probably the Eagles' greatest achievement. It also marked the beginning of the Henley/Frey writing double act, and the launch of Henley as a significant rock-and-roll vocalist, giving him the performing platform he missed on the debut album, where his input was largely limited to the drums.

Not many young groups offer a record company what they refer to as a concept album as their second release. The Eagles proposed an album with an Old West gunfighter and outlaw theme that would draw parallels between life as an outlaw and life as a musician. In retrospect, however, calling *Desperado* a concept album may be stretching the definition a little. It's certainly no rock opera; it's more a collection of songs connected by a theme and an image. Henley and Frey were, at the time, sincere in their belief that the album's themes of outsiders and outlaws reflected their own position in the music business, but only those in the industry could really appreciate those connections. For the public and critics, this was more a collection of songs connected by mood, feel, theme, and time. The cowboy metaphor reflected in the album artwork certainly gave the project the look of a concept album, and Geffen, who prided himself in being in touch with the artistic community, supported the venture when many executives would have reasonably passed on the idea. Bands like the Who, the Beatles, and the Rolling Stones were all mainstream stars who could afford a risky venture. The Eagles were in less of a position to push the boundaries of rock and roll. But Geffen, as was his wont, supported the band's ideas, recognizing that his talents lay in selling, not creating, music.

15

New Kid in Town

Revolving Doors

T he absence of hit singles on the *Desperado* album gave Henley and Frey less leverage than they would have liked to make Asylum listen to their requests for a new producer. Then again, Johns' failure to recreate the commercial zing of the band's debut on their second album could be used against him, too. But for a while, at least, the Eagles chose to go with the flow.

The band's third album would again be recorded with Glyn Johns at the helm, and again in London. Almost a year after they had assembled at Island Studios for *Desperado*, they were back to record what would become *On the Border*. It would not be a pleasant experience for anyone, however, and despite cutting recording short to support Neil Young on a series of U.K. dates, which gave them some much-needed respite from the control room, the Eagles were ready for a change of producer. Six weeks in the studio had produced just two songs, "You Never Cry Like a Lover" and "Best of My Love."

This time around, Frey and Henley had an ally in their management company. The band's new manager, Irving Azoff, was still proving himself to them, and this was his opportunity to show his worth. The Eagles had been particularly unhappy when told that at the end of 1973 there were no profits for the band to share. Besides the money, they felt that they were no longer a priority to their management. This was a crucial issue, and a matter that was reinforced when Elliot Roberts told Frey to take a taxi to a concert instead of getting him a limousine. Frey snapped. That was disrespectful, as far as he and the other Eagles were concerned, and it would not be forgotten. The Eagles had been slighted.

Azoff wisely took care of the immediate problem and found the band a limo. He also threw his full support behind replacing Johns, even connecting them with an alternative candidate: Joe Walsh's producer, Bill Szymczyk.

Big Shorty

The twenty-two-year-old Irving Azoff who asked Geffen and Roberts for a job at their über-cool offices on Sunset was a far cry from the man who would later take Geffen's confrontational, artist-first management techniques to a completely new level and wind up as one of the most powerful men in entertainment business. Azoff was an inexperienced but eager young artist manager working tirelessly out of a small Los Angeles apartment to promote his first two clients: Dan Fogelberg and Joe Walsh.

The diminutive Irving, who at five feet and three inches would be nicknamed "Big Shorty" by the Eagles and "Poison Dwarf" by others, had given up on a career in medicine after attending a Yardbirds show when he was seventeen years old. That cemented his love for rock and roll, which had begun earlier when he started booking local bands. As a non-musician with a serious passion for music, pursuing a job in the business side of the industry seemed obvious to him. "I used to sit and read my *Rolling Stone* about David Geffen and Bill Graham, and to me, they were gods," he told *Rolling Stone* in September 1978.

While still at high school, Azoff found local rock group Shades of Blue somewhere to practice and booked them some shows. The kid had a knack for it, and soon he was running the college circuit, making and breaking bands as he built connections across the Midwest. As his influence and confidence grew, Azoff helped REO Speedwagon secure a major-label deal. He then figured it was time to leave Illinois behind and seek his fortune out on the left coast. Management would become his next step after he came across another artist he believed in, Dan Fogelberg, a singer/songwriter with plenty of talent who was also ready to travel west.

The Odd Couple

Azoff and Fogelberg shared a small Los Angeles apartment as they began their musical journey. Then Azoff ran into another old contact playing in an L.A. club: Joe Walsh. Walsh was despondent after it seemed his career had stalled and was ready for encouragement and direction. Azoff, showing an innate understanding of the artist ego, cajoled and supported Walsh, signed him as a client, and would go on to play a significant role in the continuation of Walsh's crazy adventures in rock and roll.

Walsh helped Fogelberg in the studio after Azoff scored him a solo deal at Epic Records. Walsh produced the 1974 *Souvenirs* album, chipping in on guitar, bass, and vocals. Azoff took Walsh and Fogelberg with him to Geffen and Roberts at a time when Geffen's attention was turning elsewhere. (Unknown to most, Geffen was readying himself to make a huge financial deal with Warner Bros.)

Like his musician friends the Eagles, singer and songwriter Dan Fogelberg (August 13, 1951–December 16, 2007) was inspired by Native American culture and imagery. As he is quoted as saying on his Facebook page, "The Navajo and the Hopi communicated with their god, the Great White Spirit, by wishing on an eagle feather. They would pray over it, bury it, and hope the message would ascend with the feather up to the god. That is essentially the same thing as recording an album."

As Asylum Records merged with Elektra to become part of Warner Communications, Geffen pocketed a couple million dollars, as well as millions more in Warners stock. Now the president of Elektra/Asylum, Geffen would no longer be involved in artist management, and the new guy found himself with a much larger workload than he'd expected. From having a couple of talented but low-profile clients, Azoff was thrown into a hive of activity, guiding the careers of Joni Mitchell, David Crosby, Graham Nash, and America.

Another part of his role was to check in on the Eagles, who were out on the road in support of *Desperado*, an artistic statement that had proven less popular than its more commercial predecessor. Glenn Frey and Don Henley had lost faith in Geffen and felt they were being neglected. Promises weren't being delivered on, and the band were being deprived of the kind of input and control they felt they deserved, especially as far as recording was concerned. It was disconcerting, too, for the Eagles to discover that their management company had signed two bands, Poco and America, without informing them. They found out instead from the British music press.

Azoff and the Eagles got along well, slowly building a trust that would result in Azoff taking the management reins from Geffen's company.

Bill Szymczyk

While there's a huge technical aspect to making a record, especially in the post–George Martin/Phil Spector era, the majority or top rock-and-roll producers have a background in playing musical instruments. Even if their musical pursuits were amateur at best, many have dabbled fairly seriously with being a musician/artist/performer. The Eagles' first producer, Glyn Johns, was a choir singer and semi-pro musician before opting for life behind a mixing desk; George Martin was a classically trained pianist; Dann Huff was a session guitarist before becoming Nashville's top producer.

By contrast, Bill Szymczyk, who by the time he was working with the Eagles was an established rock producer, had never lifted a guitar in anger—at least not in the musical sense. His music path began with a childhood fascination with crystal radio. Back in the pre-digital age, many kids were entertained for hours by crystal radios—rudimentary radio kits that run without a power supply and involve some wood, nails, a crystal diode, an earphone with a solenoid, a thin metal plate, and a small antenna. Crystal radios are still made today, but in the '50s they came in kits that advertised in children's comic books. When Szymczyk discovered how to pick up more than one station on his radio, he discovered the raw blues and country and rock and roll that was busting out of radio stations in the Southern states, and he loved the sound.

ABCs

In 1960, seventeen-year-old Szymczyk signed up for a stint in the United States Navy, where his natural pitch perception saw him ushered off to sonar training. The navy also gave him a basic understanding of electronics. He left the service in the winter of 1964—the year the Beatles launched themselves on *The Ed Sullivan Show*—determined to work his way into the music business.

Unafraid to work his way up, he began his music career as "Mr. Fixit" at a recording studio in New York, turning down a place at New York University's Media Arts School to take the job. The studio he worked at, Dick Charles Recording, happened to be contracted for all the demo work for music publishers Screen Gems, the company that provided many of the hits for the Monkees, with ace hit songwriters like Neil Diamond, Gerry Goffin, and Carole King.

The eager and enthusiastic Szymczyk worked on folk music and R&B (even engineering some Quincy Jones sessions) before moving to a full-time engineering job at the Hit Factory. From there he took a substantial pay cut to move from engineer to producer when he found himself a job as a staff producer at ABC Records. But the move led to an opportunity to make his name. By revamping B.B. King's sound with some young pop and rock musicians, he played a key role in relaunching the blues legend with the crossover hit "Why I Sing the Blues." B.B.'s career was suddenly in overdrive; Szymczyk rose quickly at ABC and was given license to find some new acts for the label.

James Gang

It was during an ABC Records scouting trip to Cleveland that Szymczyk stumbled across Joe Walsh & the James Gang. He recalled seeing them play in a high-school gym and presuming, as he walked toward the gym, that they were a five-piece, from the amount of noise generated. Bill was impressed. "I thought, 'Damn, this guy's pretty good,'" he told *Goldmine* in October 2012. "I watched the set and then afterwards I talked to Joe and I said, 'Joe, I'd like to maybe think about producing you guys and signing you.' They

Walsh, who brought much-needed guitar grit and steel to the Eagles, forged his gunslinger reputation with the James Gang.

had cut some demos, and I took them back to New York and I studied them. I really wanted to sign them, so I talked to the bosses and they said, 'Bring them out.' I signed them and they got a total advance of $2,000. The entire album only cost something like seven grand. We knocked out the first album in about a week or so, and we were off and running."

Unfortunately for Szymczyk, when ABC Records became part of Dunhill in 1969, most of the old ABC staff was let go or transferred to the West Coast office. And so it was that Bill Szymczyk arrived in Los Angeles on January 1, 1970.

Who's Next

The next month, California was hit by a sizeable earthquake. Szymczyk figured that one quake was enough, so he moved instead to Denver, Colorado, determined to establish himself there as a freelance record producer. The opportunity soon came for him to work with Joe Walsh again when a bored Walsh, on tour with the James Gang, found time to catch up with his old producer when the band played Denver. Several drinks later, Walsh had chosen to pursue a solo career, with his next album to be produced by Szymczyk in Colorado.

Meanwhile, Glenn Frey and Don Henley had reached their limit with Glyn Johns. Johns still wouldn't buy the Eagles as an R&B/rock-and-roll band. This time, the Eagles won the battle to remove him and decided to scrap the recordings they'd made in London, except for a couple of tracks they were actually happy with, "Best of My Love" and "You Never Cry Like a Lover." While looking around for someone to replace Johns, they listened to Joe Walsh's solo work at Irving Azoff's suggestion. Walsh set up a meeting, and Henley and Frey decided to work with Szymczyk.

This placed the producer in a tricky situation, however, as he explained to *Sound on Sound* in November 2004: "They started the third record with Glyn in London and had completed most of it when they decided to work with me. They were willing to start all over. I agreed, but on one condition: that I check with Glyn and that he was OK with it. He was one of the producers I had looked up to for a long time. I called him in London and I guess the feeling was mutual, because he said 'Better you than me, mate!'"

Borderline

A rejuvenated Henley and Frey resumed recording for what would become *On the Border*, with Szymczyk piloting the ship. Szymczyk's personality could not have been more different from Johns'. He was laid-back, affable, and prepared to let the band have plenty of input and direction.

For a while, at least, the new kid in town brought some much-needed harmony to the Eagles' recording sessions. When one track sounded like it needed some meatier guitar, Bernie Leadon said he had the perfect man for the job. The band had already met Don Felder, an old guitar-playing friend of Leadon's from Florida, at various gigs; now, when he came by to visit with Leadon, Felder reacquainted himself with the guys and played the heck out of "Good Day in Hell."

Frey invited Felder to join the band the next day, but Felder wasn't too sure about it. Knowing Leadon well, he was well aware of the frictions in the Eagles camp, and was under the impression that they were constantly on the point of breaking up. Then again, they were a pretty great band. Weighing his options was difficult, so Felder simply asked his current boss, Graham Nash, for advice. Nash—one of the most decent men in rock and roll—advised Felder to join the Eagles for career reasons, despite Felder being an integral part of the Crosby and Nash band.

Felder had a difficult decision to make. His wife was pregnant with their first child, and he was making excellent money—around $1,500 a week. But as Nash had pointed out, he was just a sideman—a musician for hire. To be part of a major rock-and-roll band, and one that wanted his particular skills and style, could be career-changing. But would it last? Would the arguments and in-fighting break up the band? Obviously, Felder voted yes to joining, and once he became attuned to the internal dramas, the addition of some new blood brought a huge uplift in spirits in the Eagles camp.

Eagles Ltd.

In the spirit of camaraderie and bonhomie, the band members started a company, Eagles Ltd.—a corporation of Don Henley, Glenn Frey, Bernie Leadon, Randy Meisner, and Don Felder. It was fair, simple, and democratic, as Felder told Macleans.com in November 2008. "We each owned 20 per cent of this company that owned the Eagles. It owned the T-shirts, the touring, everything, it was all divided equally. This band was going to be different, there were going to be no sidemen involved with this organization."

Felder could hardly have joined at a better time. New blood gave fresh impetus to the band, and being free of Glyn Johns' control improved Frey and Henley's moods considerably. They were also back on home soil, recording at the legendary Record Plant, which was more conducive to partying than being at Island under Johns' watchful eyes in chilly old London.

On the Border proved that Henley and Frey had a good sense of where the band was heading. The tougher, rockier sound that Felder's extra rock guitar gave them worked brilliantly, more so, perhaps, on the rowdy "Already Gone" than even on the biting "Good Day in Hell."

16

Border Control

Tom Petty's Guitar Teacher

Don Felder joined the original members of the Eagles in 1974 after dazzling them with some beefed-up guest slide work for the "Good Day in Hell" sessions. But he was hardly an outsider, having previously been in a high-school band with Bernie Leadon.

Felder grew up in modest circumstances in a one-level house with a tin roof in the swamplands of Gainesville, Florida. Nothing came especially easy—except his gift for music. "I grew up in a really impoverished circumstance in Gainesville, and I had nothing to begin with, so I had nothing to lose as far as pursuing my dreams," he told the *Broward Palm Beach New Times* in June 2012. But seeing Elvis on *The Ed Sullivan Show* had a profound effect on the young Felder, who imagined a way out of poverty via music and the entertainment business.

Music was already in his soul, thanks to his jazz-loving father, who played Benny Goodman and Tommy Dorsey records every evening after work. "I grew up in a house where my father loved to listen to big-band music," Felder told me in 2010. "Listen to a horn player and they can only play so many notes—usually [they] play very melodic notes and then stop for a breath. Their phrasing is not an ongoing spew of notes. It's not an assault—it's a phrase. I learned so much from a jazz saxophone player who was in one of the jazz-fusion bands I was in. He had beautiful phrasing and he taught me about melodic phrasing."

Felder's father had a deep connection to music, and Don recognized its importance to him. After working a tough sixteen-hour day, he'd get home, filthy from working on cars, and, after cleaning up, his most simple pleasure was to listen to cassette tapes he'd made from a friend's records. He taped the albums because records were too expensive for him to buy, but the end product was the same.

Like any kid, Felder wanted to impress and connect with his father, and he recognized that one way to his heart was through music. It was seeing

Elvis on *The Ed Sullivan Show*, however, that ensnared him in the rock-and-roll trap. He decided there and then to become a guitarist and play guitar for a living. Felder traded some Cherry Bomb firecrackers for a neighbor's beaten-up guitar and bought some new strings from the local drugstore.

When he wasn't at school, Felder worked a newspaper delivery round and taught himself to play guitar. He had a natural aptitude for guitar, and was a good enough guitarist to form his own band when he was fourteen years old. At the time, the group was just one of many local bands playing clubs and frat parties in the north Florida area. But, in retrospect, Felder's first band had a fascinating lineup. The Continentals also featured future guitar legend Stephen Stills, and when he left to further his career, another future Rock and Roll Hall of Famer replaced him: Bernie Leadon.

Felder worked at a music shop in order to obtain equipment and traded guitar lessons for music-theory lessons in order to learn how to write. One of his students was none other than Tom Petty. "One day this kind of scrawny, scraggly blond-haired kid came in and wanted guitar lessons," Felder reminisced to Gibson.com in 2010. "I started teaching him guitar and we became friends and I went over to his house a couple of times. He had actually set up a microphone in one of the rooms in his house and he was playing bass in this little band. He wanted to learn guitar so he could play guitar instead of just bass in the band. So I went over to his house and was hanging around and he would play songs."

Skydog

It would be Felder's astounding slide-guitar playing that wowed the Eagles when he guested on the *On the Border* recording sessions in 1974. And little wonder, because he had been taught those slide tricks of the trade by the very best in the business: Duane Allman of the Allman Brothers band.

Legendary Southern-rock guitarist Duane "Skydog" Allman was actually born in the home of country music, Nashville, but grew up in North Florida, where his and brother Gregg's band the Allman Joys was one of the best outfits in the region. After trying his luck in Los Angeles—without much success—Allman moved back south, working as a session guitarist at the world-renowned Muscle Shoals Sound Studio in Alabama, adding his deft touch to a series of rhythm-and-blues classics from the likes of Aretha Franklin and Wilson Pickett. Bored with session work, Duane headed back to Florida and put together a new project, the Allman Brothers Band,

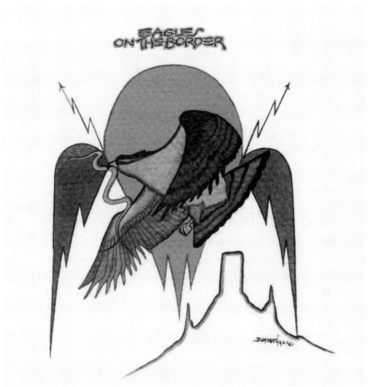

Released in 1974, the Eagles' third album, *On the Border*, exhibited more rock and roll, thanks in part to the impact of guitarist Don Felder, who joined half-way through the recording sessions. The record features two Top 40 singles: "Already Gone" and the band's first-ever #1 record, "Best of My Love."

alongside Jaimoe Johanson, Dickey Betts, Berry Oakley, Reese Wynans, and brother Gregg. The first Allman Brothers Band album was released in 1969.

The Allman Brothers Band toured heavily, improving all the time and developing a style all their own based on mixing jazz, blues, and country within an improvisational rock-and-roll framework, presented with lashings of fiery slide guitar. They became known as one of the finest live acts in America. By the time the Allmans recorded the live *At Fillmore East* album in 1971, they had already started the whole Southern-rock genre, and Duane himself had ascended to "guitar great" status alongside the likes of Hendrix, Clapton, and Jeff Beck. An original stylist on his trademark guitars—a 1959 cherry sunburst Les Paul, a '57 Gold Top, or a cherry Gibson SG—Allman had a magical tone and was a beautifully melodic player who drew on blues and jazz for ideas and inspiration even when playing the most routine downhome rock-and-roll riff.

Tragically, Duane died aged just twenty-four on Friday, October 29, 1971, in Macon, Georgia, after suffering massive injuries in a horrific motorcycle accident. Fresh from critical acclaim and great touring success, the band had decided to take a mini-vacation. On the Friday evening, Duane took his motorcycle for a spin and was forced to swerve to avoid a flatbed truck that had turned in front of him. His motorcycle spun out of control, skidded, and pinned Allman underneath it as it slid across the road. Duane was in a bad way and had to be revived several times during the ambulance ride to the emergency room. He died not long after arriving at the Macon Medical Center. His funeral was more like a gig than a solemn religious goodbye. Three hundred people showed up, and Gregg, fighting back his emotions, sang with the band in tribute to his brother.

"Allman was simply the best player," Felder told me in 2010. "I'd go to his house and he's show me how he played these amazing licks. He was a wonderful man and I was blessed just to know him, never mind learn slide from him."

For a small Florida town, Gainesville had a stellar rock-and-roll cast during the years Felder was growing up. Petty, Stills, the Allmans, and Felder would all go on to play major parts in rock-and-roll history, but in Florida they were just young, music-mad kids, hanging around in hole-in-the-wall cafes in the early hours after playing their weekend gigs.

All the Gainesville bands knew each other and helped each other out. There were plenty of gigs available locally, especially in the summer months, where bands played the strip and the pier in the thriving vacation resort of Daytona Beach. At one point, Felder offered some assistance to Petty's band the Rucker Brothers. Petty played bass fine but the two guitar players had no concept of teamwork and played too loud and over each other. Felder helped arrange the two guitars so the band had some shape and sounded more professional.

When Leadon departed Gainesville, Felder had begun to think about taking his music career to another level, but he wasn't yet convinced that music would offer him a career—at least not on that level. But when his girlfriend left for Boston and he began traveling to see her, the notion of moving away from Florida seemed less daunting. Soon after, the Maundy Quintet—the band that had started out as the Continentals—broke up when another member went to college, leaving Felder at a crossroads. He took jazz and improv lessons locally, and through word of mouth began to play with a band in Ocala, Florida, called Flow.

Flow were a complex jazz-blues fusion band based on improvisation that called for dexterous playing and a quick, open musical mind. Felder loved the experience, and when the band was set up with a prestigious gig at New York's iconic Fillmore East, it seemed his career path was being mapped out for him. Out of the gig came a deal with the CTI Records label, started by one of the key men in the New York jazz industry, Creed Taylor. Taylor had produced Quincy Jones and was a leading light in both jazz and fusion.

Felder and Flow made one album, but it failed to find an audience. Felder was growing tired of the rest of the band's nonchalant attitude, and New York was beginning to wear on him too.

Harvard Blues

Reconnecting out of the blue with his ex-girlfriend, Susan, who was now working at Harvard University in Cambridge, Felder realized that he needed to be with her, not scraping a living with a band that however good musically was never going to succeed commercially. Susan offered him a place to stay, and Felder found work in a recording studio in Boston.

Everything was perfect—except for the wages. Felder played guitar for singers and bands making demos, produced the vocals, engineered all the tracks, and essentially learned the art of making records. In the evenings, he would ride a train to Harvard Square in Cambridge and play classical guitar at the Holiday Inn for the hotel restaurant's diners. After playing standards for a couple of hours, he would join up with a covers band and play until the early hours whenever they had a gig. It was a lot of work, but Felder was gaining an incredibly diverse musical education.

Every now and then, Leadon would pass through with one of his bands, get together with Felder, and try to convince his old friend to move to California. Felder kept saying no until one time, fresh from Eagles success, Leadon came with an offer of somewhere to stay and some great contacts for work in Los Angeles. Felder decided to make the move. It was 1972.

Go West

In California, Felder, with his guitar skills and experiences with different styles, picked up studio work immediately. He then went on the road with

David Blue's band. Blue was a member of the Geffen stable, and was sent out on tour with Crosby & Nash (CSNY having broken up in the summer of 1970). Aside from playing guitar, Felder sang the Stephen Stills parts on a number of songs. He continued to do a great deal of session work, and it was as a session player that he was drafted in by Frey to work with the Eagles on "Good Day in Hell."

17

The Last Resort

The President's Daughter

On the Border was proof that the Eagles could rock, and rock they did, with the help of a producer more sensitive to the kind of sonic boost they had in mind. Looking back on the conversations between the two camps, it's clear that Johns was sitting defiantly in one corner, stubbornly but passionately believing that the Eagles were a harmony vocal act, while Henley, Frey, and Meisner had grouped themselves in the opposite corner, desperate to take their music to the world's biggest stages and have the sound carry them round all corners of the biggest stadiums and venues on the planet.

Johns had never been onstage with the Eagles. He had not felt the sense of powerlessness when the band came up against louder, fuller, bigger rock-and-roll machines like the British prog-rock bands they had played with recently, Jethro Tull and Yes. The Eagles were not willing to feel that embarrassment again. It was not that they were ready to throw away their interest in country music, or their passion for blending it with rock and roll. It was more that they felt justified in having some freedom to push their stylistic boundaries—and, most crucially, to have access to a bigger sonic arsenal available to them when needed.

It certainly wasn't that the Eagles were having Zeppelin envy. Frey did not want to out-Plant Robert Plant, and Henley was no John Bonham. Looking lightweight in contrast to the rest of the bands onstage, however, was quite another matter.

Of course, rock and roll cannot be an exact science, and while On the Border did change the band's sound and perception with radio, venues, and audiences around the world, the switch of styles was not without its contradictions. It was deeply ironic, for one thing, that Leadon's major contribution to the record that blasted the Eagles into the rock-and-roll orbit was a tribute to the founding father of country-rock, Gram Parsons.

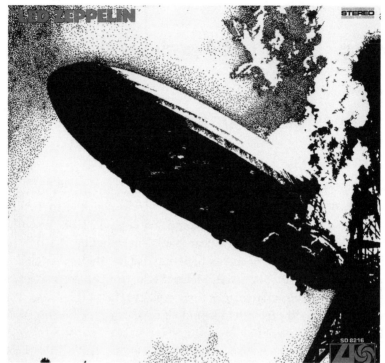

The kingpins of hard rock released their genre-shattering debut album in 1969. *Led Zeppelin* was produced with a very loose and live feel by guitar god Jimmy Page in tandem with future Eagles producer Glyn Johns.

Joshua Tree

Originally, "My Man" was an ode to another rock-and-roll immortal, Duane Allman of the Allman Brothers, who was tragically killed in a motorcycle accident in 1971. Allman was part of the rock and blues crowd in Florida that Felder, Stills, Leadon, and Tom Petty were involved in as musically advanced teens, and would always greet Leadon with "Hey, My Man," hence the title, but when Gram Parsons died of a drug overdose at Joshua Tree in September 1973, Leadon was inspired to turn the tribute toward him instead.

After that, when the first two singles from the album, "James Dean" and "Already Gone," managed only to bubble under, it took an older, Glyn Johns–produced country-rock ballad, "Best of My Love," to crack the charts and give the Eagles their first-ever #1. Johns must have enjoyed that moment, back home in London. Frey and Henley may have had their way regarding the creation of a tougher, rockier sound—and, in the long run, one that brought them world superstardom—but there was no small irony in the realization that it was a heavily country-tinged song from the London sessions that provided the Eagles with their breakthrough to the next level.

The Eagles' take on Tom Waits' classic "Ol' '55," meanwhile, is nothing exceptional, but it does showcase some fine pedal steel from another country-rock pioneer, Al Perkins, the guitar prodigy Shiloh recruited shortly before leaving Texas for Los Angeles. But when the Eagles did rock, as illustrated by Felder's thunderous but glistening slide work on "Good Day in Hell," it was clear that their early-'70s sound had been transformed beyond recognition. The bluegrass-meets-folk-meets-Byrds approach was still valid, but to be able to dip into the furnace of Southern-rock fire courtesy of a player taught by the slide king, Duane Allman, himself, was a game-changer. The extra pace and extra musical depth and urgency drove all of the Eagles to an extra level of sonic power and expression. The other element that's crystal clear on this record is the coming of age of Henley as a songwriter and vocalist with remarkable variety and depth, as well as an instinctive ability to deliver a lyric.

On the Border sold better than both *Eagles* and *Desperado*, climbing to a creditable #17 in America and galloping into the Top 30 in England. The U.K. breakthrough was the result of some dynamic live shows, some BBC airplay, and a recognition in Britain of the deep country-rock bloodline in the band's music. Country-rock was—and indeed still is—highly respected in Europe, far more so than mainstream country and mainstream rock and roll. Singer/songwriters, folk singers, and country music with an edge had long enjoyed both popularity with the general public and, unusually for a music genre that has broad appeal, a swath of genuine support among the press and media.

The pop-friendly sound of "Best of My Love" brought the Eagles a brand new audience. Azoff's relentless work with radio and television promotion ensured that the group had the best possible chance of success. If the creative unit could just deliver a catchy, memorable, and quickly identifiable record that would fit the fairly stringent requirements of the radio programmers in key markets, then the Eagles were well equipped for future chart domination and massive commercial returns.

Money, Money, Money

Even as the Eagles grew more successful in 1974, the cracks in the band were getting deeper. Henley and Frey gathered more and more control while Leadon and Meisner retreated, oftentimes feeling ignored and isolated

Gram Parsons
GP

After years fronting various musical combinations, Gram Parsons, the fragile and troubled poster boy of angsty country-rock, released *GP*, his first solo album, in 1973. By September of that year, Parsons was dead, killed by an overdose of morphine and alcohol.

from the decision-making process. But the money was flowing in like vintage wine, and Henley and Frey were determined to make the most of their first flush of fame and fortune. The pair had been around the music scene long enough to be acutely aware that there were no guarantees of longevity in rock and roll. More than that, there were no guarantees of short-term success in music, either. If things are going well, don't stop.

Leadon wanted to slow down and enjoy the experience more than the others. He suggested taking a break every now and then, to recharge and maintain the drive over a longer, more sustained period, but Henley and Frey were focused simply on driving the Eagles tour bus—or, more accurately, the increasingly luxurious Eagles plane—as fast as they possibly could.

Teamwork was still the order of the day when it came time to record the band's next album. If *On the Border* had proven that the Eagles could rock, then this album would show the doubters that the Eagles were an accomplished all-round band. Significantly, as Henley and Frey observed the revolution occurring in pop music and were witness to the widening chasms of conflict tin American society, they were also determined to produce lyrics that stood up with the best.

18

One of These Nights

How a New Sound Sent the Band Global

n some ways, *One of These Nights* was an appetizer for the great album to come. Moving together to a cool pad high in the Hollywood Hills with a panoramic view of the city they loved and hated in almost equal measure, the songwriters were priming themselves for producing songs and stories that dealt with their own reality, be it good or bad. And if that reality somehow struck a chord with America, then it was all to the good.

Night Moves

Released on June 10, 1975, *One of These Nights* was the album Henley and Frey—as well as Meisner, to a lesser degree—had been waiting for. It was their first #1 album, and a record that combined strong deep album cuts with catchy and commercial but still top-drawer singles.

"One of These Nights" was released as a single and followed "Best of My Love" to the top spot, shimmering as it did with a delicate falsetto from the brilliantly in-form Henley. The more traditional country-meets-rock sound of "Lyin' Eyes" won them a Grammy (Best Pop Performance by a Duo or Group with Vocal) if not another #1. And then, just in case anyone had forgotten about the Eagles' most affable and steady bass player, Randy Meisner took center stage and owned every inch of it for his performance on the astounding "Take It to the Limit," a group co-write by Meisner, Henley, and Frey. Meisner's extraordinary vocals were haunting, the free-flowing harmonies were irresistibly sublime, and the song sold in excess of half a million copies in America alone.

Meisner was hanging in there; despite the rapid flowering of Henley and Frey, the old Poco and Stone Canyon Band guy could still stand and deliver. Leadon's contribution was not nearly so commercial. Leadon, perhaps reflecting his discomfort with the whole rock-star trip that he and the rest of the band and their management were riding along on, fashioned himself an odd piece, "Journey of the Sorcerer," which might have been inspired by those long nights supporting Jethro Tull.

The Hitchhiker's Guide

One of the great trivia questions in the "pop and rock" category is the connection between Bernie Leadon and Ford Prefect. Nothing to do with a motorcar, the Ford in question is Arthur Dent's friend, and the context is their journey through the universe as key protagonists in *The Hitchhiker's Guide to the Galaxy*.

The Hitchhiker's Guide began life in 1978 as an off-the-wall BBC radio series, a blend of sci-fi with English eccentricity and silly whimsy that found itself a global audience in the multimillions (if you count the hordes who bought copies of the spin-off novels). The connection between Leadon and a character in the series? The theme tune to the radio show.

Ask your average punter for a handful of Eagles songs, and the obvious tracks always come up—usually "Hotel California" first, followed by a selection from "Witchy Woman," "Take It Easy," and "Desperado." Most of those songs—thanks to the Eagles and related artists like Jackson Browne and Linda Ronstadt—have been given an extended pop life, but there's another track, less well known by name as those other commercial smashes, that has taken its own cultural hold by way of the *Hitchhiker's Guide* franchise (franchise being the operative word, since the music, in one format or another, has appeared across a slew of media from the original radio series to two records, a television series, a computer game, a stage show, a video game, and a movie). An unusual minor-key banjo-heavy tune from Bernie Leadon on *One of These Nights* that's seven minutes of off-the-wall prog-rock meets folk meets heavy rock that was always at odds with the song selection on the album. But put in another context, as a theme song, it takes on another life as one of the strongest and longest-lasting tracks in the Eagles canon, and that only makes it that much cooler.

In the early 1970s, Douglas Adams was a struggling writer looking for his own creative niche. He tried comedy, unsuccessfully, with Monty Python's Graham Chapman, but then found himself working with some BBC producer friends who asked if he had any fresh ideas for them. A product of his generation, Adams took music quite seriously, and once *The Hitchhiker's Guide to the Galaxy* became a production reality, he envisioned as more of a rock-and-roll concept project than a sedate and cozy radio program.

Now a rock band rather than a country-rock group, the Eagles became an international act with the 1975 release of *One of These Nights*. With its three hit singles—"One of These Nights," "Lyin' Eyes," and "Take It to the Limit"—this was very much the precursor for the Eagles' crowning glory, *Hotel California*.

Adams explained his vision in *The Hitchhiker's Guide to the Galaxy: The Original Radio Scripts*, published by Pan: "Though it was now ten years since *Sgt. Pepper* had revolutionized the way that people in the rock world thought about sound production, it seemed to me, listening to radio comedy at the time, that we still hadn't progressed much . . ."

Already very familiar with "Journey of the Sorcerer," Adams picked it out as the perfect theme tune for his radio baby. Interestingly, the Eagles' original cut, as found on *One of These Nights*, appeared on every episode of the radio show across five seasons, but issues with publishing rights, royalties, and copyright meant that the subsequent television series and album releases featured a reworking by Tim Souster. Later CD issues contain a version by Philip Pope, while it was another take—this time by Joby Talbot, once a pop star alongside Neil Hannon in the U.K. group the Divine Comedy—that featured in the 2005 movie.

Hollywood Globetrotters

It was the populist and more sophisticated sound and subsequent global appeal that *One of These Nights* brought that allowed the band to turn into a truly international act. The years 1974 and 1975 were critical in pop and rock history in both the United States and Europe. The 1970s—a much more challenging and spiteful decade than the swinging, peaceful '60s—saw an array of social and economic setbacks around the globe, from a nasty new trend in airplane hijacking to gas and oil price increases that caused serious inflation everywhere. In Europe, workers went on strike and at times brought the social fabric of their nations to a perilous halt.

Despite—or maybe because of—the upheaval sweeping the Earth, rock and roll suddenly grew up. While the Eagles found their feet, working their way up the rock-and-roll totem pole via producer Glyn Johns' rock cred and some terrific material (plus some superlative business deals, marketing, and promotion, courtesy of David Geffen), they had to move fast to keep up with some seismic changes in the rock landscape.

Rock and roll got loud in the early '70s, persuading the Eagles to add volume and energy, with some additional guitar weaponry to supplement Bernie Leadon's light and melodic ouch. When British blues-rock mainstays the Yardbirds broke up, lead guitarist Jimmy Page resurfaced with a new band, Led Zeppelin. Page, John Bonham, John Paul Jones, and the Adonis-like front man Robert Plant changed the rules of rock-and-roll power and intensity, making Eagles precursors like CSNY, the Byrds, and Poco sound lyrically whimsical and musically gentle by comparison. Zeppelin ushered in a new genre, heavy metal, and opened the doors for thunderous bands like Black Sabbath, Deep Purple, and Uriah Heep.

And so it was that the Eagles, with Don Felder in their armory, campaigned to match up with the rapid movements and changes in rock and roll and test themselves in Britain. The U.K. had been a second home to the Eagles, with the band embroiled in a complex and inconsistent love/hate relationship with their foreign cousins. The U.K. was hip, and it was always looking for the next big thing. American music changed slower, and ever since John, Paul, George, and Ringo changed the world, American bands revered the British pop and rock culture—sometimes forgetting that the English rockers they so admired were themselves drawing inspiration from the home of the Eagles: America.

Midsummer Night's Dream

The 1975 Mid-Summer Music concert that took place at Wembley Stadium on June 21 (hence the title of the event) was one of the most important gigs the band played as they transformed from top-notch country-rock band to international rock-and-roll superstars. The lineup featured Elton John, the Beach Boys, Eagles, Joe Walsh, Rufus featuring Chaka Khan, and Stackridge, with the overall show billed as being "presented by Radio One DJ Johnnie Walker."

Headliner Elton John was promoting his new album, *Captain Fantastic and the Brown Dirt Cowboy*, now considered one of the greatest albums in pop history. In the liner notes to the album's deluxe reissue, Elton calls it his and co-writer Bernie Taupin's "finest" record. At Wembley, he was about to play the new album in its entirety—a risky prospect—and, to ensure maximum publicity, had recorded a promotional trailer film in Los Angeles in which he hailed the U.S. artists on the bill as "some of my favorite American bands."

Stackridge—Britain's answer to the Eagles, perhaps—kicked off proceedings with a robust fusion of folk, bluegrass, '60s pop, and British eccentricity, followed by funk outfit Rufus, which at the time "featured" a young singer called Chaka Khan. Then it was Joe Walsh, whipping the crowd into festive mode with a wild version of "Rocky Mountain Way" before his new cohorts, the Eagles, took their turn to mix some California rays with London's hot and sunny summer-festival vibe.

With their new album only recently released, the Eagles (unlike Elton) played it safe with a mix of tracks from their first three albums. But the band were in transition, and their 1975 sound was more rock and roll than country—something the Wembley audience latched onto immediately, as the band played amped-up versions of "Already Gone" and "Witchy Woman." Future Eagles mainstay Walsh added more guitar firepower alongside the Eagles via a Chuck Berry cover and finally a super-smooth rendition of "Best of My Love." Glenn Frey dedicated "Peaceful Easy Feeling" to "G.J." (producer Glyn Johns) and the band, realizing that British audiences were partial to Byrds/Poco/Springfeld/Burritos–style country, while Bernie Leadon was allowed to let rip on banjo on a couple of songs, "Blackberry Blossom" and "Midnight Flyer."

Despite this vote of confidence, however, Leadon was becoming increasingly marginalized from the rest of the Eagles outfit. And, by 1975, he was having difficulty coming to terms with the rocket ride of success he had experienced with the Eagles. He'd offered up a hint in song with the soon-to-be prophetic "I Wish You Peace," co-written by the love of his life at the time, Patti Davis. It's a beautiful song about letting go of acrimony and parting peacefully. Leaving was presumably on his mind.

Unlike so many other country-rock outfits Leadon had been a part of, the Eagles had found the kind of fame and financial success that most other artists and bands only dream about. But he was concerned that the concerts they played were becoming more like business deals than musical expressions. On top of that, the whole rock-star lifestyle—complete with elite hotels and limousines—was beginning to bother him. A bluegrass folkie by nature, Leadon aspired to a simpler lifestyle. He told *Rolling Stone* in September 1975 that he disliked limos because "it feels like you're thumbing your nose at your audience."

Girl Trouble

The "old lady" Leadon referred to was another complication in his life. Patti Davis was the daughter of Nancy Reagan and Ronald Reagan, then the governor of California and later, of course, president of the United States. Patti used the name Davis in an attempt to distance herself from her parents' conservative ideals and politics. She was a free-spirited liberal who first rebelled at the age of fourteen, when she got hooked on diet pills, and was seen taking pills from her mother's medicine cabinet. Moving in with a long-haired, T-shirt-and-jeans-wearing rock-and-roller was hardly on the menu for the governor's daughter. But that's what she did as she and Leadon lived together between 1974 and 1975.

The relationship did not bother only the Reagans; the Eagles camp—notably Don Henley—was none too keen on the pairing, either, especially as it began to encroach on the work of the band. Like John and Yoko just a few years earlier, Leadon wanted Davis with him in the recording studio. Henley did not appreciate this, and was further irritated when Bernie insisted that his girlfriend be given a co-writing credit on "I Wish You Peace."

Whether Henley thought the song was weak or it was more a culmination of Leadon's behavior that upset him is unclear, but tensions grew to breaking point. Leadon would disappear for a couple of days, releasing the pressure, but only temporarily.

Historians have presumed that it was the band's move away from the country and bluegrass with which Leadon is always associated to a heavier R&B sound on *One of These Nights* that was the reason behind the original Eagles guitarist's dissatisfaction with life in the fast lane in 1975. But when

Leadon recalled those days to *Rolling Stone* magazine in 2008, he said it wasn't about musical direction at all. "It implies that I had no interest in rock or blues or anything but country-rock," he said. "That's just not the case. I didn't just play a Fender Telecaster. I played a Gibson Les Paul and I enjoyed rock and roll. That's evident from the early albums."

Leadon wanted some respite from the pressure of being an Eagle, and he had asked the band to take a break in 1975. The idea was rejected by Henley and Frey, who refused to halt the money-making machine they had built—not even for a few months. With nothing having been resolved, the frustration and disagreement continued until one night before a show in Cincinnati. Leadon and Frey got into a heated argument that ended with a glass of water dripping over Frey's head.

That was it for Leadon. The band's management denied rumors he had quit for a while, but it was finally confirmed just before Christmas 1975 that Bernie Leadon was no longer an Eagle. In true "show must go on" tradition, Irving Azoff, who had already been talking with Joe Walsh about joining the group, announced to the world that the flamboyant ex–James Gang guitarist would be replacing Leadon in the Eagles.

Hey Joe

Azoff had worked too hard with the Eagles to let one member's departure break the band. He didn't recommend Joe Walsh because the ex–James Gang guitarist was a client. He had too much to lose for that kind of short-sighted self-interest. After all, the Eagles were big business. *One of These Nights*, their fourth album, had gone #1, and their two most recent singles, "Take It to the Limit" and "Lyin' Eyes," had both made the Top 10, while the band's concert tickets were selling like the proverbial hot cakes. The new album that Henley and Frey were planning would be the group's pinnacle of achievement—a continuation of the direction they had taken with *One of These Nights*, but with a lyrical focus, creativity, and musical mastery that few bands have ever matched.

19

An Eagles Los Angeles

A Guide to the City of Angels

The Eagles all came to California seeking fame and fortune, just as the pioneers who settled the American West had, a century and more before. So it's only correct to begin looking at key Eagles landmarks in Los Angeles with a visit to the Paramount ranch, the Wild West movie set where the original Eagles shot their *Desperado* album cover in 1973.

Wild West

Throw away the "homes of the stars" flyer and head instead to 2903 Cornell Road, Agoura Hills, California, 91301. It's a simple drive on Route 101 (Ventura Freeway) to the Kanan Road exit. From there, you head south for a half-mile, take a left on Cornell, and a couple of miles down the road, slightly to the right, you'll see the entrance to the ranch.

Nothing captures the maverick outlaw image like the photo shoot for what became the cover of the Eagles' second album. Photographer Henry Diltz and the album's art director, Gary Burden, took the band to a Hollywood rental store called Western Costumes and kitted them out. Then they bought 1,500 rounds of blank ammunition and on December 18, 1972, they drove the band plus Jackson Browne and J. D. Souther and some other gang members out to the Paramount Ranch.

Back then, the ranch was still owned by Paramount; now it's a public park, but you can still sense the glory days of Hollywood, back when it all started—1927, to be precise, when Paramount Pictures bought 2,700 acres of the old Rancho Las Virgenes in Malibu Canyon to use as "movie ranch." The studio built a complete, authentic western town with a typical main street, a sheriff's office, a Wells Fargo depot, and of course a saloon. The set was used for hundreds of western movies, including some of the best of the genre: the Bob Hope classics *Paleface* (1948) and *Son of Paleface* (1952),

Gunfight at the OK Corral (1957), *Fancy Pants* (1950), *The Virginian* (1946), *Whispering Smith* (1948), *The Forest Rangers* (1942), *The Miracle of Morgan's Creek* (1944), *The Perils of Pauline* (1947), *Geronimo* (1939), and *The Streets of Laredo* (1949).

Laurel Canyon

In San Francisco, they had Haight-Ashbury, the neighborhood that spawned so much music and countercultural activity. In Hollywood, the Canyons were home to the back-to-nature hippie movement, and Laurel Canyon was a shrine for anyone involved in the music scene. This was due primarily to its closeness to the party and music scene of West Hollywood. It's a rustic, mountainous area that connects the San Fernando Valley on one side of the hill to the Sunset Strip on the other.

With their first Eagles cash, Glenn Frey and Don Henley moved into homes in Laurel Canyon, a teeming community of musicians, artists, and eccentrics. Frank Zappa had a house there; so did Joni Mitchell and Graham Nash. Peter Tork of the Monkees threw outrageous parties at his house and David Crosby took free love to new heights.

At the heart of the 1960s Laurel Canyon community was the Country Store. This is the place where Glenn Frey famously saw David Crosby, cape and all, sitting on the steps when he arrived in Hollywood the very first time. Mama Cass Elliot of the Mamas & the Papas lived in the basement. Like the ranch, it's not hard to drift back to the '70s while you're there. It's much the same as it was back then. Head down Sunset Boulevard past the Comedy Store and the notorious Chateau Marmont and you'll reach Laurel Canyon. Go left, and after a mile you'll see the Country Store, at 2108 Laurel Canyon Boulevard. It's a quaint, hippie-flavored general store that would make a fascinating visit even without the rock-and-roll history contained inside its walls.

Jimmy Cagney

While on Laurel Canyon, take a trip to Ridpath Drive, where both Henley and Frey lived, after the Eagles made enough money from record sales and touring to get out of their tiny apartment in 1972. Take a detour to Coldwater Canyon, and 1740 La Fontaine Court in particular. This is the house Glenn Frey bought from old Hollywood movie star James Cagney. Then spin the car around and pop down to the site of the old Asylum

Records building at 9120 Sunset Boulevard.

You can't do any kind of Eagles-landmarks tour without dropping from Sunset to Santa Monica Boulevard to find the small but perfectly formed Troubadour. It's at 9081 Santa Monica and is easily spotted thanks to the unmistakable font of its signage. The Troub, as the regulars call it, is one of the longest-lasting music clubs in Los Angeles. In the 1960s, it was at the very center of the folk and country-music boom, with everyone who

Numerous establishments in Hollywood and New York might claim to be *the* place where the stars eat and drink, but in the case of Dan Tana's, it's true. So cool was this establishment among Hollywood circles that the main character on the TV series *Vegas* was named Dan Tanna in tribute. *Courtesy of Elisa Jordan, Lawomantours.com*

was anyone turning up for Monday's audition or "Hoot" night. Perhaps only the Cavern Club in Liverpool is more famous in rock history—and that club only launched the Beatles. The Troubadour launched so many acts to worldwide attention that the list sounds ridiculous. Elton John played his first breakthrough U.S. shows there, the Eagles met there, Neil Young and Stephen Stills hung out there with the likes of Joni Mitchell, Linda Ronstadt, Lowell George, and Bonnie Raitt, Cheech & Chong started there, and comedian and movie star Steve Martin learned his stand-up craft in front of the Troubadour crowds.

The club may no longer be singer/songwriter central, like it was in the '70s, but it's still a terrific place and great value for an evening visit—but only after visiting Dan Tana's Restaurant, just a couple of doors down the street. Henley and Frey liked to eat here—at table number four at the front, near the bar, they'll tell you—before taking in a show, or just hanging out in the front bar at the Troubadour. Before the rock stars moved in, it was an old-time movie-star haunt, complete with checkered tablecloths and a downhome Italian vibe.

Henley and Frey wrote some major hits sitting in Dan Tana's, notably "Tequila Sunrise" and "Best of My Love." If you do visit, expect to see some A-listers munching on lasagna and gnocchi. It's that kind of place.

I Love Lucy

When the Eagles started out, Frey liked to insist that they were "Eagles," not "the Eagles." A minor point of semantics, perhaps, but in another Frey/Henley haunt, Lucy's El Adobe on Melrose, a photo of the band from their Rock and Roll Hall of Fame induction sits behind the register. The photo is signed, "To Lucy, with love, Eagles (all of us)."

The restaurant is near Paramount Studios at 5536 Melrose Avenue, between Beachwood Drive and Plymouth Boulevard. The owner, Lucy Casado, opened the restaurant in 1964 and still loves the musicians she helped back when they were poor, and who stuck with her through thick and thin. Fifth Eagle Jackson Browne is a particular favorite, as she told *Hollywood Patch* in September 2011: "Jackson! What can I tell you about Jackson? Everyone knows—he's a great man. Of all the rock stars and musicians, nobody does more for other people—more benefits, more charities—than Jackson. Nobody. He's brave. He will march on picket lines. He will protest. He will be there. There aren't many like him. He cares, and he shows up."

Echo Park in central Los Angeles is these days a cool, hip community. In the early '70s, it was less so, but it was cheap—which is why Frey and his songwriting buddies lived there. As Frey would later tell Cameron Crowe, he lived in an Echo Park building with Jackson Browne and J. D. Souther, sharing a cramped apartment with the latter for $60 a month.

Talking of the less than salubrious, be careful visiting another must-see Eagles scene, the Lido Apartments lobby. This is where they shot the inside photos for the *Hotel California* album. The location, at 6500 Yucca Street in East Los Angeles, is run-down and shady, but if you can get inside the building (be careful!), you'll see why the lobby was chosen for the photo shoot. It has a Moorish look, but it's dark and sinister and definitely evokes the darkness of those eerie Henley lyrics.

It's probably best to counter the seediness of the Lido with a trek to the location used on the front of the *Hotel California* album: the famous Beverly Hills Hotel. Head back to Sunset Boulevard, near Rodeo Drive, and you'll see the Pink Palace, a Hollywood staple for celebrities, movie stars, and industry movers-and-shakers since it was built in 1912.

20

Pretty Maids All in a Row

All You Need Is Love

Don Henley, Glenn Frey, Randy Meisner, and Bernie Leadon were hardly rock-and-roll virgins when they formed Linda Ronstadt's backing band at Anaheim in the summer of 1971. Frey and his friend Souther had a reputation as sexual athletes for most of their time in Los Angeles, while Meisner and Leadon had been through several band implosions due to drugs. Henley had seen a fellow band member die in an accident, while Leadon had been part of the Flying Burrito Brothers, who had fired their leader, Gram Parsons, due to the effects of acid, alcohol, cocaine, and heroin abuse on his behavior. In fact, Parsons' addiction was so bad that when he followed his friend Keith Richards to France, the other Stones had him removed for being a bad influence on Keith.

There's really very little that the individual Eagles did as they "took it to the limit" in their own rock-and-roll fast lane that millions of Americans weren't doing as well. It was really just a matter of degree. Bands like the Eagles and Led Zeppelin and the Rolling Stones and Fleetwood Mac could shell out millions of dollars on the finest alcohol, pills, and drugs. It was a life of extravagant excess. If they wanted hamburgers from a vendor in a different city, why not send a plane to pick a few up? If a girlfriend was out of town, why not fly her in on a Learjet for a romantic interlude? This was one of Don Henley's favorite moves, and the reason for the "Love 'em and Lear 'em" tag that was mostly aimed at the band's king of romance. Rumor has it that if experience told them—or the rock-and-roll telegraph indicated—that the groupies and hookers in a particular town were below their usual grade, arrangements were made to fly some favorite California ladies to the hotel in question.

Wall Street

The Eagles' behavior was extreme, yes, but not so different from that of the Wall Street bankers, business executives, or politicians stopping off in five-star hotels across America. Before the real dangers of addiction were widely understood, when smoking was allowed almost everywhere, and long before America had multiple TV series about celebrities in rehab, drugs were accepted and tolerated in many circles. In fact, LSD (or acid) had only been illegal in California since 1966, and in America as a whole since 1968.

Sure, there were pockets of moral disdain, but in the major metropolitan centers there was an underlying acceptance of marijuana, alcohol, and cocaine. In April 1973, *Time* magazine described a fashionable dinner party on Manhattan's East Side in New York as including all the "chic refreshments." It began with perfectly mixed martinis, followed by a fine vintage French wine with the main course. With dessert guests puffed the finest marijuana. Then, after coffee and cognac, the young hostess presented the evening's pièce de résistance: a glass jar filled with white powder. "Would anybody like a hit of coke?" she asked casually, as if offering another drink.

As Don Henley noted to the *Daily Mirror* in March 2008, "It was something that practically everyone was doing. It was a time when there was a generation that was coming of age and experimenting with whatever they could get their hands on. But in our case—luckily—not a great deal of damage was done. We managed to remain productive through that period, making albums, touring and being successful."

The first thing David Geffen did with his select band of country-rockers was send them off to Aspen, Colorado, to rehearse and become a tight musical entity. Besides learning to play as a unit and developing those immediately identifiable vocal harmonies, the Eagles learned how to party. Aspen was their rock-and-roll lifestyle training session. "Our label, Asylum, booked us into a club in Aspen, Colorado, because we needed to play to people," Henley told the *Daily Mail* in May 2013. "It was a wooden shed, but we had some wild times there. It was a hippie town, and everybody was on drugs."

Almost Famous

If Hollywood ever painted an accurate picture of rock bands on the road in the 1970s, complete with drugs, booze, "old ladies," dealers, and groupies, it was *Almost Famous*. It was realistic because the writer and director, Cameron Crowe, had been a rock journalist as a teenager. Crowe's enthusiasm, age, and innocence endeared him to several heavyweight rock bands of the early

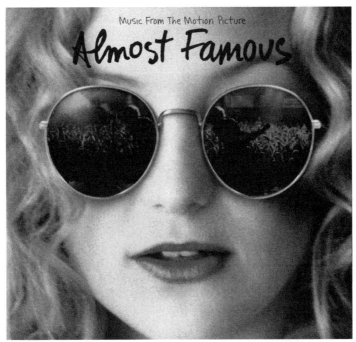

MUSIC FROM THE MOTION PICTURE
Almost Famous

Almost Famous director Cameron Crowe had interviewed the Eagles at length while a music reporter, and he based the Russell Hammond character, played by Billy Crudup, on Glenn Frey. This soundtrack album from the film, however, contains no Eagles tracks.

1970s, notably the Eagles, Led Zeppelin, and Lynyrd Skynyrd. He toured with the Eagles in their early days, and is as good a witness as there is to the sheer roguery of the band on the road.

In the September 2003 issue of *Rolling Stone*, Crowe explained why Glenn Frey was his inspiration for the rock-and-roll star in the movie, guitar whiz Russell Hammond. "I realized that so much of Russell is Glenn. He was the coolest guy I had ever met in 1972. I was backstage at a concert interviewing everybody—the Eagles, King Crimson, Ballin' Jack, Chaka Khan. In the Eagles' dressing room, everyone's talking about Glenn—the one guy who isn't there. He's out looking for babes. Everyone's like, 'The thing about Glenn,' 'Oh, one time Glenn and I . . .' And then, like a one-act play, Glenn appears. He walks in a little buzzed, he's got a long-neck Bud, and he's like, 'How ya doing'?' Just classic."

Don Henley, in retrospect, feels that a self-destructive phase in young rock-and-rollers is just part of the deal. It comes with success. "There was a lot of braggadocio about intake and behavior," he told the *Daily Telegraph* in November 2007. "The fact is, we were sort of a binge and purge kind of band. In between the benders, I remember jogging and going to the gym and taking vitamins. When you think about it, we managed to accomplish quite a bit given the shape we were in."

Third Encore

As the money flowed in, so did the parties and exploits become more outrageous. It was really just a matter of scale and price. During the *One of These Nights* tour in 1975, the Eagles decided to limit themselves to just two encore songs. The third encore would be saved for something a little more titillating and adult in nature than performing another Eagles hit. As at most rock-and-roll shows of the era, roadies were sent into the audience to scout potential guests for the after-show parties—those guests being attractive and unattached women. Those interested typically received special backstage passes—a passport to the rock-and-roll good-time hour. So there could be no confusion with regular crew laminates, the Eagles used buttons: a classy and discrete "3E," in yellow type, which was short for "third encore," the after-show hotel-suite party for specially invited female company.

Henley's excesses tended to involve women, and he would appear to have had quite the reputation as a ladies' man. Connie Hamzy, a well-known groupie, wrote a book about her exploits in the 1970s and told Howard Stern on his radio show that Henley was one her top two rock-star lovers.

According to another of the women he wooed with extravagant gestures, Stevie Nicks, Henley loved to spend his Eagle cash. "The Eagles had it down," she told *Uncut* in May 2003. "They had the Learjets and the presidential suites long before we did and so I learnt from the best. And once you learn to live like that, there's no going back. It's like, 'Get me a Learjet. I need to go to L.A. I don't care if it costs $15,000. I need to go now.'"

Chainsaw Massacre

Things became more extravagant and outrageous when party-loving wild man Joe Walsh joined the band. Walsh was exorcising some demons of his own—mainly the tragic death of his daughter Emma in a car accident when she was just three years old. Drink, drugs, or both; Walsh used them in excess, to have fun, or to medicate the pain, depending on which way one chooses to look at his history.

Walsh, a longstanding friend of the Who's drummer Keith Moon, learned plenty from one of rock music's most extreme and outrageous characters. Like Moon, he took to destroying hotel rooms, perfecting his own destruction style with the frightening cutting power of a chainsaw. As he explained to *Men's Journal* in June 2012, there are specific requirements to such activity: "Two things: superglue and a chain saw. You can superglue a toilet seat down or glue stuff to the ceiling. You can superglue somebody in their room, and they're there for at least a day. I had a chain saw for a while. You find if you have a chain saw, you really don't need to use it very often—just walking up to the front desk holding it will usually get a lot done. One of the most terrifying things that ever happened to me was that Keith Moon decided he liked me. He taught me the finer arts of hotel damage."

Walsh did things his own way. Chicago DJ Bob Stroud was at WLUP in the '70s and later recalled Joe Walsh showing up at the station dressed in just a bathrobe bearing the logo of the hotel the Eagles were staying in. One night in 1978, at a hotel in Chicago, Irving Azoff could only grin and watch while Joe Walsh wrecked a hotel room with a chainsaw, causing Azoff and the Eagles to be billed for $20,000 worth of destruction.

Eagle Poker

And then there was the gambling. The Eagles became renowned for their poker games. Frey was the protagonist, inventing a game he called "Eagle poker"—essentially a derivative of acey-deucey, a game that's more about chance than skill. Frey got the Eagles playing when they traveled to London in the winter to record the *Desperado* album. With not much to do, stuck miles away from central London in a country where the bars and pubs closed their doors two hours before midnight, the band spent a lot time playing Frey's game and became quite skilled at it. Eagle poker became more and more popular, and was introduced to new band members and crew alike.

On tour with Neil Young in the United Kingdom, Henley used the game for some payback on Young's producer, David Briggs, who had been giving the Eagles a hard time on the bus. Henley took Briggs for $7,000, a large amount of money in 1972, as guitarist Don Felder reports in his book, *Heaven and Hell.* (Felder quit the poker games himself after losing $2,000 to a roadie.)

Back in the United States, Frey hosted regular high-stakes poker games at his Laurel Canyon hacienda on Kirkwood Drive, where the Frey gang amused themselves betting thousands of dollars on hands of poker and piling up hundreds of bottles of their favorite Mexican beer into unusually creative structures.

Frey came up with a term of his own to describe the use of illegal substances. He called it "monstering," inspired by Robert Louis Stevenson's classic tale of split personality, *The Strange Case of Dr. Jekyll and Mr. Hyde*, in which the title character periodically changes from good to bad. Frey explained the connection to *International Musician and Recording World* in September 1982: "It's when you take foreign substances and chemicals into your body and slowly, but surely transform yourself into the party person that you are. So your monster is who you are when you're high or when you're drunk."

21

The Player You Get

U nlike Don Felder, a guitarist's guitarist generally unknown to the public, Joe Walsh was already a hit-making axe-man of note, celebrated and feted in hard-rock and mainstream rock-and-roll circles. He was mates with Pete Townshend and Jimmy Page, and his prior band had opened for the Who at their frightening peak.

Walsh was a showman, a rock-and-roll guitar-slinger, and a feisty character who liked nothing more than popping music-biz balloons of pomposity and creating havoc and amusement around him. He once said that Pete Townshend taught him how to play guitar and Keith Moon showed him how to wreck a hotel room. He was truly larger than life and a daunting prospect for any band to accept into their ranks. But Irving Azoff figured it would work out. Felder, Frey, and Henley worked on his live album *You Can't Argue with a Sick Mind* (released in 10976) and liked what they heard.

Walsh had more credibility in rock-and-roll circles than all the other Eagles put together. With his trademark guitar slung low like a Wild West gunfighter, he played with an aggressive tone but combined it with his natural bent for melody. He looked dangerous but sounded sweet—at times. He was a guitar god, Slash before Slash was born. He would naturally bring a rougher and tougher element to the Eagles sound, clearly marking their move away from their mellow beginnings.

Roots

Joe Walsh was originally from Wichita, Kansas, but grew up in Columbus, Ohio, before moving east to New York City and New Jersey. It was John, Paul, George, and Ringo who got Walsh started in music, as with so many other musicians in the 1960s. Walsh saw them on *The Ed Sullivan Show* and was as impressed by the band's cool factor as he was by their music.

The Walsh family moved to New York when Joe was eleven years old. Initially, they lived in a third-story, two-bedroom apartment in the city. It was serious culture shock for a kid who had enjoyed the typical eleven-year-old's outdoor pursuits in Ohio. One day, horribly bored in the apartment, he discovered an antenna on the building's roof. He traced the wires that led from it to an apartment and inquired at the door as to what they were all about. The owner was a ham-radio operator. Walsh was transfixed, and has been a serious ham-radio fan ever since.

The family soon moved to Montclair, New Jersey. Being close to Manhattan and the new music of the day had its uses, as Walsh remembered to the *New Jersey Monthly* in June 2012. "I was not old enough to get in, but I would go to the Village and stand out front [of the Bitter End] and listen to the Lovin' Spoonful. I'd go stand in front of the Peppermint Lounge and listen to Joey Dee and the Starliters. I would go to Manny's Music Store,

The original James Gang trio lineup—Joe Walsh, Tom Kriss, and Jim Fox— released *Yer' Album* in March 1969. They'd been signed to ABC and produced by future Eagles recording maestro Bill Szymczyk.

and I would look at all the guitars and all the amps and dream. Didn't have money to buy 'em. And then I would take the last bus back out to Montclair."

Walsh went to high school in New Jersey. He joined the school marching band, where he played the oboe, of all things. Discovering that he could play anything he heard in his head on guitar, he switched instruments and got a gig playing rhythm guitar in an instrumental band with Bob Edwards, the G-Clefts. "Even though we could hardly play anything, we had plans to be the next Ventures," he told *Rolling Stone* in February 1975. "All those great instrumentals like 'Wipe Out,' 'Wild Weekend,' and 'Walk, Don't Run' were coming out, and we learned them all. We were terrible; but it was cool. I never got any shit 'cause I only played rhythm."

Walsh then took to bass guitar in his senior year with the Nomads, a covers band that played gigs in the area. When it came time for college, he was ready to quit school and become a professional musician, but his parents had other ideas. Fortunately for Walsh, he was enrolled at Kent Sate, a freewheeling school at the time, and while studying—or at least attending—he played in a rock band called the Measles. The eighteen-year-old guitarist had found his calling.

When one of the Measles was called up to the army, the band broke up, and Walsh knocked on the door of Jim Fox, the drummer of another well-respected local band, the James Gang.

The James Gang

The James Gang were good, and Walsh knew he had to take this gig seriously. He studied the guitar like he hadn't before, which included learning some B.B. King licks after he read about the blues pioneer in an interview with Eric Clapton. Playing as part of a three-piece meant the guitar carried a bigger load than normal. On top of that, he was also the band's singer. But the commitment to improve brought a new focus to Walsh's playing. The James Gang were so good, in fact, that they soon scored a recording deal, plus support gigs with one of the most respected rock-and-roll bands in the world: the Who.

Initially, the band played covers, but Walsh's originality soon shone through. As he told *Guitar World* in 2013, "The James Gang started out doing cover songs. And then the next thing for us was to do the beginning of a cover song and then do a five-minute jam in the middle that was different every night. And 'Funk #49' was actually a groove that we'd come up

This 1973 release put Walsh on the rock-and-roll map, thanks mainly to the hit single "Rocky Mountain Way."

with—one of our tools that we would throw into the middle of cover songs. And finally we just wrote some words for it."

The James Gang's manager, Cleveland concert promoter Mike Belkin, got the band a recording contract with ABC/Bluesway, and they recorded an album, *Yer' Album*, with producer Bill Szymczyk. The local favorites became a major draw in the region, and were especially noted for their fast, loud, and sonically dynamic live shows. One night in Pittsburgh, they were booked as the local act to open for the Who. Headliners don't often see the support bands perform, but on this occasion, Pete Townshend watched the James Gang with admiration. He later said that Walsh's guitar playing was unusually fluid and intelligent.

Townshend pulled a few strings, and the James Gang opened for the Who again in the spring of 1970, even supporting them on some European dates. And, aside from impressing the Who, they now had another new fan in Led Zeppelin guitar god Jimmy Page. "The James Gang opened for

Led Zeppelin a couple times right at the end of the Yardbirds, when Led Zeppelin was together," Walsh told *Guitar World*. "Before their first album really hit, they came over and played shows. It was Jimmy Page's new band. So I started a friendship with him at that time."

In May 1970, Walsh returned to the Kent State campus from a road trip to hear that there had been trouble on campus. The next day he was witness to violence himself, as he told *Rolling Stone* in 1975. "People started to scream and cry. I even saw a National Guardsman throw down his gun and sob, 'What the fuck have we done!' The whole town went into shock. Nobody was allowed downtown, all the bars closed. The whole scene totally fell apart. Everybody gave up, and so did I. It was too heavy to have been there."

Fortunately, Walsh had his music career, and with the James Gang he put out two more studio albums, *James Gang Rides Again* and *Thirds*. But the band would not be the future. Walsh had tired of the restrictions of being in a three-piece. He wanted to do more musically, but the band couldn't recreate his ideas onstage with just three instruments. The loud, metal power of the James Gang was becoming restrictive, and Walsh wanted a change.

They did find time to play Carnegie Hall in New York in May 1971, resulting in a live album, *James Gang Live in Concert*, released in September 1971, four months prior to Walsh's departure. But he still wasn't happy. The rock-and-roll lifestyle had taken over from music, as he explained to *Rolling Stone* in 1975. "The band began to turn into a big group preoccupied with bucks. Everybody started buying big cars. The emphasis came off good music and creating; that was all left behind. I got fed up with the whole flash guitarist, heavy metal thing we were going toward. They money was great, but I felt like a whore. I played the remaining dates and quit."

Free at Last

Once the word was out, various offers came in for Walsh's guitar-playing services. Humble Pie wanted him to move to England. Instead, Walsh chose to head west, to Boulder, Colorado, with his wife Stefany and baby daughter Emma. In the spring of 1972, he worked with bassist Kenny Passarelli and drummer Joe Vitale as Joe Walsh & Barnstorm. Their album came out in October 1972, and it was a radical departure from the James Gang.

The album *was* lovingly textured and heavily produced, with synths and acoustic instruments taking up as much space as his trademark electric guitars. But stylistic departures typically satisfy artists and confuse fans. Thus it was with *Barnstorm*. The album failed to set the charts alight. Maybe it was the name, because the following year, Walsh used most of the same musicians on a follow-up album, credited simply to Joe Walsh, called *The Smoker You Drink, the Player You Get*, which made the *Billboard* Top 10. Much of the success was down to one song, the magnificent "Rocky Mountain Way," which had been inspired by the stunning landscape of Colorado.

Song for Emma

While Walsh was in the studio making records, Stefany and Emma liked to take a walk every day from their home in North Boulder Park to a playground that Emma enjoyed. It was a safe, simple life. Walsh had been away during the spring of 1974 but was due to arrive home on April 1. That morning, Stefany was driving her daughter to playgroup when tragedy struck. A

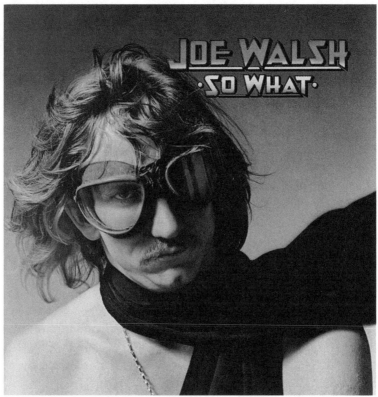

The title of this 1974 LP, *So What*, came from Walsh's attitude toward life at the time. He'd recently lost his young daughter in a car accident. Thanks to management connections, several Eagles—namely Don Henley, Glenn Frey, and Randy Meisner—sang harmony on some sessions.

car drove through a stop sign and hit Stefany's Porsche hard enough to spin it across the street. Stefany was not hurt, but Emma, just three years old, suffered serious brain injuries. She died in the hospital that night. Walsh was devastated; he and Stefany never recovered emotionally from the accident, and were divorced not long after the terrible event.

While he couldn't admit it for a long time, Walsh almost went under. Years later, he told radio presenter Redbeard, on an episode of *In the Studio*, how deeply he was affected by his daughter's death. The presenter asked Joe a question that he had been asked many times before: why did he join the Eagles? Walsh would usually talk about admiring the group, or, if he was feeling flippant, he might say he was recruited for his sense of humor and fun, so as to stop the Eagles beating each other up. But on this occasion, he told the truth.

"At that time, I was coming off of the death of my daughter Emma, who was killed by a drunken driver in 1974," he said. "Some senile drunken lady ran a stop sign, and I lost my family. And I tried to kill myself for two years. That's why I called my album *So What*. I didn't care about nothing. I didn't have any emotions, and I was not strong enough to continue a solo career. On *So What* is a song called 'Song for Emma.' She died . . . nobody knew that. I didn't allow it being in *People* magazine or Associated Press. I kept that very quiet. But that squashed me like a bug and I tried to kill myself for eighteen months. And I still wasn't dead. So I forgave God and joined the Eagles, just to get going again."

22

Funk #49

Guitar Talk

While the Eagles were blending country music and rock and roll, the band's main guitarists through the years—Glenn Frey, Don Felder, Bernie Leadon, and Joe Walsh—have employed an array of instruments to craft the group's distinctive six-string interplay.

As with many musicians—and guitarists in particular—these men have picked up and played hundreds of instruments. Don Felder, for instance, owns over 300 guitars and claims to have kept every one he has ever owned. But within this huge arsenal of instruments, there are some distinctive guitars that play an intrinsic part in the musical history of the Eagles.

Glenn Frey

The guitar Glenn Frey is most associated with is "Old Black," the '50s Les Paul Junior he's been playing since at least 1974. Read the numerous guitar forums and blogs on the web, and there are some who suggest that that the guitar came to him by way of Little Feat six-stringer Paul Barrere, but Frey himself told *International Musician and Recording World* in September 1982 that it was a gift from songwriting pal Jackson Browne, from their Echo Park days. Browne could not get the guitar to tune properly, so when he got a new Telecaster, he passed the Les Paul to Frey.

"Old Black" was loud, which was to Frey's liking, and its thick neck suited his workmanlike guitar style. "I play it hard," he continued. "I'm not an artful player, so I need something I can grab onto." Frey's a better guitarist than he claims, though, and while some fans have called him the Keith Richards of the Eagles, due to his rock-steady rhythm work, some of his solos, on songs like "Witchy Woman" and "Already Gone," reveal him to be an underrated lead player as well.

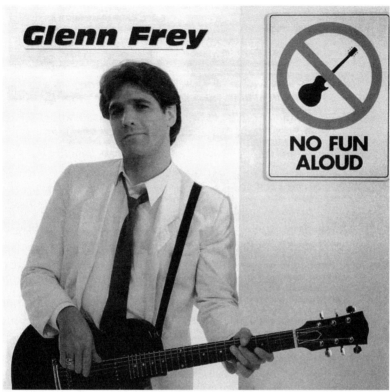

Glenn Frey, on the cover of his 1982 debut solo album *No Fun Aloud*, with "Old Black," the '50s Les Paul Junior that his pal Jackson Browne gave him in the early '70s.

Aside from "Old Black," Frey used a Gibson SG Junior with the Eagles for a short period in the '70s, and a Gibson ES-335 in the late '70s and early '80s, mostly during his solo years. In the 1990s, he moved away from Gibson for a while and associated himself with Rickenbacker, which made him the Glenn Frey Limited Edition (only one hundred ever made), about which he said in a 1992 Rickenbacker statement: "The shape is contoured for ease and comfort, the appearance striking, but subtle. The high output humbucking pickups provide a wide range of tones, from the warmest to the brightest, with a simple combination of tone and volume controls—in other words, a guitar for everybody to enjoy. This guitar truly represents a return to simplicity. I can get all the sounds I want, and more, from these instruments without clutter or complexity."

Most recently, as on the band's 2013 tour, he's played a Les Paul Cherry Sunburst.

Bernie Leadon

As a multi-instrumentalist with a bluegrass background and an uncanny sense of harmony, Leadon was integral to helping shape the band's early country-rock sound. The band's original guitarist, he is less associated with a special guitar than with a brand and a particular style and technique.

Leadon was a Fender Telecaster player during his tenure with the Eagles, and he continues to be today. A disciple of Byrds guitar great Clarence White, Leadon often used a "B-Bender" to simulate pedal steel—most notably on "Peaceful Easy Feeling" from *Eagles*, widely considered to be the first Top 10 hit to feature the effect.

Developed on White's old guitar back in 1965, the B-Bender immediately gave guitarists the ability to imitate pedal steel bends mid-flow on a standard guitar, and played a significant part in the development of country-rock guitar. The Parsons/White Pull-String, to give it its formal name, has been an essential part of the Nashville sound ever since White and his drummer friend Gene Parsons came up with it. Their radical invention is a mechanism in the back of the guitar attached to the strap button, connected to an internal lever-and-gear system that bends the second ("B") string anywhere from a half-tone to a full tone, by simply pulling down on it.

Parsons and White were hardly businessmen, and they sold their idea to Fender, which never actually released any product. They then licensed the design to Dave Evans, who developed and sold his own version from 1969 to 1973. Bernie Leadon was one of his very satisfied customers.

Don Felder

The peerless twelve-string part Felder plays on his Gibson double-neck guitar to begin "Hotel California" is absolutely one of the most iconic moments in rock-and-roll history, but there are actually two legendary Gibson electrics that figure into his history with the Eagles: a '59 Les Paul Standard and an EDS-1275. Felder has often spoken about the unique sound he achieves playing the '59 Les Paul through a narrow-panel Fender Tweed Deluxe. "That combination is a very common sound of mine," he told *Guitar World*, explaining that he used the setup for "One of These Nights" and for his solo parts in "Hotel California."

Although Felder's acoustic intro for the studio version of "Hotel California" was played on either a Takamine twelve-string or a Martin twelve-string (he's cited both, in separate interviews), in live performance, he famously turned to the Gibson EDS-1275 double-neck. His original EDS-1275 is now in the Rock and Roll Hall of Fame, while his '59 Les Paul is locked away in a secure location.

From a young age, Felder was a Gibson man, as he told Anne Erickson of Gibson.com in 2012. "I've been a Gibson advocate since the first Les Paul Jr. that I ever got to play in high school," he said. "I scraped together some money working at a music store and playing in a band, and I finally ordered a 355, which was my dream guitar."

Felder is a serious musician, so the guitar's mechanics and musicality were important factors to him, but image counted pretty highly, too. "I was in a band and everybody in the band had cherry red guitars," he told me in 2010. "So the bass player had a cherry red EB-0, which is a thin line, hollow body bass, the other guitar player had a 330 and I wanted to have the 335, so we all had matching Gibson guitars—really a great look." Within four months, sadly, that cherry-red guitar was stolen from Felder during a gig in Miami. "I was heartbroken," he said. "It destroyed me."

As a mark of respect toward Felder's guitar legacy, the Gibson Custom Shop has produced Felder Signature Models of both his iconic guitars, replicating their exact specifications. "They're just incredible," he told *Guitar World*'s Damian Fanelli in March 2013, describing the EDS-1275 and '59 Les Paul reissues. "I use them on the road because they feel so much like my originals, right down to the stains, rust and tarnish. Seriously, when I put both guitars side by side, I have a hard time telling them apart. Even all the scratches and nicks are there. When I went to Gibson's Custom Shop, they had Billy Gibbons' Les Paul there. I asked them, 'How do you put these scratches in? They look so identical.' They opened a drawer and took out a rhinestone Elvis Presley belt buckle and said, 'This is what we use.'"

Other noteworthy guitars in Felder's collection include a Taylor acoustic (for songwriting and for practice, prior to live shows) and a Les Paul Special (used on the studio version of "Already Gone," among others). "I have guitars that are always sitting in my studio, ready to go," he told Erickson. "I have a Sunburst Les Paul, a '59 Les Paul, a Goldtop Les Paul, Gibson acoustic guitars and on stage, I play my Don Felder 'Hotel California' EDS-1275. Those are my first go-to guitars, and I use them on the road or in the studio. I have a little under 300 guitars in my collection, and Gibsons are usually the ones I go to first when writing and looking for certain sound. It's just a great instrument."

Joe Walsh

Walsh sometimes seems as famous for the guitars he's parted with as he is for the guitars he plays—not least Jimmy Page's "Number One," the 1959 Les Paul Standard that's been integral to Page's work from *Led Zeppelin II* onward. "Jimmy was having trouble finding a good Les Paul back then," Walsh recalled at the Guitar Center launch of the 2008 Gibson Les Paul Standard. "I had two, so I sold him one of mine. He used that Les Paul on the bulk of his work with Led Zeppelin. Once you get used to a Les Paul it becomes your axe from then on. Les Pauls are like that. Once you find your personal Les Paul, that's it."

Walsh also gave Pete Townshend the 1959 Gretsch 6120 famously used during the recording of *Who's Next*. "The James Gang opened for the Who

When Joe Walsh released his *Analog Man* album in 2013, he kept technology at bay and relied on old-fashioned methods, like the Gibson acoustic guitar pictured on the front cover.

when they performed *Tommy* in England and in Europe for the first time," he told *Guitar World*'s Alan Di Perna in 2012. "So Pete and I started hanging out. After Tommy, he was playing a Gibson SG and Hiwatt amps . . . But he was kind of stuck in that, and I think he wanted to move on. So I figured, well, a Bigsby should fuck him up pretty good! And that Gretsch was a great guitar. . . . So I gave him my 6120 and a 3x10 Bandmaster, an old Fender amp that I had. And said, 'Here.' And *Who's Next* is that."

As regards Walsh's own collection, the veteran rocker possesses a monumental stash of instruments. On the Eagles' most recent tour, he's been playing a Music Man Axis Super Sport, a Music Man Silhouette (for "Hotel California"), a Les Paul Standard (for "Rocky Mountain Way"), and a Gibson Explorer, among other instruments. When push comes to shove, his all-time favorite setup is a '58, '59, or '60 Standard, a wah-wah pedal, a tube-model Echoplex, and a pair of Fender Super Reverbs. He also prefers a Les Paul with a raised action for slide work. "I always come back to my 1958 Les Paul Goldtop and a 1956 Stratocaster," he told *Guitar World*, when asked about his must-have gear. "They were two of the first electric guitars ever designed, and I am not sure anybody has topped them in all these years."

You can't discuss Walsh's guitars without mentioning his trademark talk-box—the immediately identifiable sound heard as his "Rocky Mountain Way" roars out of the radio. Essentially, the talk-box is an effects unit that lets the guitarist change the sound of the guitar using his mouth via a plastic tube running from the effects unit. Speaking with *M—Music & Musicians* in 2012, Walsh revealed how he stumbled across it. "The James Gang used to play in Nashville, and I became good friends with Dottie West, the famous classic country singer. Dottie's husband, Bill West, was a pedal steel player. He actually invented the Talk Box that was used on Pete Drake's album. One day, while I was at Dottie's house, Bill went out to the garage and got it and gave it to me."

It took a couple of months for Walsh to become proficient with the device. "After I got the hang of it, I then figured out how it was built. I went to a hardware store and got some parts and made one for myself. 'Rocky Mountain Way' was the first time I used it on record."

23

Hotel California

Check Out, Never Leave

T he Eagles did not receive the kind of critical recognition they felt they deserved (and, in retrospect, absolutely *did* deserve) through the 1970s. Somehow, too many critics felt they were a sellout Flying Burrito Brothers, or a too-slick Poco. Gram Parsons slammed them, but then he slammed almost everyone else attempting to fuse country music and rock and roll. The press understood Jackson Browne, who was stylistically very similar and certainly cut from the same denim-and-cheese cloth, but Browne had a political edge that lined him up with the hipper, cooler acts of the day. Neil Young, Stephen Stills, Lowell George, and Harry Nilsson, for example, had street credibility; Bruce Springsteen was blue-collar rock and roll and always a critic's darling. But Bread, America, and the Eagles were considered lightweight—a huge misconception, in the case of Frey's band. Then, while Henley, Frey & co. were working on ideas for what would become *Hotel California*, rock and roll went through a ground-level revolution.

New York, New York

The New York Dolls (whom Frey had famously dissed back in '72) were breaking down social, gender, and musical barriers, upsetting the rock-and-roll establishment, and creating a movement. In the U.K., the pop world was shocked by the outrageous and anarchistic Sex Pistols as a new music emerged from the streets. Punk was becoming significant in both America and Europe. The minimalist, "anyone can do it" philosophy radically challenged the accepted wisdom of what defines musicianship within the boundaries of rock and roll. Punk was homemade, raw, and spontaneous. It was, on the surface at least, the polar opposite of slick, smooth studio bands like Fleetwood Mac and Steely Dan—and, yes, the Eagles.

The Write Stuff

In the shape of Don Henley and Glenn Frey, however, the Eagles had a secret weapon. Their songs were as good as anything in rock and roll in the '70s, and in Henley they had a writer who was a wry and increasingly experienced observer of his world, and a sharp social commentator. Henley had lived through personal and professional turmoil, and he experienced it on a micro and a macro level. He and the Eagles *were* America; they had moved quickly from the warm cozy idealism of the 1960s to the chilled, steely self-indulgence, excess, and materialism of the 1970s. The Eagles' shared experience was vital. They had all migrated from small-town America to the vice capital of the world, Los Angeles.

Not only did this album sell a cool sixteen million copies in America, its three hit singles ("New Kid in Town," "Hotel California," and "Life in the Fast Lane") were all radio classics, all very different, and all showed Henley, Frey, and the rest at the absolute top of their game.

For all Hollywood's magic and wonder, there was a tangible taste of despair and darkness blowing down Sunset Boulevard. Like novelist and hypocrisy-buster Nathanael West in the 1930s, Henley lived and breathed the dangerous air in Los Angeles, at once drawn to and repelled by the sin, the excess, the hedonism, and the pursuit of pleasure. Henley's intellect fought against the narcissism of being a rock star in a world where "no" just doesn't exist. He loved it and he hated it. And it was that conflict, tied to Henley's gift of expressing astute social observations in three-minute pop songs, that gave the Eagles a chance to stay relevant, despite the revolution happening down on the streets in cities around the globe. Whether 1970s critics would buy into Henley's concept or savagely pillory him for his pomposity and hypocrisy was never the point. Henley had opinions to air, and as he has proved quite adeptly many times during his long career, he will have his say, one way or another.

On the Record

Fittingly, since the album was going to focus on California and L.A. as a metaphor for the United States, much of the recording was done in Hollywood, at the Record Plant. But the Eagles also agreed to do some sessions in Miami (where Bill Szymczyk made his home) at the legendary Criteria Studios.

With the band hot off a hit album, their record company spared no expense in recording facilities or studio time. This was the era of massive and luxurious recording studios that housed bands and their too-large entourages as they spent hours "creating" in the studio. Just like the world around them, the recording process was indulgent and excessive, especially in contrast to the way "independent" records were being made in the punk and new wave scenes of New York, Los Angeles, and London. The Eagles were products of their environments, and they simply adopted the studio culture of the day.

It was loose—in terms of taking the time to get a riff or a lick correct—and relaxed enough for plenty of substance breaks, but never did any of the band members forget about making music of the highest possible order. That was why they were a band: it was what the Eagles did.

Time was split pretty evenly between Miami and Los Angeles. It was a "bits and pieces" album, as befits a group containing several perfectionists. Someone would come in with a title or a riff; ideas would be kicked around. Melodies would be worked on and finished in the studio, and then words written and vocals added at the next block of sessions. They would work for a month at a time in Miami or Los Angeles, with several weeks in between to perfect lyrics.

Mexican Reggae

It was Felder who invented and developed the original musical idea that became "Hotel California." Brought into the band for his audacious slide-guitar skills, the other Don was an accomplished all-round musician who felt he could throw different musical textures and ideas into the Eagles mix: a crucial role as they set about finally breaking ties with the country-rock tag that the majority of the band believed had kept them locked into a past that they had never been entirely comfortable with.

That summer, Felder had found himself a beach house in Malibu, and one fine California day, while enjoying the weather and spectacular ocean view, he picked up a twelve-string acoustic guitar and began expressing his relaxed contentment with some chiming chords. Liking what he heard, he recorded the chord progression on the small TEAC four-track recorder that he kept set up and ready for inspiration. With the basic chords down, he added bass and a drum-machine beat before layering more twelve-string guitar on the top, bouncing tracks around on the recorder. "When I came up with the 'Hotel California' progression," he told Gibson.com in 2010, "I knew it was unique but didn't know if it was appropriate for the Eagles. It was kind of reggae, almost an abstract guitar part for what was on the radio back then."

Felder made some cassettes of the song and gave a copy to each of his bandmates. Some time later, Henley made a phone call to Felder to let him know that he really liked the "Mexican bolero" tune. "I knew what track he meant," Felder told me. Then Henley set about writing the lyrics that would cause quite a stir, both positively and negatively, as the "Hotel California" saga played out in America.

If any track proved that the Eagles had been wise to bring in both Felder and Walsh (and that's not to say that Bernie Leadon could not have played at the same level, had he stayed around longer), it was "Hotel California." With its breezy acoustic intro, cod-reggae beat, and atmospheric, cinematic imagery, the song is a departure from their country/bluegrass past. And when Felder and Walsh launch into the twin–lead guitar passage, it's imme-diately obvious that the Eagles had morphed into a more intense, more dynamic, but still multi-layered musical machine. And magically, all of

The lobby of the Lido Hotel in Hollywood, as featured on the back cover of *Hotel California.*

them, despite the intensity of nine months in the studio, are playing at a creative peak that few would be able to reach again. It really is the Eagles' finest moment.

Twin Peaks

To record the twin-guitar outro, producer Bill Szymczyk had Felder and Walsh set up to play in the control room, so they could hear everything that came out of each other's guitars. They improvised and created on the spot, a technique Szymczyk refers to as "search and destroy."

It was a career highlight for the producer, as he told *Sound on Sound* magazine in November 2004. "Just overdubbing all those leads was a basic two-day process, and man, what a ball that was. They're both great, great players, and the two of them were on fire."

Don Felder discussed his interplay with Joe Walsh in an interview with Gibson.com in August 2010: "Joe and I had great respect for each other to step back and have the courtesy to allow the other player to play and that's really something you learn over the years. It's something that you do between two guitarists and also with the keyboard player, so everyone has an area where they shine and then step back and take a supporting role. Both guitarists have to dance together and have the grace to allow each other the space. Joe and I did it from the start; it was very easy to play with Joe."

Felder was surprised when Henley told him at the record's playback party that his bolero song was going to be the first single from the album. It was hardly formatted for AM radio, where hit singles lived and breathed. It was more of an FM, album-track sound. After all, the song was antithesis of a commercial radio hit. It had challenging lyrics, an unusual tropical sound, and, with its brilliant but extended guitar solo, was way too long for radio. Felder was happy to be wrong, of course. "It had a two-minute guitar solo on the end, it wasn't really rock and roll and the drums stopped in the middle," he told me. "I was really happy to lose that argument and be proven wrong. But Don's instincts on that track were just brilliant."

There was no hiding the serious intent behind the Eagles' new album as it launched at the end of 1976. "Hotel California" was a culmination of everything Henley and Frey had been cooking up for the past couple of years, and it was a great representative of the whole album. "We figured it was time for another concept album," Frey told radio presenter Redbeard, in a 1992 episode of *In the Studio*. "Not a 'cowboy' concept album, but the dark side of success, the underbelly of Hollywood and L.A. Someone described it as dark songs from paradise."

Henley also talked about *Hotel California* being a concept album when interviewed by *ZigZag* magazine in 1976. The motive, he said, was looking at America as it celebrated 200 years as a nation: "It's our bicentennial year, you know, the country is 200 years old, so we figured since we are the Eagles and the Eagle is our national symbol, that we were obliged to make some kind of a little bicentennial statement using California as a microcosm of the whole United States, or the whole world, if you will, and to try to wake people up and say, 'We've been okay so far, for 200 years, but we're gonna have to change if we're gonna continue to be around.'"

But while many marveled at the song's sound and message, others whispered that it was too close for comfort to "We Used to Know," an old tune by Jethro Tull. This was the band the novice Eagles had supported on several road dates on their first tour as a band, as Ian Anderson of Jethro Tull later told Songfacts.com: "We didn't interact with them very much because they were countrified laid-back polite rock, and we were a bit wacky and

English . . . [but] they probably heard us play the song, because that would have featured in the sets back then, and maybe it was just something they kind of picked up on subconsciously, and introduced that chord sequence into their famous song 'Hotel California' sometime later. But, you know, it's not plagiarism."

The Internet is filled with intellectual and pseudointellectual analysis of the musical basis for the Eagles lifting the song from the British prog-rock pioneers. It would have been totally innocent and so very easy for Felder to have heard Tull play the song so many times on those shows back in the early 1970s, and for it then to have filtered into his musical memory. Except that Felder would have had to have been in the audience, or backstage, since he didn't join the Eagles until 1974. He was of course friends with Bernie Leadon, and perhaps he was with the band when they all heard Tull play that distinctive chord progression. Asked whether he was familiar with the song during promo interviews for his 2012 album *Road to Forever*, Felder said he did not know the song but did recall that Jethro Tull was the band that had a guy with a flute. Or maybe, as many musicians will attest, there are only so many chord progressions, and sometimes several songs will have the same chords. Check out Lady Gaga's "The Edge of Glory," Pink's "F**kin' Perfect," and Rihanna's "California King Bed." Same four chords for all four songs.

There is no filler on *Hotel California*. If the title track was an eerie warning about America's social issues, "Last Resort" was the beginning of Henley's lifelong fight for environmentalism and ecology. As Frey told Redbeard, "It was the first time that Don took it upon himself to write an epic story and we were already starting to worry about the environment . . . we're constantly screwing up paradise and that was the point of the song and that at some point there is going to be no more new frontiers. I mean we're putting junk, er, garbage into space now."

Frey's vocals on his and J. D. Souther's "New Kid in Town" recall the early, classic Eagles country sound, but the production is miles away from Glyn Johns' more delicate treatment. This time around, the country-rock feel is tough and focused, allowing Felder's fiery guitar to impress and Frey to steal the show. Similarly, new boy Joe Walsh shines on his "Life in the Fast Lane." The track features a heavy guitar riff by Walsh, with lyrics that are a bit on the edgy side. Frey explained the song's genesis in the 2013 film *History of the Eagles: The Story of an American Band*. "I was riding shotgun in a Corvette with a drug dealer on the way to a poker game. The next thing

I know we're doing ninety. Holding! Big-Time! I say, 'Hey man!' He grins and goes, 'Life in the fast lane!' I thought, 'Now there's a song title.'"

Felder and Walsh combine powerfully again on "Victim of Love," a track that began with guitar from Felder before Souther, Henley, and Frey worked on lyrics. It's a feisty song, but more than its sonic boom, it's an early indicator that cracks were beginning to appear within the Eagles camp. Felder wanted to sing lead on the tracks, and was allowed to cut several versions. He was unhappy—from a democratic, "team player" point of view—that Henley later cut a new vocal that was used on the final record. But while it is understandable that Felder would feel passed over, Henley was the superior vocalist, and was 100 percent committed to *Hotel California*'s sound. Quality control outweighed any notions of fair play or sensitivity to Felder's ego.

Talking of vocals, Henley's work on "Wasted Time" is proof indeed that he had developed into one of the finest interpreters of lyrics in the business. The song is a low-key drinking ballad, somewhat akin to "Desperado" but tinged with a world-weary sadness that only experience could have delivered with such integrity.

"Try and Love Again," written and sung by bassist Randy Meisner, is another heart-wrenching ballad from a man who had proved himself capable of consistently high-quality musicianship via bass and backing vocals, and who could chip in with songs of his own that were as good as anything on any album. He had reached the top with his performance on "Take It to the Limit," but this song is almost as moving, and almost as memorable. In fact, it may be more memorable, since "Try and Love Again" was Meisner's last contribution to the Eagles catalogue. He rode off into the Nebraska sunset after the *Hotel California* project, worn down by the pressures of fame and success and exhausted by the internal personal politics.

Hotel California is the seminal Eagles album. The band had learned their craft well, developed as players and musicians and writers, and knew their way around the recording studio. Aware that they had a lot to live up to, after *One of These Nights*, they were inspired rather than daunted by the pressures of the challenge. According to Frey, he and Henley were supremely confident in their songwriting and musical abilities at that point. They were on a roll.

The album was released in December 1976, and was at #1 by January 15, 1977. It kept hold of the top spot for eight weeks and went on to sell more than sixteen million copies. "Hotel California" is one of the most recognizable songs in America—and almost every other country in the world. The first measure of a classic is whether other artists cover it, and in this case, hundreds have given it a go, from Nancy Sinatra, the Killers, and Rascal Flatts to the Gypsy Kings, Wilson Phillips, and Marilyn Manson.

Nielsen SoundScan has recorded that the Eagles' Mexican reggae tune is played on the radio somewhere in America once every eleven minutes. And that's almost forty years since its release. And the album continues to make headlines. To celebrate the Eagles' six-night residency at the refurbished L.A. Forum in 2014, a large rendering of the *Hotel California* LP was constructed to sit atop the venue. The rotating structure was made of vinyl, with a 470-foot diameter, and turned at a rate of seventeen miles per hour.

24

Take the Devil

The Darkness Behind the Glamorous Veneer of Hollywood

The music contained on the thin black vinyl of the Eagles' *Hotel California* album may have surprised and/or delighted many millions after its release, but there was more to the package than just what blasted from the turntable or washed gently over the radio waves.

As with *Desperado*, the Eagles had expended plenty of time, thought, and money on the album artwork—$60,000 to be precise, a small fortune in 1976. Henley had a concept, and he and manager Irving Azoff presented it to art director John Kosh, whose album covers for Linda Ronstadt and James Taylor they so admired. Norman Seef, the top rock-and-roll photographer who did the images for *One of These Nights*, took the pictures.

The visuals reinforce the themes explored in the songs, with the two sides of Hollywood presented as a microcosm for America in the mid-'70s. The title song's narrative was intriguing but vague, as a tired traveler sees a lonely hotel in the distance, discovers unbelievable beauty and luxury inside, but then finds that the paradise is tarnished by the knowledge that he can never actually leave. It's classic horror-movie fare, but it's compelling, asking the listener to fill in the gaps, providing prime material for waves of interpretation that varies from the rational to the bizarre.

The artwork fits beautifully with the story the lyrics partly tell—so much so that fans, non-fans, and casual observers began to analyze the album sleeve, struck by the contrast of the front cover—a glorious shot of the splendor of the prestigious Los Angeles landmark, the Beverly Hills Hotel, exuding history in soft, grainy, pastel tones, having been shot from a crane some 150 feet in the air for maximum otherworldly effect—with the interior imagery of a far more down-to-earth Los Angeles.

The artwork was designed to reinforce the dichotomy between good and evil, darkness and light, although as Don Henley later told the *Daily Mail*, "Some of the wilder interpretations of that song have been amazing. It was really about the excesses of American culture and certain girls we knew. But it was also about the uneasy balance between art and commerce."

Beverly Hills Don

For the inside gatefold artwork, Norman Seef shot a collage of characters. Henley wanted to visually represent a demographic cross-section of American society. The Eagles were hardly that by themselves, so a gang of their employees and friends gathered in the lobby of a run-down downtown L.A. building that had once been the towering and elegant Lido Hotel.

Today, the Lido is in a neglected part of Los Angeles, and is even more eerie than it was in 1977.   *Courtesy of Elisa Jordan, Lawomantours.com*

It was all very well thought-out, as Henley told *ZigZag* in June 1976. "Once upon a time, it used to be very elegant, now it's a home for old people, some pimps, and young starting actors. . . . That represented to us what happened to California and to the country in general, so we got a lot of our friends and we hired a bunch of people to come in and stand there. Then the back of the cover is the same lobby, except its empty. The poor Mexican janitor is all alone packing it up at five o'clock in the morning . . . the Spanish people are left to clean up. It's a symbolic sleeve, and it's not very pretty."

Devil in Disguise

On the upper balcony stands a half-lit character looking down on the crowd. This image, which is almost impossible to make out clearly with the naked eye, triggered a series of rumors that spoke of hidden messages, secret codes and ciphers, and even that ultimate in rock and roll debauchery: Satan worship.

According to the Satan-watchers in the know, the man in the shadow on the album cover is none other than Anton LaVey, leader of the Church of Satan. LaVey was the archetypal misfit, a loner whose life before forming his church was more than a little unusual. He was a low-paid, part-time musician who played Wurlitzers in various establishments around the city. Nothing too unusual about that, but at various times he also worked as a circus trainer, owned a pet lion (which he took for long walks on the nearby streets—with a leash, of course), and found employment for a while as a crime photographer with a San Francisco newspaper.

LaVey's religious beliefs were formulated while playing organ in a series of sleazy downtown nightclubs. He witnessed what he recognized as the power of lust in men's eyes and its ability to make outwardly respectable people behave like louts. He recognized many of the clientele personally as upstanding members of town society, often well connected within the Christian church.

LaVey smelled a rat and turned to different philosophies to explain the human condition. Playing organ at seedy burlesque, he recognized some well-to-do churchgoing members of local society lusting after half-naked women. He formulated a philosophy that was based more on understanding human nature's instinctive drive toward and desire for pleasure than actually worshiping the devil. It was probably a poorly named church, since the title was on the surface objectionable and inflammatory to many. Then again, LaVey's other constant personality trait was an uncanny ability for self-promotion. His Church of Satan did not recognize Satan as a being but instead accepted the carnal desires of human beings. LaVey established the church in a property on California Street in San Francisco—the "Black House" as it was dubbed in 1966, or A.S. 1, the first year of Satan, as the church called it.

The media was fascinated by LaVey at a time when the works of Aleister Crowley and the occult were also filtering into mainstream America. The local media referred to LaVey as the "Black Pope," and his church's unusual rituals and beliefs led to regular appearances for LaVey on popular TV shows, including *The Tonight Show* with Johnny Carson and *The Phil Donahue Show*. LaVey wrote *The Satanic Bible* in 1969, a year after Roman Polanski's devil-themed *Rosemary's Baby* movie had shocked audiences around the world and brought the occult and black magic into the public consciousness. The book has sold millions of copies ever since, and has never been out of print. "Satanism is the only religion which serves to encourage and enhance one's individual preferences, so long as there is admission of those needs," wrote LaVey in *The Cloven Hoof*, Issue #127, Year XXXI A.S.

The fact that LaVey was a celebrated bad guy in the early '70s, that the Church of Satan had its headquarters on California Street, and that it appeared that LaVey himself was on the *Hotel California* album cover, must clearly have meant the Eagles—and Henley in particular—were signaling their support for LaVey's Church of Satan. Throw in a couple of Henley lines about Heaven and Hell and 1969 and killing the beast with steely knives, and the amateur and professional culture-analysts went crazy.

Whoremongers and Communists

Church groups denounced the Eagles as yet another satanic rock group. Even today, the website Jesus-Is-Savior.com states, "The Eagles are one of thousands of rock bands who've sold their souls to Satan in exchange for worldly success and worldly prosperity. For those who are older, if you notice the bands from decades ago that are still popular today on the radio, most of them were either homosexuals, whoremongers, Communists, occultists, Satanists, feminists, or witches. This is why the Doors, Elton John, Mannford [*sic*] Mann, Blue Oyster Cult, the Beatles, Ozzy Osbourne, Gene Simmons, Jefferson Starship, Madonna, the Beach Boys, the Rolling Stones, Van Halen, Fleetwood Mac, and thousands of other bands sold out to Satan are still being promoted today." You might want to thumb through your record collection for evildoers.

Similar sites and forums quote a newspaper article that "proves" that the Eagles were members of LaVey's Church of Satan. The band's publicist, Larry Solters, was interviewed by the *Waco Tribune-Herald* in 1982 and supposedly admitted that the Eagles were involved with the dark church, but the interview cannot be found online, and the original does not appear to exist, despite in-depth searches by numerous researchers.

Get Back

There also arose a theory that "Hotel California," like tracks by other rock stars (the Beatles and Led Zeppelin, to name just two), used "back-masking" (that is, placing a message in the record that only becomes clear when the song is played backward) to convey satanic beliefs. Play "Stairway to Heaven" backward, and the golden-maned singer Robert Plant supposedly sings, "It's my sweet Satan . . . Oh I will sing because I live with Satan."

To be fair to the occult "outers," some high-profile rock-and-roll bands were indeed dabbling with black magic and the occult, and the writings of Aleister Crowley had become popular and fashionable in some circles. Crowley is even featured on the cover of the Beatles' *Sgt. Pepper* album. Before his death in 1947, he espoused the use of psychedelic drugs like heroin and opium, and worshipped via sadomasochistic sex-based rituals.

Led Zeppelin's genius guitarist Jimmy Page took a genuine interest in Crowley's writings on the occult and even bought the former Scottish home of the writer in 1970—a home that some anti-Satan campaigners believe was the actual inspiration for Henley's hotel. Listening to "Hotel California" backward, however, the message is most unclear and very, very open to interpretation. Plus, how many fans are able to listen to their records in reverse? But then, supposedly, there's a line in Henley's lyric that, when played backward, says, "Yes Satan, he organized his own religion."

That wasn't all; the lyrics were all codes for Satanism. For example, the "Captain" in Henley's tale is Anton LaVey; the wine he asks for is of a satanic sacrament variety, and then lyrics say they haven't had that spirit since 1969, which obviously refers to the year LaVey first published *The Satanic Bible.* Proof indeed.

Of course, it could just be a beautifully constructed piece about the dangers of luxury living in California during the hedonistic 1970s. Henley did say as much to Steve Kroft in a 2007 interview on *60 Minutes*, in which he called "Hotel California" a song about the "dark underbelly of the American dream and about excess in America, which is something we knew a lot about." And it was a theme that Henley would examine over and over throughout his songwriting career.

Obscure interpretation for hidden meanings in "Hotel California" doesn't end with Anton LaVey and the Church of Satan. Several other theories about the meaning(s) have sprung up with their own equally sincere and committed groups of followers and believers around the world.

First up is the notion that Henley was actually writing about a mental hospital, cryptically disguised as a hotel. The story goes that the words actually refer to Los Angeles' Camarillo State Mental Hospital, an unsettling treatment center that was dubbed, by some, "Hotel California." The hospital ran for around sixty years as a secure long-term facility for the mentally ill before closing in 1997. The lyrics and story could indeed fit this scenario, but what would the Eagles' purpose be in hiding the basis for their biggest song? Was it a subtle way of admitting one or some of them had been in rehab or had mental issues? Probably not. Any top-ten list of rock stars not afraid to speak their mind, however unpopular, would always include Don Henley. Whether you agree or disagree with him, he has never shirked from expressing his truth, so it would be odd for him to have hidden this real meaning for the past forty or so years. Then again, if he were a member of LaVey's Church of Satan, perhaps . . .

There are also stories that suggest that there was in fact a real Hotel California (a hotel, not a mental hospital). One such story claims that there was a Hotel California in El Centro, California, that fit the description in the song quite perfectly, but burned down in February 1969, leaving no trace and no records. There's a Hotel California in Palo Alto that some hail as "the place," but it's actually just a small bed-and-breakfast and doesn't fit at all. Sorry.

Then there's the Hotel California in the Mexican Pacific coastal village of Todos Santos. Ray Di Genaro bought the hotel in 1986 and told the BBC it was a run-down hippie place when he took it over. He said that locals had told him that Don Henley was a regular visitor in the early 1970s. "When we purchased it we were told by some of the locals that this was the hotel that the Eagles sang about," he explained, in February 2001. "We never really promoted it as such but the legend was there and it just grew. It fits the description of the hotel in the song, you know, desert highway and church close by."

In the mid-1990s, a U.S. travel writer, Joe Cummings, became curious about the story after it appeared in several mainstream American publications. He had spent a night there and was intrigued to find the truth. He went to the source of the song and faxed Don Henley at his then Vicente Boulevard Los Angeles office. The Eagle replied the next day, August 4, 1997. Henley said he believed that the hotel was using the song's popularity for commercial purposes and denied that he had ever stayed in the establishment. "I can tell you unequivocally that neither myself nor any of the other band members have had any sort of association—business or pleasure—with that establishment." (The full fax can be read at the Todos Santos web pages, in an article called "Hotel Where.")

Hundred of tourists have their pictures taken outside the front of the hotel every day, according to eTurboNews.com, but the current owner says the hotel is not marketing the Eagles connection. "We are very happy that the legend of the Eagles' song brings people here every day. But it is not what we are selling."

25

After the Thrill Is Gone

Another One Bites the Dust

The Eagles enjoyed 1977. The *Hotel California* album sold in vast quantities, and the title track took the #1 spot in February of that year. Irving Azoff worked the band hard, though, refusing to let them bask in the glory of what was obviously their finest recorded achievement. He knew it was wise for his fun-loving boys to be busy, so he kept the Eagles on the road, with Jimmy Buffett in support. He also made hay while the sun shone and negotiated the band an unprecedented royalty rate from their label.

The Eagles had played internationally before, but the four nights at Wembley in April 1977 were among the best shows I witnessed in London in the 1970s. Frey and Henley had instinctively known that the Eagles, no matter how accomplished they became musically, would never be able to compete with the top rock acts on the live stage with their original lineup. In London, armed to the teeth with Felder and Walsh, the Eagles were loud and direct while also being musical and magnificent. It was a stunning return by a band at the top of their game. Confidence oozed from every note the band played after they opened the show with their #1 hit "Hotel California"—a track that an act with less ammunition in the belt might have saved for last.

The Meisner/Henley rhythm section performed to perfection, while Felder's laid-back approach disguised a technically gifted player who was easily the best musician in the band. Joined by the dynamic and explosive Joe Walsh, the Eagles of 1977 were as powerful a live band as any to come out of America. They may have lacked the onstage visuals of Kiss or Alice Cooper, the sheer raw energy of Springsteen, or the charisma of Lou Reed, but for millions of new stereo owners in the late 1970s, this was one of those magical moments when a live rock band sounded exactly like the record. Musically, it was as good as it got—to Eagles fans, at least.

On the strength of the instant classic "Hotel California," which held the top spot on the U.S. singles charts for fifteen weeks, the new album sold hundreds of thousands of copies every week. The Eagles were at their peak, life was good, and the dreams they had believed in back in a cold, depressing London recording studio years earlier had been delivered. The only thing that could knock the Eagles from their perch was the band members themselves; excessive living, excessive rewards, and too much ego and power for a bunch of alpha males could clip their wings at any time.

Meisner Alone

There always seemed to be a correlation between Eagles success and Eagles friction and infighting. The underlying resentments and frustrations of Felder and Meisner, who essentially felt increasingly like bit part players in a Henley and Frey movie, were causing divisions between the band members.

Randy Meisner didn't feel good. He was tired, and he wished the others had listened to Bernie Leadon's advice to take a break and recharge. Meisner had stomach ulcers, so life on the road ranged from uncomfortable to severely painful. Everyone knew he was ready for a change, but trooper that he was, the bass player stuck the tour out before announcing to the band and management that he was tired of being an Eagle.

"After *Hotel California* I had been on the road so much and I was married and going then going through a divorce," he told RockHistoryBook.com. "I thought this whole thing has taken its toll. . . . Glenn and I got into a little fight but it's something that just happened . . . we kind of got mad at each other and took a swing at each other in Knoxville, Tennessee. At the time to me it was just like two guys fighting but it got really bad, so at that point I just decided to leave, because I just didn't like what I was doing anymore."

Irving Azoff took care of the press and announced that Randy was suffering from exhaustion and intended to leave the band.

Replacements

With Timothy B. Schmit replacing Meisner, the Eagles finally had a native Californian in their lineup. The ultimate California band was now complete—on a demographic and geographic level, at least. But seriously, the Eagles could not have chosen a better singing bass player to replace Meisner.

Poco's twelfth album, *Indian Summer*, appeared in 1977 and was Timothy B. Schmit's Poco swan song. With Schmit's departure, the record company halted the planned release of a Poco live album.

There wasn't much risk: they could simply ask old Poco pals Richie Furay and Rusty Young how Timothy B. did filling Meisner's shoes the last time, since when Meisner quit Poco, Schmit replaced him, and fit in remarkably well.

Easygoing and calm by nature, Schmit understood the volatile nature of creative and nomadic musicians and easily found his own space within the band dynamic. Having played in bands since he was fifteen years old, he was ready for it.

The son of a road musician—violinist Danny Schmit, who was part of a trio called the Tune Mixers—Timothy B. didn't see much of his father in the early days. Then, when he was five years old, the family bought a trailer and hit the road together for weeks at a time. When he wasn't traveling, Schmit excelled at gymnastics and music, playing the Encina High School band and then forming a folk trio with two pals. Tim, Tom & Ron turned into the Contenders after a while, first moving up to playing Beach Boys–influenced material and then, just like all the other young American musicians in 1964, changing tack completely when they saw and heard the Beatles.

In May 2011, Timothy B. told LegendaryRockInterviews.com that the Beatles "just upped the ante on what could be done on all levels, it was big. I was actually able to see them twice, both times in San Francisco. The show at Candlestick Park turned out to be their last concert and I am really happy that I was able to do that. I don't know any Beatles songs I don't like; they're pretty much all just amazing. I pretty much learned to sing from listening to the radio and they were of course, all over the radio. I would listen and I started getting a lot of my vocal stuff down from listening to those guys and some others but the Beatles were big."

The group revamped their image, grew their hair, and named themselves the New Breed. They were not bad at all, and in 1965 they recorded and released a single, "Green Eyed Woman," which was a local radio hit and got the band some TV spots in Los Angeles. They then recorded enough material for an album and achieved some minor local success—enough, at least, to warrant having their own fan club.

In 1966, still very influenced by the Liverpool sound, the New Breed released "Fine with Me" on their own label, World United, but it failed to get much industry or radio traction. Byrds producer Terry Melcher signed them to his new independent label Equinox in 1968, and the New Breed morphed once more, this time into Glad. Melcher overproduced the resulting album, *Feelin' Glad*, however, and none of the band members were especially happy with the sound. The public wasn't too interested either, and Glad fizzled out.

Schmit had been playing L.A. clubs long enough to be well connected and respected as a bass player and vocalist when he heard on the musician grapevine that country-rock outfit Poco needed a bassist. It was a huge step up for a musician who still wasn't of the legal age to drink, and in the end Schmit, despite auditioning well, missed out to another bass player, Randy Meisner. Timothy B. was devastated and considered quitting the Los Angeles music scene, but fortunately he didn't, and just a few months after being rejected by Poco, Meisner left for Rick Nelson's Stone Canyon Band, and Timothy B. was back in.

Schmit was an essential part of Poco for over eight years, but despite remaining a critic's favorite since the 1960s, and scoring a few modest hits, the band could never find another gear, especially in contrast to that other country-rock band, the Eagles. At the same time, their Eagles cohorts were getting more popular by the day, evolving and developing musically and writing incredible material—all factors Schmit was fully aware of when he received word from a friend, J. D. Souther, that Meisner was out and he should be hearing from the Eagles very soon. Schmit received a call from Frey, offering him the chance to replace Meisner one more time.

It was a great opportunity for him. "I knew it was a very big thing being put in front of me, one of the biggest in all of music," he told *Music Radar* in November 2011. "But I knew I could do it. I knew I could fit. In my heart, I knew I was the right guy. I'm pretty sure they thought everything through before they even called me. They knew I was playing a similar style of music in Poco, and they knew I was a singing bass player. The whole thing wasn't a big stretch. Plus, they knew I could hit the high notes. If my voice wasn't the right fit, I don't think I would've gotten the call to join."

Schmit soon hit the road with the Eagles and performed on the group's 1979 album *The Long Run*, co-authoring one of the album's signature tunes, "I Can't Tell You Why," which also featured his lead vocal.

26

Busy Being FAB-ulous

America's Beatles?

B ut Paul would go like 'one, two, three, four' and then they would launch into 'I Saw Her Standing There' or something and then the crowd would get soooo loud and people were like hysterical," Glenn Frey told *Uber Rock* in July 2012. "There was a girl in front of me who fell in my arms almost catatonic just saying 'Paul, Paul' and I'm just thinking to myself 'this is awesome, this is what I need to do.' It really was a huge influence on me."

It doesn't take a lot of Googling to find forums and fan sites dedicated to both the Beatles and the Eagles. In fact, both have large armies of fans dedicated to every era of their careers. Some Beatle fans prefer the early "mop-top" era, others the psychedelic flower-power days of the later 1960s. The same goes for Eagles fans. According to some, the original lineup is the only true Eagles band. The Felder and Leadon teaming is the best for others, while many prefer the late-1970s *Hotel California* lineup with Joe Walsh.

Nowadays it's commonplace for a fan, particularly a dedicated to fan, to see the world very much in black and white. *Their* band or artist is the best . . . and then there's everyone else. Every now and then, even in a rock-and-roll universe that 99 percent of the time hails the Beatles as the greatest pop group of all time, some online chatter will challenge that assumption. It doesn't happen too often, but occasionally fans will claim the Eagles to be better than the Beatles, or Henley and Frey as better than Lennon and McCartney. It's difficult to argue that one, however, no matter how highly Frey and Henley are regarded, and I doubt very much that Don or Glenn would sign up for that team.

Sometimes another debate appears, this time over which group or band is America's answer to the Beatles. Now, presuming that there is such a thing is one thing, and offering up a champion is another. The Beach Boys, say some; the Byrds, the Doors, R.E.M., say others. Some will always offer up Bruce Springsteen, who of course is not a band. And then there are the Eagles.

Is it crazy to suggest that the Eagles might indeed be the United States' answer to the Fab Four? That is not to argue that the Eagles are as musically magnificent or creatively diverse as John, Paul, George, and Ringo, but there's no doubt that on several levels there are some very compelling points of comparison.

Both bands were incredibly popular in their own right, blending different musical styles into their own distinctive sound. Both bands enjoyed success and fame beyond their wildest dreams and came to represent something cultural with their history and experiences. The Beatles were very much a band of their time. That is, a history of the Beatles through the 1960s is in many ways a social history of the decade. Want to study the Summer of Love? Read about the Beatles. What was it about Eastern philosophies in the 1960s? Read about the Beatles and the Maharishi. Want to learn about police corruption? Study the illegal drugs busts and harassment of John Lennon. And on and on.

The same goes for the Eagles. They too represented a generation—a generation deflated by the failure of the promises made to them as teenagers in the 1960s. They were Pete Townshend's "Won't Get Fooled Again" generation. Want to understand free love? Check out the Troubadour and Laurel Canyon story, and how the Eagles took that lifestyle around the world in jet planes and five-star hotels. Want to understand the cynical '70s? Study the Eagles' approach to making money and its relationship to art. And on and on.

The Beatles symbolized the naïve and simple love-fuelled Swinging '60s perfectly. The Eagles, operating in a decade that had seen the promise of the previous ten years turn sour, typified the self-indulgence and self-gratification of an excessive decade. And more than that, both bands wrote about their own lives within those changing worlds with such universal understanding that they both, in their own different ways, provided the soundtrack to the decades they dominated with record sales and their songs.

'62 and '72 Vintages

There are some fascinating connections and parallels between the two bands; some meaningful for understanding the connections between music and society, others just fascinating because they are fascinating. And both groups had pretty similar runs, at least in their original incarnations. The Beatles started having hits in 1962 and ran through to the end of the decade. And then, just as the Beatles faded into lawsuits and solo land, the Eagles first hit the charts in 1972 and enjoyed success until 1980, when frictions and egos drove the band apart—something that also happened with the famed breakdown between Lennon and McCartney and the ensuing mini-feud.

Mersey Beat, California Dreamin'

The Beatles may have honed their craft, discovered their artistic selves, and become a real band in Hamburg, Germany, but they'll forever be associated with the northern English seaport of Liverpool. It was their hometown—the place they came back to in order to really attempt a serious launch of their music careers.

Liverpool had a long tradition of folk and country music. This mixed with rock and roll would play a part in the formation of what became known as the Mersey sound. Liverpool was home to a new phenomenon, probably before England's capital city, London: a visible rise in the young generation who suddenly found themselves possessing voices that counted, and that were actually being heard. Liverpool teemed with teenagers—the original postwar baby-boomers—looking for entertainment. Clubs, pubs, and coffee shops were filled with kids, and it was kids making the music. Bill Harry, the founder of the *Mersey Beat* newspaper, guessed at one point that there were probably 500 different bands in the Liverpool region in the early 1960s. And, of those, the Beatles were not necessarily the best—certainly not in all facets of making music—but they did become the most popular, a skill in itself when it comes to becoming a pop sensation.

And this, in a London-centric entertainment business, was shocking to many and inspirational to many more. Entertainers were supposed to come from the south, speak the Queen's English, and behave accordingly. Obviously, regional artists had had careers in England before, just not on the scale of the Beatles and the movement they created.

That's how the record business was in America, too, until the late 1960s and early 1970s, when Los Angeles began to challenge New York. Before then, the *real* music industry in the Big Apple used Los Angeles and Hollywood for movie connections and the occasional act, but generally the power was in the east.

That all changed with the folk-rock, country-rock, and singer/songwriter boom that came out of California, headed by the economic powerhouse the Eagles with able support from the likes of Fleetwood Mac, Jackson Browne, and Linda Ronstadt. It was a scene, just like Liverpool. There was the Cavern Club in England, and the Troubadour and Laurel Canyon in Hollywood. Kids tried their hand at writing songs and crafting lyrics, and wanted desperately to be part of the in-crowd. That goes for Liverpool and for Los Angeles. There was a youth movement in both cities—a movement that saw two groups of four young men rise to the top, both with a dynamic songwriting duo driving the engine.

Aleister Crowley

Critics started dissecting popular music, particularly its lyrics, soon after Bob Dylan threw away the "Moon in June" rulebook, and by the time the Beatles came along, there was enough of an academic approach to analysis to frighten fans and artists alike. What was the hidden meaning? How did the artist intend the song to be heard? What were these musical phrases really telling us? What did those complex chordal progressions signify?

The Beatles were famously analyzed by the *Times* of London's music critic William Mann, who wrote a discourse on the band's music during the early days of Beatlemania. The December 1963 article became notorious for its references to pandiatonic clusters and Aeolian cadence, and signaled the point at which Lennon and McCartney's songwriting began to be seriously considered by established critics. "But harmonic interest is typical of their quicker songs, too," Mann wrote, "and one gets the impression that they think simultaneously of harmony and melody, so firmly are the major tonic sevenths and ninths built into their tunes, and the flat submediant key switches, so natural is the Aeolian cadence at the end of 'Not a Second Time'."

It wasn't something the Beatles themselves took too seriously. In fact, they found it somewhat amusing. "We had no idea what Aeolian cadences were, you know," Paul McCartney told me in 1989. "Me and John just made the songs up. Up until *Sgt. Pepper*, pop music had never been taken seriously as art, but suddenly there were people writing theses on the stuff and analyzing our chords and progressions, which was pretty stupid, since we usually made them up as we wrote the songs. The Beatles never had a grand design for changing pop music or whatever, but sometimes I think people want us to have that role. As far as spotting if something'll sell or not, I haven't a clue. No chance. I just do the album when I feel a need and put it out. I leave it for the critics to analyze and the public to decide if it's what they want to hear."

Don Henley—a shade more prickly than the always-diplomatic McCartney—has equal disdain for over-analysis of his material. "Hotel California," with its obscure and surreal lyrics has, of course, been dissected to death. Interpretations vary from "treatise on Satanism" to "prophetic metaphor of society as a mental institution." Yet Henley has explained, over and over, that it was simply an essay, in pop-song format, on what he felt was happening in America in the mid-1970s. Henley's dismissal of a critic who wanted to take his analysis to a level beyond what Henley thinks necessary got short shrift in this discussion in the *Cleveland Plain Dealer* in 2009.

The writer, John Soeder, begins, "I realize I'm probably not the first to bring this to your attention, but wine isn't a spirit. Wine is fermented; spirits are distilled. Do you regret that lyric?" Henley's response says it all. "Thanks for the tutorial and, no, you're not the first to bring this to my attention—and you're not the first to completely misinterpret the lyric and miss the metaphor. . . . But that line in the song has little or nothing to do with alcoholic beverages. It's a sociopolitical statement. My only regret would be having to explain it in detail to you, which would defeat the purpose of using literary devices in songwriting and lower the discussion to some silly and irrelevant argument about chemical processes."

The Boss

Top groups tend to also have top managers. Sometimes that manager rises to the top on the coattails of the superstars he or she is taking care of, but more often the manager manipulates and steers, directs and drives the musical unit to the very top. The Eagles had exactly that in the shape of David Geffen in the early days and later Irving Azoff. Geffen and Azoff were young, direct, and obnoxious when they felt it necessary, and they achieved their goals.

Brian Epstein, the Beatles' manager, was—outwardly at least—quite unlike the brash and bold Geffen and Azoff. But he was tough. Behind the polite "English gentleman" façade was a man of character who dedicated himself to making the Beatles the biggest and most successful group in the world. That he was unaware of the power of global marketing and merchandising and branding is not a result of him lacking the necessary drive or the skills. It's more that a provincial shop manager was pioneering the whole concept of pop group as product or brand. The imaging, styling, merchandising, and marketing of a musical act were all in their infancy in Epstein's hands, but it was still there. Epstein admired the Beatles' rough-and-ready rock-and-roll image, but he knew it needed harnessing for the general public. So he put them in suits, cleaned them up, and polished some of the rough edges.

Geffen's band were not going to wear uniforms or have matching haircuts—those days were long gone. But he did help them find a common look in the Western/outlaw themes they all bonded over. Geffen saw that the mystical desert, Americana, and Western themes were perfect branding for a band that could be directed to symbolize far more than just one individual group. Like the Beatles, the Eagles stood for a sound and a movement. They created and refracted back a lifestyle and an "opinion" of the times to the fans.

Like Geffen and Azoff, Epstein was young, a contemporary of the band he managed. He may not have had the cool charisma to be in a band himself (ditto Geffen and Azoff) but he truly loved music and being part of the burgeoning youth movement. And, like Geffen, Epstein passionately believed in his artists and starting with a core group allowed his enthusiasm to spread to a flock of other, similar artists. Both built rosters of acts and both then struggled to maintain the focus that their original discoveries really deserved and needed.

Both groups recognized the importance of their managers, too. Lennon and McCartney both commented on Epstein's value, with Lennon later lamenting that Epstein's death in 1967 marked the beginning of the end for the group. "I knew that we were in trouble then," he said, as reported by Peter Brown and Steven Gaines in their 1983 book *The Love You Make: An Insider's Story of the Beatles.* In a 1997 BBC documentary, McCartney also lauded Epstein's impact, saying, "If anyone was the Fifth Beatle, it was Brian."

As for Henley, he gave Azoff—whom the *Wall Street Journal* called the most powerful man in the music industry—his due at the band's induction into the Rock and Roll Hall of Fame in 1998, remarking, "He may be Satan, but he's our Satan."

Paperback Writers

So, the Beatles had Lennon and McCartney, and nobody in their right mind is going to challenge that duo as the ultimate pop writing team of all time. Whether judged on quantity or quality, dollars or sheer impressions, they win every time. But Henley and Frey developed into quite a formidable pairing. And with that centralization of musical control came dissent in the ranks. George Harrison and Ringo Starr were "allowed" only a track or two on the Beatles' albums, and as Harrison grew and developed as a bona-fide songwriter and performer in his own right, he came to dislike the assumption that Lennon and McCartney's songs came first, his second.

Similarly, in the Eagles, the democracy was originally much more equally spread, but as the band rose in prominence, and Henley developed further and quicker than the others (lyrically, at least), a sense of quality control came into being, and non-Henley/Frey songs were turned down or changed by the main two. Henley felt it was a big part of his job to maintain standards. But for the other songwriters in the band, his level of control—even if correct—was artistically frustrating, and reminiscent of Harrison's weary temperament regarding working with McCartney toward the end of the Beatles' career, as witnessed throughout the *Let It Be* movie.

Henley has said that he admires the Lennon/McCartney way of working, especially in the early days, when they sat knee-to-knee, guitars in hand, in a bedroom in someone's house. "In our heyday, we wrote them together," he told *Classic Rock* in May 2014. "And to make this an authentic Eagles project, Glenn and I are going to have to co-write at least three or four songs together. I know how the Beatles did it in the final days. And that's fine. That's still my favorite group in the entire world. But I hope that we can do it in a more authentically collaborative fashion than that. But if we have to do it that way—separately—by God we will!"

Eagles and Cold Turkeys

Both bands fueled their crazed lifestyles and creativity with vast supplies of legal and illegal substances. Amphetamines such as Benzedrine and Preludin were the order of the day (and night) for the Beatles during their Hamburg days. As Lennon explained in the Beatles' *Anthology*, "In Hamburg the waiters always had Preludin—and various other pills, but I remember

Preludin because it was such a big trip—and they were all taking these pills to keep themselves awake, to work these incredible hours in this all-night place. And so the waiters, when they'd see the musicians falling over with tiredness or with drink, they'd give you the pill. You'd take the pill, you'd be talking, you'd sober up, you could work almost endlessly—until the pill wore off, then you'd have to have another."

Later, when Dylan turned them on to marijuana, pot became an essential ingredient in creation. Then it was acid, and its resultant psychedelia, before some of the foursome dabbled with hard drugs, notably heroin. Lennon, always prepared to push a little harder than the others, found himself addicted. He later admitted he was addicted to heroin at the time of the Plastic Ono Band's performance at the Toronto Rock and Roll Revival festival on September 13, 1969.

Fortunately, Lennon and his wife, Yoko Ono, avoided needles, as she recalled when speaking to the BBC Radio 4 program *Desert Island Discs* in 2007. "Luckily we never injected, because both of us were totally scared about needles. So that probably saved us. And the other thing that saved us was our connection was not very good." In the summer months of 1969, Lennon and Ono decided to withdraw from heroin, and Lennon, being Lennon, documented the process and his views on the drug in the disturbing and powerful song "Cold Turkey."

The Eagles famously took drug use to its limit in the 1970s. As Henley told the *Daily Mail* in May 2013, "I'd drink and take drugs all weekend, but I'd go to the gym on Monday morning to clean it all out. We had a survival instinct—every current and former member of the Eagles is still alive."

The Eagles had their own Lennon in the shape of take-it-to-the-absolute-limit Joe Walsh. Walsh used all kinds of narcotics, as well as copious amounts of alcohol, as he pushed everything thrown at him to the limit. Coming into the band with a reputation as a wild man of rock gave him license to be outrageous. Indeed, it was expected. Some of his drug-fueled antics were even encouraged by the Eagles team, including their manager. But once the fun was over—once the drugs faded—Walsh faced a dark future. Like Lennon, he would document the recovery process in an unsettling but moving and candid song, "One Day at a Time," which appears on the Eagles' 2005 live DVD/CD *Farewell 1 Tour—Live from Melbourne*.

Walsh cleaned himself up in the mid-'90s, and now likes to help others to get their lives in order. In fact, in 2011 in an interview with the Australian *Herald Sun* newspaper, he said, "I'd love to speak to leaders and politicians in Melbourne and around Australia about addiction. Addiction is a disease and, with help, people can get back to being responsible members of the community. I hope to give your leaders that message."

Family Affair

In 2012, Paul McCartney was asked to perform at the prestigious Grammy Awards ceremony. Who did he ask to join him onstage for some tasteful guitar accompaniment? Correct, he asked Ringo's brother-in-law, Joe—Joe Walsh, that is, since Ringo and Joe have been legally related since 2008, when Joe made Marjorie Bach, sister of Ringo's wife Barbara, his fourth wife. Ringo and Joe go back much further than 2008, of course, with Joe

The level of musician Ringo Starr has managed to attract for his various "All-Starr" groups is testament to the esteem the Beatles were held in by the generation of musicians who came of age in the wake of the Fab Four. Joe Walsh was part of the first two All-Starr bands, and this 2001 anthology includes Walsh's guitar and performances of the Eagles' "Desperado" and "Life in the Fast Lane."

appearing in the first two of Ringo's All-Starr Bands (Timothy B. Schmit played in the second version as well), filling in with some nice classical guitar for a performance of Macca's then-current single "My Valentine."

Walsh's 2012 album *Analog Man* includes a song he wrote called "Family" about the experience of finding a new family. In a June 2012 interview with *Guitar World*, he said, "When I married Marjorie, along with her I got this very large family and a bunch of family friends. . . . It's a dynamic I've never been around. I've always been kind of a loner, and my attempts at domestic life failed miserably. So the family dynamic is a great thing."

27

Witchy Woman

Kiss and Tell

The more successful and powerful the top rock bands of the 1970s became, the more their lives spiraled into plots that would have been too extravagant for even the most fantastical soap operas. Superstar lives based on indulging the senses in the pursuit of pleasure led to impulsive decision-making and tempestuous personal relationships whose drama was heightened with copious cocaine use. The two biggest bands in America—both of whom came to symbolize the California FM sound despite not hailing originally from California—were the Eagles and Fleetwood Mac. And both lived entirely without limits.

In March 2011, Fleetwood Mac's Stevie Nicks told the *Guardian* newspaper, "In '75, '76, we were beautiful, fast, and sexy, love was everywhere, and we were moving from person to person. That's it. Love was around every corner." And so were drugs. Nicks estimates that she spent millions on cocaine, given that even in the 1970s it was going for $100 a pop. Like the Eagles, Nicks and her bandmates lived outrageously, drove fast cars, bought houses like most people buy groceries, and sold millions and millions of records. Fleetwood Mac had *Rumours*; the Eagles had *Hotel California*.

And they moved in the same circles. In the summer of 1976, the two bands played a huge show together at Schaefer Stadium in Foxboro, Massachusetts. The Eagles were the headliners, having released a greatest-hits album earlier in the year. Fleetwood Mac were still touring in support of a self-titled disc that was the first to feature Stevie Nicks and Lindsey Buckingham. Within a year of that show, both bands would release the albums that elevated them to superstar status—*Hotel California* and *Rumours*, 1977's hottest records.

While recording *Rumours*, tensions between the band—and between Stevie and her lover, Buckingham—led to them breaking up, and while her relationship with Buckingham was on hiatus, Nicks succumbed to the charms of Don Henley. She recounted the romantic beginnings of her time with Henley in an interview with Courtney Love for *Spin* in October 1997. "He is sexy. He is such an interesting guy. . . . We are all in Miami, Fleetwood Mac and the Eagles. They're recording at this gorgeous house they'd rented on the water. It's totally romantic. So I started going out with him. And this is not popular. Sure, Lindsey and I are totally broken up; I have every right in the world to go out with people, but . . . I spend most of my time with the band, and it's not real conducive to having a relationship. So, I went out with Don for awhile."

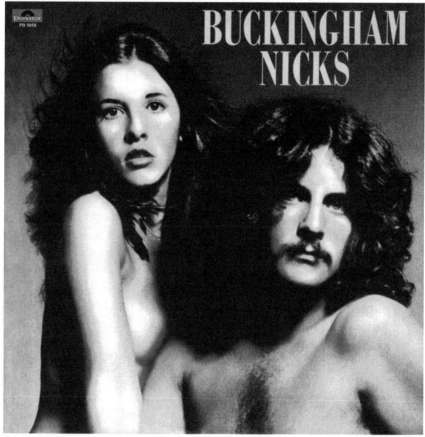

Buckingham Nicks, recorded in 1971, was the first studio pairing of Lindsey Buckingham and Stevie Nicks, released several years before they found mega-success with Fleetwood Mac.

Nick of Time

Some artists are simply born to be stars. Stevie Nicks was driven by two passions as a child: one was singing, the other was dress-up. She put the two interests together in the 1970s to worldwide acclaim, rocking out onstage in her trademark nouveau-hippie dresses with chiffon scarves and big, flowing hair as she became one of the biggest stars of the 1970s and '80s.

Nicks grew up middle class and wealthy, the daughter of a business executive whose work took the family all over the United States while she was growing up. She aspired to be Janis Joplin or Grace Slick, and while living in San Francisco in 1966, she ran into a handsome young Lindsey Buckingham singing "California Dreamin'" at a high-school party. Nicks was smitten. She joined in on harmony and told him her name. Later, he called her, as she recalled to MTV in October 2009. "I never saw him again for two years, until he was in a band and he remembered that night and he called and asked me to join their band."

The band was called Fritz, and Nicks did indeed join. Within weeks the unit had gigs opening for the likes of Jefferson Airplane and Nicks' heroine Janis Joplin. This was 1968, and Fritz played gigs for three years while Nicks and Buckingham became a solid couple. In 1971, they decided that San Francisco was not going to deliver them their prized recording contract, so they moved to Los Angeles, center of the record business, to fulfill their dreams.

What they found was the harsh reality facing any wannabe moving to Tinseltown. Los Angeles was a tough place for a young couple with little money and few friends. Both quit college, with Nicks supporting the pair with waitressing and cleaning jobs. Buckingham, they decided, needed to be free to develop his guitar technique. Nicks found work as a housekeeper for a recording engineer/aspiring producer Keith Olsen, who listened to some of the duo's material and worked to secure them a recording contract with Polydor. Lindsey and Stevie appeared topless on the cover of the *Buckingham Nicks* album (which used some clever camera placement and lighting to disguise the nudity).

The record did very little, and for the most part Polydor ignored it. Visiting with her father, Nicks agreed to give the music career six more months, at which point he'd pay for her to go back to college. Three months later, having been tipped off by Olsen, Mick Fleetwood invited the pair to join Fleetwood Mac. It worked. Buckingham and Nicks gave the discordant band some much-needed personal and musical harmony, and enough mainstream commercial appeal to finally crack the U.S. radio market.

In 1975, the new configuration released *Fleetwood Mac*. The record went to #1 and sold over five million copies. The British-American band had started out in the U.K. as a cerebral hardcore-blues act, a vehicle for troubled guitar genius Peter Green. Now, after numerous lineup changes, internal marital discords between band members Christine McVie and John McVie, and record company interference, they needed a new direction. New blood would be an asset—or at least Mick Fleetwood thought so. He was introduced to Buckingham by Olsen after the producer played him a track from the *Buckingham Nicks* album. Fleetwood was impressed, and invited Buckingham to join the band. Buckingham insisted Stevie be part of the deal.

The addition of Buckingham and Nicks brought a pop sensibility and a clutch of exhilarating songs that rejuvenated the group. The eponymous album went to #1 in America; the follow-up, *Rumours*, became a phenomenon. By then, Nicks and Buckingham were breaking up after five years together. The seven-year marriage of John and Christine McVie was almost finished, too, and Mick was getting a divorce. So while Nicks may have been cautious about embarking on an inter-band rock-and-roll romance with the now very Afro-haired Eagles drummer, her colleagues in the group were hardly in a position to judge her behavior.

Henley and Nicks

Henley and Nicks enjoyed an impetuous and passionate romance for a couple of years, but it never looked like being more than a series of luxury booty calls between the two superstars. Both bands were peaking, and consequently always on demand for interviews, promotion, meetings, tours, rehearsals, photo shoots, recording sessions, and all the other "glamorous" chores rock stars endure on a day-to-day basis. So it was an affair consisting of late-night phone calls, meetings in cities where itineraries combined, and Don sending for Stevie via Learjet. It was the romantic move of a Southern gentleman with cash, which describes Henley to a "T" in the middle part of the 1970s. The romance was never likely to end in marriage and a house in the hills. Both were too busy with their careers—too involved in themselves as artists—to truly commit at that point. Had they tried, they would more than likely have been doomed by the sheer scale of success they both experienced when sales of *Hotel California* and *Rumours* went crazy in 1977.

The romance cooled when Nicks became pregnant but chose to terminate. It was a desperate situation, and one she'd face again in the future,

Fleetwood Mac's 1977 tour de force, *Rumours*, set the group up as the kings and queens of soft rock. Nicks' whimsical vocals and rock-goddess persona played a huge part in the band's popularity. Only the Eagles could match them in FM radio smoothness and record sales in the late 1970s.

but, as she told *Vox* in February 1992, she was too busy and had too many commitments to have a child. She realized, too, in retrospect, the impact of those decisions on her relationships. "Eventually their hearts couldn't take it. They couldn't understand quite enough how deeply embedded in all this I was. And so it eventually hurt them too much, and they had to leave, or face devastation on their own."

Henley and Nicks was an intense but short affair that may have ended with sadness but which developed into a lifelong musical and personal friendship that culminated in the successful Two Voices, Henley & Nicks tour of 2005.

Wild Hearts: Nicks and Joe Walsh

Nicks would have affairs with several rock-and-rollers after Henley, but it was another Eagle who truly stole her heart. She fell in love with Joe Walsh, she told the *Daily Telegraph* in 2007, during the 1983 *Wild Hearts* tour on which Walsh was the opening act. It happened one night in a bar in Dallas. "I fell in love with Joe at first sight from across the room, in the bar at the Mansions Hotel in Dallas. I looked at him and I walked across the room, and I sat on the bar stool next to him, and two seconds later I crawled into his lap, and that was it."

Walsh was at his wildest in the mid-1980s, but Nicks saw through the drugs and drink to the heart of a rock star in pain. And somehow, maybe through the shared loneliness of life as a celebrity on the road, Walsh managed to communicate that pain to Nicks. She even wrote a song for him, "Has Anyone Ever Written Anything for You."

The song came as a result of Walsh tiring of Nicks' complaining about some trivial—but at the time very annoying—tour frustration. They were staying in Denver, not far from where Walsh had once lived, so he rented a jeep and drove Stevie to Boulder. On the way, he told her about losing his daughter Emma in a car accident when she was just three years old. He told her about how his daughter loved to visit a local park every day but was always upset that she was too short to use the drinking fountain. Walsh took Stevie to the park, where he showed her a tiny silver fountain. It had a dedication.

> *This fountain is given*
> *in loving memory*
> *of*
> *Emma Walsh*
> *April 29, 1971–April 1, 1974*

It was a profound moment for Nicks—a reminder that even the wildest men of rock and roll have a sensitive side, or, in Walsh's case, a broken heart that had never completely healed. As she wrote in her liner notes to the *Tie Space* compilation album, "He wrote a song for her ['Emma's Song'] and I wrote a song for him."

Drugs got in the way of Walsh having a long-term relationship. "Joe and I broke up because of the coke," Nicks told Sylvie Simmons in *Q* magazine in May 2008. "He told my friend and [backing] singer Sharon, 'I'm leaving Stevie, because I'm afraid that one of us is going to die and the other one won't be able to save the other person, because our cocaine habit has become so over the top now that neither of us can live through this, so the only way to save both of us is for me to leave.'"

Settling Down

Ever since the infamous "Yoko breaking up the Beatles" mythology started around 1969, romance and relationships have haunted rock-and-roll bands on differing levels. The dynamic of the tightly knit male unit is eventually changed by wives and girlfriends, and levels of commitment and seriousness come and go. Henley and Frey were happy-go-lucky single guys in the early days, while Felder came into the band a married man. But his experience on a romantic level was rooted more in guilt and betrayal than fun and simple debauchery.

Don Felder was married to his first wife Susan for nearly thirty years. She supported him during his rise to the top and turned several blind eyes to his on-the-road antics during the Eagles' heyday. Their marriage broke down around the time Felder was fired from the band, but he recovered, examined his behavior, and found a new partner in life. He told UltimateClassicRock.com in May 2013 that he and his first wife are still great friends. "We have grandkids, we have hundreds of friends together, we see each other at weddings and at parties. She's got another guy, and she's completely happy. I'm re-connected with another woman, and I'm completely happy. We maintain that relationship of twenty-nine years of being married, and didn't just let it wither on the vine and die. I'm a firm believer that people that have been such a substantial part of your life should not be slashed out. People that are good people, I like to keep in my life."

Joe Walsh was married in 2008 to Marjorie Bach, sister of Ringo Starr's wife Barbara. The union—and the security it brought—has been a blessing for the often self-destructive guitar legend.

As for Don Henley, he too finally settled down, marrying ex-model Sharon Summerall in 1995, with the wedding performers including Bruce Springsteen, Sting, Billy Joel, Sheryl Crow, and Tony Bennett. The writer of the "Hotel California" lyric no longer lives in Los Angeles, having decided to go back to Texas and live with his family in a Dallas suburb. "Sharon grew up here, her father grew up on a farm like mine did, so we have a lot in common," he told the *Daily Mirror* in March 2008. Sharon suffers from multiple sclerosis, which brings its own domestic challenges, but the family remains strong. These days, Henley is the ultimate family man, as he told RGJ.com in June 2012. "My children fill the entire spectrum—they bring me inexpressible joy and profound heartache. It's all there in one package. They're the Big Mirror, reflecting the best and the worst of myself."

And then there's free-spirit Stevie Nicks. "I'm single, I don't have children, and I've never been married except for three months a long time ago," she told the *New York Times* in February 2014. "And that doesn't matter; it wasn't a marriage of reality. I live a single woman's life and yes, I spend a lot of time by myself. I have a few very close friends, most of them I've known forever, and I kind of like it."

28

The Long Run

Running on Empty

n many ways, *Hotel California* was the end of the Eagles. Infighting, emotional burnout, physical exhaustion, and cliques within the camp had begun to take their toll a couple of years before, and were not so different from what occurs in most rock-and-roll bands. Petty jealousies are magnified by fame, misunderstandings become feuds, and arguments turn into full-scale knock-down fistfights.

It's happened with them all in different forms. Think of Oasis, with two rock-star brothers publicly denouncing and slamming each other. It's reminiscent perhaps of the Kinks brothers, barely able to speak to each other and staying in separate floors of their hotels, lest they run into each other in the corridor. Which is the same as the sad story of the Everly Brothers, who only spoke to each other onstage during concerts—and there were only two of them in the group! The Rolling Stones have gone through long periods of Mick Jagger and Keith Richards ignoring each other, and moments of nastiness with other members who have been forced out or quit. The Beatles—the ultimate band of brothers in rock and roll—may have patched things up by the end of the 1970s, but their breakup was horrible, ugly, and unpleasant. When the two bandleaders, Lennon and McCartney, began turning their God-given songwriting talents to writing hate songs to each other, pop music was the real loser.

So the bickering and disputes between the various Eagles were hardly an occurrence peculiar to Henley and crew. It's the nature of the rock-and-roll beast. What's clear, looking back, however, is that since the Eagles did "resume" (or reunite) some years later, there was enough common ground among the warring members to keep the unit alive. If the breakup could be resolved then, clearly it was an outside force that caused relations to snap. In the case of the Eagles, that force was the ridiculous success of the *Hotel California* album.

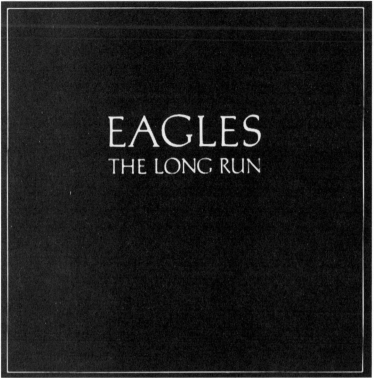

The Eagles' 1979 LP *The Long Run* was the end . . . almost. Despite intense internal friction, musical fatigue, and general weariness at being rock stars, the band pulled it together and scored three more hits with "Heartache Tonight," "The Long Run," and "I Can't Tell You Why." It was the band's final studio album for nearly three decades.

First it fed into their already bloated egos. How could it not? Few albums are both critically acclaimed and massively successful in the marketplace. The sheer scale was historic—and, for a while, it was a blast. But then, as the dust settled, Timothy B. replaced Randy M., and *Rumours* took the top spot and Fleetwood Mac the ascendancy, the Eagles felt a pressure to perform. Now it was their turn to topple Fleetwood Mac and regain the crown they'd been given with *Hotel California*. But how on earth do you follow such an impeccable and startlingly original album? How do you find pure pop songs for radio and dark subtle album tracks for reviewers—and make them all so good they are interchangeably beloved?

The Eagles, naturally enough, were tired, and they needed a break—a break that Bernie Leadon had recommended a couple of years previously, only to be turned down flat. But resting only takes so long—not the two years the Eagles spent in the studio working on the follow-up to *Hotel California*,

The Long Run. In May 1982, Joe Walsh told Robert Hilburn of the *L.A. Times*, "We ended up on the next album in Miami with the tapes running, but nobody knowing what was going on."

Conflicts during previous album sessions had resulted in better work, with the will to prove Glyn Johns wrong about their rock limitations spurring some terrific songwriting and playing. But now, for the first time, the long, drawn-out sessions for the new album became tedious and lacking in inspiration. Henley did not enjoy the process. Neither did Frey. And if the engine room is slowing down, there's little the rest of the crew can do to steer the ship.

Every note was debated over. Debates turned into arguments. There were too many unresolved issues and resentments festering under the surface for the band to really work in any kind of harmony. Henley, in confessional mood, told *Rolling Stone* in 1987 that the "romance had gone" when the band came to record *The Long Run*. "We were having fights all the time about the songs—enormous fights about one word—for days on end. That record took three years and cost $800,000, and we burned out."

It's ironic then that "The Long Run," a quite moving story about keeping relationships alive over a long period of time, should both title the album and say so much about the inner workings of Henley and Frey's personal and professional relationship—a relationship that, despite a willingness to compromise, refused to be anything but volatile and unpleasant over the two years they spent on this project.

"It was hard to cope with it rationally," Frey told the *Independent* in July 1992, "because we'd been living this lifestyle of limos, private jets, first-class hotels and people doing what you told them to. Plus, both Henley and I had developed drug habits, which didn't help matters. Going to the studio was like going to school—I simply didn't want to go. But most importantly, during the making of *The Long Run*, Henley and I found out that lyrics are not a replenishable source."

That the musicians were able to make sincere and meaningful music at all is a testament to their sheer professionalism, and a suggestion that underneath the anger and hostility there was still some sense of shared experience and musical brotherhood. There was nothing bad or half-baked on the album, but the inspiration and creativity seem lacking—in contrast to the previous two albums, at least. On the plus side, Timothy B. Schmit rides in for his first album and debut vocal ("I Can't Tell You Why") with all guns blazing. The other truly notable and Eagles-standard track was the single "Heartache Tonight," which was contemporary, with its masterful blend of rock meets dance, and blessed with as catchy a hook as you can get outside of the Archies' "Sugar Sugar." "Sad Café" is almost as good a song—albeit very different in tone, with its melancholy feel—and shows that Henley's writing was as sharp as ever in a bittersweet lament for the past that's autobiographical and all the more poignant for it.

The power and strength of the Eagles had been apparent from the outset, when Leadon offered up a "take it or leave it" approach to Geffen, through going to war with Glyn Johns over a belief in their own ability, to expanding the band when they'd already found a nice winning country-rock formula. Henley and Frey had been resolute and sure about what the Eagles were and what they were not. But for the first time, on this record, there was a sense of them looking to the pop and rock mainstream and wondering where they fit as a band. They may have lampooned punk and new wave but disco was also now having a major effect on the charts, and for the first time the Eagles seemed aware and concerned. The confident young Eagles of 1973 would have watched the new sounds with interest but never felt compelled to match them, or even try to go in that stylistic direction themselves. But that's exactly what they did on "The Disco Strangler," a track best ignored and left to rest in peace.

When the album appeared in the fall of 1979, the band were sensitive to criticism, mostly because they knew deep down that the record was not up to scratch. What had started out in their heads as a dynamic, hit-filled double album shrank in time to a weak single album with filler material that Henley and Frey would have absolutely rejected a couple of years before. It's not surprising, then, that Henley allowed his defensiveness toward the album to get him involved in spats with members of the press who, understandably, were disappointed with the record and said as much in their reviews. He didn't like what the *Village Voice* or *Rolling Stone* said at the time, but with hindsight he would admit publicly that the album was not up to standard—certainly not by comparison to its brilliant predecessor.

Critics had seen the beginning of cracks in the band, but the public was still in *Hotel California* mode and bought *The Long Run* by the million. The record debuted on the *Billboard* album chart at #2 but found the top spot the next week and remained there until the end of November. It didn't sell as many copies as the *Hotel* record, but that would be impossible. *Hotel California* was an exception—the kind of classic album that comes along once in a decade. No band could match that level of artistry or sales in the space of couple of years. Perhaps, if Henley and Frey had accepted that, they might have produced a fine follow-up, instead of reaching too high and breaking under the pressure.

In the meantime, the band that barely got along in the studio—and who were already down at heel at the initial press reception—had to tolerate each other once more as they hit the road for another giant tour. Luckily, they kept themselves to themselves, but the tensions were still there at rehearsals, and at soundchecks, dinners, and meetings.

A break might have been a better idea, but instead the Eagles zapped around the globe before playing their first Los Angeles gigs in two years: five nights at the L.A. Forum, billed as "The Eagles Come Home." For the first show, the Eagles were reunited with Elton John to rip through a handful of Chuck Berry classics, and for their final night they brought out another legend, rock-and-roller Roy Orbison. For all the studio drama, they could still have fun onstage. Or so it appeared.

29

Good Day in Hell

The End

Everyone in the Eagles camp realized that the band was in trouble. *The Long Run* saga had frustrated everybody involved, and now, instead of booking another studio album, the record label chose the safer option of releasing a live album. Recordings would be made at multiple venues during the upcoming tour, with the best tracks selected for release at a later date.

One date on the previous tour that will never be forgotten by anyone there was a July 31, 1979, benefit show in Long Beach. Political rallies had been part of the Eagles' repertoire since the beginning. Their pal Jackson Browne was one of the most active musicians in liberal causes, and the Eagles often felt compelled to support and show up for various causes themselves. They had been public supporters of California politician Jerry Brown at various times, and now Glenn Frey set up a benefit for politician Alan Cranston.

Don Felder, however, had tired of Frey deciding everything for everyone else. At least that's how it seemed to Felder. He didn't especially want to play a benefit for Senator Cranston, but he felt he had no choice. During the afternoon of the show, the Eagles held a press conference; Felder answered a question about Cranston, muttering about how the senator was not that important in his view. Frey was furious, and felt that Felder was being plain rude—and then the rest of his issues with the guitarist began to surface. The gig was going to be bumpy, as Felder recalls in his book, *Heaven and Hell: My Life in the Eagles.* "We walked onstage and [Frey] came over while we were playing 'Best of My Love' and said: 'F— you. I'm gonna kick your ass when we get off the stage.'"

Turn Down the Volume

The trading of insults grew so obvious that the sound crew had to turn their mics down during the show. It was clear to everyone that something unpleasant would happen as soon as the band stepped offstage. Frey was looking for a fight, and had been preparing for it all night. As he says during the *History of the Eagles Part 1* documentary, "We're out there singing 'Best of My Love,' but inside both of us are thinking, 'As soon as this is over, I'm gonna kill him.'"

The crew was aware of this, too, and as soon as there was a sign that Frey and Felder were going for each other, they intervened. It all started again, however, when it was time to leave the venue. An angry Felder smashed an acoustic guitar against a wall in frustration. This was not a problem in itself—he could afford to buy a replacement, after all. The problem was that he did this, intentionally or not, right in front of Frey and Mrs. Cranston.

That was it, as far as Frey was concerned; Felder, in Frey's book, was history. He couldn't really discuss the issue with Henley, since they weren't getting along either. The two listened to mixes of the live shows on the road in their own houses. Henley based himself in Miami and Frey in Los Angeles, so at least they had some geography between them. The common denominator was easygoing producer Bill Szymczyk, who listened to both artists' mixes (with Frey FedEx-ing his in from L.A.) and assembled the best possible album from the recording approved by the two maestros. "We were exhausted, and we were sick and tired of each other," Henley told *Rolling Stone* in November 1987. "We needed a vacation, and we didn't get one. So we just flamed out."

But they were both professional enough to work through the live recordings with the producer and give the record company a terrific album. Fans listening to the resulting *Eagles Live* album would be forgiven for not picking up on the destructive friction and flaming animosities within the Eagles camp. But for the musicians themselves, this final offering came with only a thin veneer of musical compatibility. Sure, their vocal harmonies may technically never have sounded better, but the spark was gone, and once Frey lost his passion the end was inevitable.

Frey had started a band when Geffen advised him that he didn't have the right ingredients for a solo career. The band Frey assembled went as far as he could have ever imagined, sitting in the Troubadour, talking a big game with J. D. Souther and Don Henley. But now the dream was over. Frey was tired, angry, and ready to call it quits. Now, having fulfilled his artistic obligations with the live album, he made a relatively easy decision, calling Henley on the phone to tell him that he was out.

Frey was simply tired of the band. In May 1982, he told Robert Hilburn of the *L.A. Times* that he had felt it was time to move on to something new:

Recorded over several dates in 1976 and '77, *Eagles Live* was the group's first live album that appeared in November 1980, after the Eagles had disbanded.

"I just couldn't see myself spending all of the '80s making just three more Eagles albums . . . three albums that wouldn't be any fun."

The record company, quite understandably, was mortified. The Eagles were not just a great band but also a massive revenue stream. The Eagles were offered a cool two million dollars to carry on, but of course by that time money was the least of Frey's concerns. He had all he could spend already. What would be the point? He and his friend and writing partner weren't speaking. He was fighting with bandmates onstage. Nobody talked to each other except when they had to. Now was the Eagles' time to stop. It was the end of a decade—a good bookend to a fabulous journey around the world.

The mixed-by-FedEx *Eagles Live* finally appeared in November 1980. Tongue-in-cheek at the time or not, in retrospect, it's amusing that the album credits acknowledge five different attorneys. It's horribly reminiscent of the end of Eric Idle's the Rutles, who broke up when Dirk sued Stig and Nasty, Barry sued Dirk, Nasty sued Stig and Barry, and Stig sued himself by accident.

The album credits also said "Thank you and goodnight"—a clue, perhaps, but not definitive. Getting everything they could out of the Eagles, Asylum then released a final single, a tremendous live version of Steve Young's outlaw-country classic "Seven Bridges Road." The song had been the band's warm-up for many years after they first heard Ian Matthews' version of the song on his Michael Nesmith–produced *Valley Hi* album in 1973. Nesmith's vocal arrangement formed the basis for the Eagles' harmony master class. The single was a marvelous riposte to the unnecessary overproduction of most cuts on *The Long Run*, and a reminder that, without any outside help, the Eagles' voices in perfect harmony was one of the great sounds of the modern rock-and-roll era.

Management and label fudged the issue for as long as they could. Nobody made an official announcement that the band had ceased to exist. That was too final, too painful—and besides, they'd had conflict before. What if . . . ?

30

The Heat Is On

Glenn Frey Goes It Alone

When a band as popular as the Eagles breaks up, there's always a sense, from the fans at least, that the split will be temporary, and that the group they have loved so much will in fact rip up the divorce papers, reconcile, renew their vows, and get remarried. It's a natural reaction to the finish of something that has been a part of someone's life for a long period of time.

Despite Randy Meisner and Don Felder dealing with the termination of the Eagles with solo projects, the band's founder, Glenn Frey, needed to release his own solo project to really make the breakup definite and real. Frey told the *Independent* in July 1992, "Once that decision was made, I experienced an overwhelming sense of relief. . . . When I gave up snorting, I found I didn't need to drink any more and started to behave like a human being again." Both for the fans, and for himself.

Frey had no radical career moves in mind for his post-Eagles life. Music would continue to be his work and passion, and while considering the exact formula for the debut solo album, he busied himself with several musical projects, produced Lou Ann Barton's debut album with Jerry Wexler, lent a hand to Karla Bonoff on her latest effort, and spent time in the studio with the L.A.-based band Jack Mack & the Heart Attack.

Reacting to what he now saw as mistakes in the making of the Eagles' music, Frey chose to do things differently with his own solo album. First off, he wanted to have fun and lose the overly serious, ponderous feel of the last two Eagles albums. He told *International Musician* in May 1982 that the album doesn't "make a statement like we're all going to blow ourselves up. That's not what I'm primarily concerned with. I'm concerned with more personal things; men and women in love, out of love, around love, near love." And with that loosening of approach and material would be a different approach in the studio. Every note did not have to be perfect.

When Frey's debut appeared in May 1982, it was indeed a departure from his Eagles past, both in sound and image. Frey co-produced it with Allan Blazek and his old Eagles arranger (and Shiloh man) Jim Ed Norman. Sound-wise, Frey embraced the synth/drum machine sound of the 1980s and dressed appropriately, in snappy suits, T-shirts, and rolled-up sleeves. It was all very *Miami Vice.*

Given that he'd been writing hit songs for the past decade—much of the time with one of the best in the business—it would have been tough for Frey to surprise with a set of startling and original songs. Aware that he worked best with trusted friends and collaborators, Frey teamed up with one of his oldest songwriter pals, Jack Tempchin, for five songs on *No Fun Aloud.* One of their better collaborations, "I Found Somebody," had a swirling Stax sound, while "The One You Love," complete with strings by Jim Ed Norman, was strong commercially thanks to a beefed-up and catchy chorus.

Just to prove that Frey was about having a good time, he cooked up "Partytown," a raucous celebration of letting rip that features a crowd of revelers in the background, including manager Azoff, Jimmy Buffett, and John McEnroe. While not comparable to Eagles numbers, the album sold a very decent 650,000 copies, rose to #32 on the charts, and scored two Top 40 hits in the Tempchin collaborations "The One You Love" and "I Found Somebody."

Peaceful Easy Tempchin

San Diego singer and songwriter Jack Tempchin first met Frey back in the Longbranch Pennywhistle days, when Souther and Frey played a set at the Candy Company club on El Cajon in San Diego. Struggling songwriters didn't have cash for motels and hotels and often crashed at the homes of local musicians. So it was with Frey and Souther, who stayed over at Tempchin's place, beginning a friendship that would last decades and produce several hit songs.

"Peaceful Easy Feeling" would become a huge song for Tempchin, setting him up financially. He wrote it as a young man coming to terms with the intricacies of romance. "It was basically about trying to get the girl, but then you realize: hey, if I don't get the girl I'm still fine," he told the *Tolucan Times* in November 2013. "That's really the essence of the song; it's only when you decide to let go of something that it's going to drop in your lap because you're not ready otherwise. I never thought of it as a love song, and it never occurred to me that it was going to be a hit."

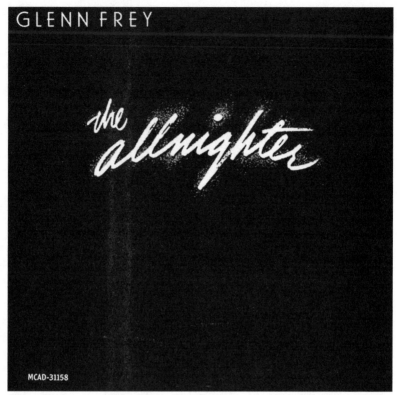

GLENN FREY

the allnighter

MCAD-31158

Glenn Frey's second solo album, *The Allnighter*, outsold his solo debut, *No Fun Aloud*, largely on the strength of its very commercial singles, "Smuggler's Blues" and "Sexy Girl." The former pushed Frey into a new career path—acting—after he guest-starred in a *Miami Vice* episode inspired by his ode to smuggling.

How the song became an Eagles hit is indicative of the loose and informal song-trading of the L.A. writing community in the 1970s. Reciprocating their friend's San Diego hospitality, Frey and Souther often had Tempchin stay with them in Hollywood. Tempchin was the next of the gang to be pushed to David Geffen, just as Browne had promoted Frey to the high-powered exec a couple of years earlier. Frey was at Browne's when he heard Tempchin singing "Peaceful Easy Feeling." He was impressed, telling Tempchin he had just put a band together and would like to play the song to them.

"Glenn made a cassette recording of me doing 'Peaceful Easy Feeling' at Jackson's house," Tempchin told UTSanDiego.com in November 2012. "He came back the next day and the Eagles had already worked it up, and he played me the tape of it, and I was blown away by how great it was. The Eagles were eight days old at the time."

In 1980, Tempchin attended an Eagles show in Santa Monica and gave Frey a tape of a new song, "Volunteer." Tempchin clearly still had the touch, and Frey invited him to co-write with him when he began working up material for his first solo album.

The different approach to songwriting Tempchin brought was the perfect medicine for an artist who had been locked into one particular way for working for almost ten years. As Tempchin explained to the *Tolucan Times*, "I think after a while with him and Henley it was really difficult; they are both such perfectionists whereas I'm just a free-flowing guy. The first time I went over we wrote 'I Found Somebody,' the next time we wrote 'The One You Love.' I love co-writing and I'm working with someone who turned out to be one of the greatest writers of our time! You've got the Beatles, the Stones, and the Eagles."

Frey was disappointed with Asylum Records—not so much with the sales of *No Fun Aloud* but with their reaction to his plans for a follow-up. When he took the tracks he'd recorded to the label, the company passed on them, telling him that he and his sound were old-fashioned.

Dropped

Frey had been caught in a radical change at Asylum. In January 1983, Warner Communications, Inc. announced that Bob Krasnow, vice president of Warner Bros. Records, had been promoted to chairman of Elektra/Asylum. Krasnow replaced Joe Smith, an absolute Eagles champion, who had resigned. Krasnow moved Elektra to New York and put all his eggs in young talent. "Some people play so as not to fail," he told *Billboard*. "There's no way to win doing that. If Elektra is to succeed, we will have to gamble heavily on contemporary talent."

Fortunately for Frey, there was another significant development in the recording industry that would prove to his benefit. It was always just a matter of time before Irving Azoff made the leap from manager to record executive. He finally got his chance to wield more control and bear more influence on the entertainment world when he was made president of the MCA Record Group and vice president of MCA, Inc. in the spring of 1982.

MCA in 1982 was a sleeping giant, waiting for an injection of new blood to awaken it from its slumbers. This was a major corporation with serious infrastructure issues that was in free fall, and it had been for some time. Its subsidiary label, Infinity, had proven expensive without yielding any real results, while other purchases left the company spending more than it made. That might be a typical situation in normal circumstances, but the industry had also been hit with increases in oil price that bumped up the cost of vinyl. MCA made a huge PR blunder by raising the price of albums by almost a dollar per unit, leading Tom Petty, an MCA recording artist, to campaign to have his album reduced from $9.98 to the old $8.99.

The MCA crisis was tailor-made for Irving Azoff. He rose to the challenge admirably, making some tough decisions, cutting back the dead wood (as he saw it), and rejuvenating the company into one of the strongest in the record business. *Billboard* called it "the most dramatic turnaround for a major label this decade."

So, for Glenn Frey, rejection at Asylum meant a quick chat with his old manager. Azoff found the new tracks totally acceptable, backed Frey to the hilt, and prepared to show the record business that he and MCA could do what Asylum dared not: make contemporary hit records with an ex-Eagle.

The record was tougher than *No Fun Aloud*, bluesier and more rock and roll. "I Got Love" and "Let's Go Home" are strong songs, and—just to prove Asylum and Krasnow wrong—very 1984 in sound and production. "Somebody Else" and "Living in Darkness" are both solid pop/rock, while Frey reaches back into his Eagles past for a moment of lyrical darkness in the shape of the crime-themed "Smuggler's Blues," a story song that fizzes with some slide guitar by Frey that Don Felder would probably be proud of.

The Allnighter would easily out-sell *No Fun Aloud*, and the record's first single, "Sexy Girl," was a Top 20 hit—a nice riposte to Asylum, which had so needlessly dumped Frey for not being contemporary.

Miami Vice

If any one item perfectly symbolizes the pop culture of America in the mid-1980s, it's probably *Miami Vice*. Indeed, check out any brochure for '80s-themed costumes, and there will be several *Miami Vice* items designed to capture the feel of the decade. It was a fast-paced show with very quick edits that visually and stylistically drew on MTV for style inspiration and flaunted the Armani/Versace pop fashion of the day with gusto. Stars Don Johnson (whose early movie *Zachariah* featured Joe Walsh and the James Gang) and Philip Michael Thomas, adorned in pale suits, no socks, and T-shirts, started a fashion trend around the world.

Miami Vice was a ratings success globally and a marvelous example of the best of American television—innovative, exciting, ridiculously expensive, and wildly unrealistic. The producers had a very sophisticated sense of their brand. Understanding the whole MTV feel, they teamed up with several record companies and music labels to incorporate contemporary pop and rock into the show. If you made records in the mid-'80s, you were featured—or wanted to be featured—on *Miami Vice*.

Glenn Frey turned actor when he played shady pilot Jimmy Cole in an episode of '80s hit TV show *Miami Vice*. Here he is in character with Don Johnson (top) and Philip Michael Thomas as the stylish detectives Crockett and Tubbs.

Photo by NBC/NBCU Photo Bank via Getty Images

The show's director and producer, Michael Mann, knew better than most the exposure power of interplay between music and television, and when he heard Frey's "Smuggler's Blues" he was immediately struck by the similarities between the song and the show. Mann had wanted to work with Frey previously, having offered B-roll footage in return for some promo on the air, but this was different. Now he came up the idea of basing a whole episode around Frey's song. It was a radical concept and strategy—and one that Frey jumped on. Frey told *Interview* magazine in April 1986 that Mann also told him, when they met at a bar to discuss the project, "You're going to play this guy Jimmy, and you'll be great."

Rock and roll had changed after the introduction of music videos and the explosion of MTV around the world. The visual formula for success affected numerous artists who were not especially recognizable, especially bands. The Eagles had an image, for sure, but did anybody really have a firm picture of Henley or Frey or Felder in their heads? The Eagles primarily sold from radio and stadium concerts, and that was in the days before Jumbotrons at 50,000-seat venues. Now, with MTV, pop stars were close up and personal and for twenty-four hours of the day.

Ironically, it was another member of the '60s Troubadour crowd, Michael Nesmith, who invented MTV. It started as a way of Nesmith promoting his solo single "Rio" around the world. Discovering that countries in Europe and Australasia had TV shows that played video clips, he set about making a full-blown mini-movie—a radical departure at the time from the cheap, lip-syncing promos bands typically used. Nesmith found a TV network to broadcast a series of videos as a show called *Popclips*, a concept he later sold to WarnerAmex, who created their own version of Nesmith's show and called it MTV.

Nesmith had envisioned artists like his Southern California contemporaries using video as an art form—an adjunct to the song and an interpretation visually of the emotion of the song. Naturally enough, when MTV exploded, it was less about expression, more about shiny, short, colorful commercials for new artists, themselves adorned in new-romantic fashion and made up to the nines.

Everyone knew who Glenn Frey ('80s-style) was after he appeared on *Miami Vice* and MTV. It was a remarkable breakthrough for an artist who rose to artistic prominence in a decade very different from the 1980s. Some, like David Bowie, managed to adapt to the new visual imagery era, but many more disappeared without a trace (at least until the invention of the CD and record companies' exploitation of catalogue artists).

Beverly Hills Cop

One afternoon, Irving Azoff called Frey and invited him to a screening of a new Eddie Murphy movie. Henley was there, too, and so were Quincy Jones, Stevie Wonder, and the Pointer Sisters. Azoff told Frey he should get one of his songs onto the soundtrack. Not too much chance of that, Frey figured, looking around at the songwriting talent in the room. A couple of months later, however, Frey received a tape of a song by Keith Forsey and Harold Faltermeyer, the masterminds behind several Donna Summer records. They wanted Frey's vocals, and for a small fee of $15,000, he agreed to perform the track.

The song was a smash hit, and Frey couldn't believe his luck, as he told Tavis Smiley on PBS in 2012. "Then when the movie came out and the record came out, (laughter) and then not only that, but they're playing 'The Heat Is On' for the Big East basketball tournament, it's playing all over all these sporting events. The record sells millions and millions of copies. It had all those great records on it, 'Neutron Dance' and 'Axle Steam,' and I was very lucky. I just happened to be in the right place at the right time."

This compilation of sixteen of Frey's best-known solo songs was released in 1995.

The song was a global smash and a #2 hit in America. Not too shabby for the second album from an artist who, according to Asylum, just wasn't contemporary. How much more contemporary could Frey be, as part of both *Miami Vice* and *Beverly Hills Cop*? How Azoff must have smiled.

Unfortunately, Frey's acting career failed to take off following its very promising start on *Miami Vice*. He had a major role in a revenge/hostage movie alongside Mark Harmon, Robert Duvall, and Gary Busey called *Let's Get Harry*, but it was a mediocre film with an above-average cast that never really made a mark. He also had a decent-sized role in the "Dead Dog Lives" episode of the TV crime series *Wiseguy*. And he was even given his own series, *South of Sunset*, which sadly was canceled after just one episode. More recently, Frey appeared on another Don Johnson cop series, *Nash Bridges*, and then scored a role on the HBO show *Arliss* in 2000. He has maintained an acting career to this day, including commercials and promotional work, but after the Eagles resumed in the 1990s, there has been precious little time for an Eagle to do anything but be an Eagle.

On top of that, Frey developed serious health issues in the mid-1980s. Perhaps as a result of years of hard living and pushing his body to the absolute limit, he began to suffer with diverticulitis (an intestinal disorder), which struck to such a degree that he was taken to the hospital just as his solo career was taking off. He responded by cleaning up his lifestyle and working out regularly, so much so that the new, buff Frey that appeared on the video for "Living Right" was even approached by a gym to do some ads.

Turning his back on the craziness of the 1970s and fixing his heath issues led Frey to the final act of settling down. In 1990, he married Cindy, whom he had met on a video set. They started a family in 1991, and Frey's turned his obsessive, driven personality toward his family rather than his music career. When he did release a record in this period, *Strange Weather*, there was less promotion, and less effort to push the album and singles to radio. Ironically, the record was one of his best, with a sophisticated sound and plenty of excellent Jack Tempchin songs, but without a full-blown promotional campaign, the record failed to deliver any hit singles, and didn't even dent the *Billboard* chart.

31

End of the Innocence

Henley Flies Solo

on Henley was hardly delighted when Glenn Frey called him, after the Alan Cranston gig, to say he'd had enough and the Eagles were over. Henley had earned himself an increasing amount of control in the Eagles organization over the past five years, and while he was just as aware as all the other parties that the Eagles were in conflict overdrive, to have it all ended by someone else was difficult to deal with.

A hit single, "Leather and Lace," with ex-girlfriend Stevie Nicks was a pleasant experience, however, and a sign that he could step out of the Eagles' shadow and create an identity and persona for himself. Whatever the internal disagreement within the Eagles, Henley always felt part of a band, and had no deep-seated ambition to fly solo. But since Frey gave him little choice in the matter, he could simply ease his way into it, should that indeed be the way forward.

Ultimately, it was Frey putting out *No Fun Aloud* that inspired Don Henley to launch his own solo career. "Well, if he's going to make an album, I'm going to make an album, too!" he told Mitchell Glazer of *Musician* magazine in 1982. Not that the decision wasn't fraught with doubt. Henley admitted as much to Robert Santelli of *Modern Drummer* in 1986. "It was pretty frightening because, as we all know, when large, famous groups breakup, a lot of the members don't survive in solo careers. . . . You can't just sit down and retire when you're [thirty-two]. So I just sucked in my gut and stuck out my chin and decided to see if I could do it."

I Can't Stand Still

Henley leaned on the musical guidance of top session guitarist Danny Kortchmar. Kortchmar had strong singer/songwriter roots, dating back to his playing in one of James Taylor's first groups before quitting while visiting

England. He later played on Taylor's seminal *Sweet Baby James*, as well as Carole King's *Tapestry* and several Jackson Browne releases.

The overall feel of the album was tentative—an ex-Eagle testing the modern-day pop waters with some old familiar sounds and a few new ones. It was mainstream rock with some updated synth and drum-machine beats to give it the '80s tone, essentially giving radio permission to play the tracks.

Lyrically, Henley continued the social commentary he had begun with the Eagles, although the first single from *I Can't Stand Still*, "Johnny Can't Read," was more obviously biting than anything he had written for the old band. It had an instantly '60s sound thanks to Kortchmar's Farfisa organ. Kortchmar explained the genesis to Songfacts.com in August 2013: "At the time I had a Farfisa organ and that's the sound you hear. That's what makes you think of the '60s, that Farfisa organ. I knocked off this piece of music, played it for Don, and he started writing lyrics for it right away."

The lyrics that came to Henley after hearing Kortchmar's swirling chords were focused on America's growing literacy problem. An English major and bookworm, Henley was speaking from the heart, but the record caused offense. It was too direct, too controversial. Indeed, some radio stations refused to play the song, even in Henley's home state of Texas.

Next up was more social commentary, but this time with more populist appeal, since "Dirty Laundry" attacked the dumbing-down of news on radio and television, especially in Los Angeles. Henley had grown up in an era of great news reporters on TV. What he saw in the 1980s were glamorous actors with too much makeup reading scripts. There was no follow-through on the stories they told, no depth and no analysis. He hated the clichéd "How do you feel?" that reporters seemed to ask victims after every tragedy and accident. An independent radio promoter got behind "Dirty Laundry" and ensured it had every chance to succeed. The track reached #3, even though the album it came from couldn't get higher than #24—a disappointing number, considering the record had a major hit single to promote it.

"I sold 650,000 copies or something, which is respectable, I guess, for a first album," Henley told *Record* magazine in February 1984. "I had a gold album and a gold single . . . I was moderately satisfied."

Geffen Reprise

By now, David Geffen had left the record business that he had so profoundly affected and revolutionized and set himself up as the head of Warner Bros. film division. It wasn't an easy period for the movie and music mogul. In

1977, he was diagnosed with terminal cancer, and decided to retire from the business and teach classes at Yale University. Remarkably, he then discovered in 1980 that he had been wrongly diagnosed, and a rejuvenated Geffen returned to his first love—records—with a brand new venture.

"I was relieved, of course," he told *Playboy* in September 1994. "I had sort of lived my life with one thing in my head, and all of a sudden there was a new piece of information. It was like a second chance. So I quickly decided to go back to work. I founded Geffen Records . . . I love the record business. It is the thing I do best, and I wanted to work."

Geffen took more of a back seat with his return to the record business. He hired street-savvy execs—people like he had been in the '70s—to find new talent, while using his own more established contacts to bring firepower to the company by signing some legendary veteran acts. First came Donna Summer, followed by Elton John. When Geffen brought across Dylan from CBS in the 1970s, he did it with a skilled wooing campaign. And while the relationship was short-lived, he did at least manage to get the man he wanted. He applied much the same tactics with his next superstar, John Lennon. Using the artist empathy he'd learned in the old days, he realized the way to Lennon was through his wife, Yoko Ono. Geffen courted Yoko, treated her respectfully, and agreed to sign them as a pair, sight unseen—or, more accurately, sound unheard. Tragically, Lennon was killed shortly after the debut of his and Yoko's *Double Fantasy* debut on Geffen Records. Such was the public outpouring of despair and affection that sales of the album soared far beyond the company's expectations.

There had been bad blood between Henley and Geffen after the Asylum Records founder left the company for new pastures. But now, with Asylum under new direction, Henley felt they could have done more with his solo debut. Geffen Records was a possible alternative destination. He may have had his reservations about Geffen, but Henley knew that the machinery at the new label was more efficient and more productive than anything Asylum could offer.

So, in 1984, Don Henley signed to Geffen Records. *Building the Perfect Beast* was the result, and was a fine solo offering. It spawned four hit records: the upbeat "All She Wants to Do Is Dance," the lilting, Eagles-influenced "Not Enough Love in the World," the world-weary and touching "Sunset Grill," and the definitive vacation tune "The Boys of Summer."

"Boys of Summer" sounded timeless the moment Henley wrote it. Inspired by guitar work from his collaborator Mike Campbell (from Tom Petty's Heartbreakers), Henley captured the sense of summer as well as

Henley's second solo album, *Building the Perfect Beast*, appeared at the end of 1984 and demonstrated his maturation as a writer and solo artist. Like his best work with the Eagles, the album contains some snappy hits: "The Boys of Summer," "All She Wants to Do Is Dance," "Not Enough Love in the World," and "Sunset Grill."

anyone since the leading expert in the field, Brian Wilson of the Beach Boys. Henley was in good spirits, as ace session drummer and longtime live foil Ian Wallace told me in 1999. "It was one of these records where everything just gelled, you know. It was a good project to be part of a good, pleasant vibe and lots of love and respect from everyone."

Henley enjoyed calling on friends, previous collaborators, and artists he simply admired from afar to contribute to the record. Helping out were teen guitar ace Charlie Sexton, Sam Moore of Sam & Dave fame, Martha Davis of the Motels, Patty Smyth, J. D. Souther, and Belinda "Go-Go's" Carlisle. ("Can you imagine, getting to work with Don Henley?" she asked me in 1988. "You know, the Eagles were just such a cool band. That was a great experience.")

Henley was back in business. The move to a new record company had given him the confidence he needed to step up his game to 1976 levels, and

Henley, consciously or not, had sent a message to Frey that he too could cut it as a personality and a solo artist. In recognition of the quality of his work, Henley picked up Grammy nominations for Record, Song, and Producer of the Year and won the award for Best Rock Vocal (Male) for "The Boys of Summer."

Once Henley made the mental switch from band member to solo artist, and had achieved success and found favor among the peers in the industry with whom he had been working in since a teenager, he was ready and able to make the finest record of his career. He didn't hurry himself, either, taking a cool five years over the follow-up to *Building the Perfect Beast.*

The End of the Innocence is classic rock meets pure pop. Henley had never sounded better, and the six different producers working closely with him bring variety and spice but never lose sense of the overall sound. Henley acts as the orchestra conductor throughout, assembling his cast of talents and then subtly overseeing every move, every beat, every nuance of the record. It's a stirring mix of electric guitars, synthesizers, layered harmonies, and sterling guest spots from sometimes expected but often quite unexpected artists, notably Axl Rose of Guns N' Roses.

Mike Campbell played a role in one of the album's finest songs, "Heart of the Matter," which also features one of Henley's oldest musical pals, J. D. Souther. "How Bad Do You Want It?" is more throwaway lyrically but fizzes sonically thanks in part to the appearance of a young Sheryl Crow on background vocals. The blues-rock of "I Will Not Go Quietly" would hardly threaten Kurt Cobain and his crew for grungy nastiness, but guest vocals from rocker-of-the-moment Axl Rose give a moderate track a suitably biting tone and delivery.

Asylum Records may have thought Henley and Frey too old-school in 1980, but clearly Guns N' Roses thought Henley cool enough to fill in for drummer Steven Adler, who was away in rehab, for a performance of "Patience" at the 1989 American Music Awards. Henley told *Modern Drummer*'s Robert Santelli in 1990 that he checked with production partner Danny Kortchmar before agreeing to do it. Kortchmar thought it a superb idea. So Henley "called Axl back and said OK. . . . I rehearsed with Axl a couple of days, although the whole band never showed up. But it was a piece of cake. There was really nothing to it."

The End of the Innocence sold in excess of six million copies in America alone, and the Don picked up another Grammy in 1990, this time for Best Male Vocalist. But there was friction ahead, this time between Henley and Geffen Records. Henley still felt the label could have done more to

Actual Miles, a Don Henley hits compilation, made its way onto the shelves in 1995 and comprises tracks from his solo albums along with some new material: "The Garden of Allah," "You Don't Know Me at All," and his pristine version of Leonard Cohen's classic "Everybody Knows."

promote and sell his records, so he began looking at alternatives. In the early '90s, publishing companies realized the worth of hit songwriters and began offering generous contracts. Henley was tempted by a huge deal with EMI and chose to sign. Unfortunately, he was still under contract with Geffen, who said he owed the label two more albums. Henley disagreed, citing an old California state law designed to stop movie actors from being trapped in long-term contracts that artists could not be forced to work under a contract for more than seven years.

Henley claimed that his seven years ran out in 1991, and that he could not be held longer just because the label said he owed them two more albums. Geffen reminded him that he had re-signed in 1988 after *Building the Perfect Beast* sold so well, and therefore the seven years continued to 1995. Henley also argued that since Geffen Records had been acquired by MCA, the contract had no legal standing.

As in all high-profile lawsuits, the two parties became embroiled in lawyer-speak and spent thousands of dollars each before both sides realized that little good could come of the dispute. The suits became increasingly unpleasant until finally a compromise was reached. It helped that the conflicts ran through the whole reunion period, and Geffen Records absolutely wanted to be involved with the Eagles. And so a compromise was reached, whereby Henley gave Geffen a compilation album, *Actual Miles*, and made a deal for the label to release the new Eagles album, *Hell Freezes Over*.

32

Flying Solo

There Goes the Neighborhood

As the clear leaders and chief songwriters of the group, it was expected that, as soon as the dust settled following the demise of the Eagles, Henley and Frey would carve out successful solo careers. They might even eclipse their band achievements; they definitely had the talent and work ethic. But what of the others? Should they find new bands, work together without Henley and Frey, or were they too destined to follow the solo path? Or perhaps it would be smart to disappear for a while, regroup, and bounce back in a year or so?

When Irving Azoff adjusted the band's contract with Warner Bros. during the *Long Run* negotiations (Azoff liked to keep things current and fresh and the label on their toes by re-jigging contracts frequently), each of the individual Eagles was also given a solo deal with Warner/Elektra/Asylum. Security in the case of a breakup, or an attempt to keep the individuals locked into the company—who knew? Either way, at some point or another, all of the ex-Eagles felt obliged to make a solo album.

Joe Walsh

Joe Walsh had had a decent band and solo career before replacing Bernie Leadon in the Eagles, so it would presumably be a case of "carry on as usual" for the guitar player. He'd really begun already in 1978 by releasing *But Seriously Folks*, which gave him a hit single with a jaunty and clever slice of rock-and-roll self-deprecation, "Life's Been Good." But with the Eagles collapsing in 1980, Walsh took his time before going solo again. There is a world of difference in pressure between releasing occasional solo projects while still a long-term member of a major rock band and existing purely as a solo act.

So, in no great hurry after the trials and tribulations of the past year or so, Walsh chose to give his time, energy, and money to his country by

Walsh's fourth studio album, *But Seriously Folks*, released in 1978, includes the wild-man guitarist's ode to the rock-and-roll lifestyle, "Life's Been Good."

running for president in 1980. He was too young to actually win; the U.S. Constitution declares that a president shall be at least thirty-five years old. But what was Walsh offering the American people if he were elected? There would be free gas for all, and "Life's Been Good" was to be the new national anthem.

Although Walsh never again captured the magic of "Life's Been Good," he spent most of the post-breakup '80s releasing albums. They ranged from the excellent (*The Confessor* from 1985, and *Got Any Gum?* from 1987) to the wayward (1991's *Ordinary Average Guy* and 1992's *Songs for a Dying Planet*).

Who Are You?

Even when the material and focus wasn't there and his addictions worsened, Walsh never lost his ability to stun with a grinding guitar riff or a poetic solo.

Consequently, some of his best musical work following his initial tenure with the Eagles came with production work or guest spots with other acts and artists.

Walsh had known the Who's bass player, John Entwistle, since the James Gang days. He contributed tasteful guitar to Entwistle's solo project *Too Late the Hero*, which, while dismissed by critics when released in 1982, is now thought of as a credible piece of work from the eccentric bass player. Walsh's playing is sensitive and empathetic throughout, allowing enough space (a Walsh trademark) for the music to breathe and pulsate. The album also gave Entwistle two hit singles, "Talk Dirty" and "Too Late the Hero."

Walsh also played guitar with several other artists, many of them friends of his, throughout the 1980s, including Graham Nash, Karla Bonoff, Steve Winwood, and a certain Don Henley. One of his better ideas was to join Ringo Starr's All-Starr band in 1989. The supergroup idea wasn't new, but Ringo, being a Beatle, had huge names clamoring to take part. The lineup for the first incarnation of the band was Ringo, Dr. John, Levon Helm of the Band, Billy Preston, Nils Lofgren and Clarence Clemons from Springsteen's band, and Walsh. Reviews were generally good, and the musicianship simply breathtaking. But life on the road was tough on Walsh. By 1991, he was in a bad way. Drinking and drug use had never previously affected his work, but now he was a professional liability and looked to be descending into his own dark cave. He didn't seem bothered about promoting his records, and he began to stumble over lyrics during his opening spots for the Doobie Brothers in 1991.

Old pal Glenn Frey came to the rescue, bringing Walsh on the road with him as Party of Two, with Walsh and Frey offering their very expensive services to corporate clients. The drinking only increased, however. Walsh needed the structure and "family" that the Eagles provided. When talk of a reunion came around, after they all recorded the Travis Tritt video, Joe was considered a problem. Once Walsh began suffering from blackouts, Frey read him the riot act. No more drinking or no more Eagles. Period.

True to his word, by the time the *Hell Freezes Over* reunion tour began in 1994, Walsh had cleaned up his act. He looked better, smelled better, and sounded better. Finally, Walsh was able to kick the habit that had plagued him for so many years. Since 1999, when the Eagles resumed their touring, he has had the Eagles' structure to keep him in check, allowing his artistic work to thrive again.

Get Bach

In 2001, Walsh was honored with an honorary doctorate from Kent State University. Having learned to keep busy and occupied, he chose to tour once more with the old James Gang. He also became enamored with Ringo's wife's sister, Marjorie Bach. The two married in 2008, and Joe Walsh, the man, has been on an upswing ever since. It was Marjorie, in fact, who pushed him into making the *Analog Man* album in 2012.

In April 2013, as the Eagles talked about the upcoming tour in support of their history documentary movie, it was Walsh who spilled the beans on Bernie Leadon's return. "I never really got a chance to play with him," Walsh admitted, "but we've been in contact. We see him from time to time, and I'm really glad he's coming because it's going to take the show up a notch, and I'm really looking forward to playing with him, finally."

Walsh also announced his next non-Eagles project: an all-star blues album featuring collaborations with Dr. John, Robert Randolph, Keb' Mo', Jim Keltner, and Jeff Beck bassist Tal Wilkenfeld. "I'll say, loosely, I've started a blues album," Walsh said. "Half of it is original, and half of it is old Howlin' Wolf or John Lee Hooker. I told everybody to bring a song in and everybody did, be it an old blues song or some idea. We went through some old Stax records from, like, the Otis Redding days, Sam & Dave stuff that were just albums tracks, and did our version of a whole bunch of stuff."

Don Felder

Don Felder, a genuinely decent man, was distraught when the Eagles crashed. "It was a difficult time for everyone, I think," he told me in 2010. "I had lived this crazy lifestyle for five, six years with these guys. I wrote about the tensions and the craziness in my book, but we were still a band, a unit if you will, that kind of band of brothers thing, you know. So when you are suddenly on your own it is a very real change. I appreciated the calm but it was definitely a major adjustment."

The timing was difficult for Felder. The band had broken down, everyone knew that, but he was also very aware that he'd played a role in the final fight that pushed Glenn Frey over the edge. He had, not too long before, just written the music for one of the finest and most popular songs in the history of popular music, "Hotel California," which now looked like the proverbial double-edged sword. On the one hand, he had finally proved

Don Felder has hardly been prolific with solo recordings, but he did return to the album business with this smart and savvy slice of mellow rock and roll, *Road to Forever*, in 2012.

himself a worthy writing peer to the band's songwriting masters, Henley and Frey, only for it to be taken away. On the other hand, his confidence was high, given the kind of rarified esteem in which the track was being held around the world.

Felder didn't know too much apart from playing music. It's all he had done since he was a kid in Gainesville. So, first up, he recorded a song for use in an animated film, *Heavy Metal*. The song was "Heavy Metal (Takin' a Ride)." It was very well received and remains a cult classic to this day. Naturally, Felder felt confident enough to start work on a solo album. After spending thousand of hours with the Eagles in state-of-the-art recording studios, he knew his way around a mixing desk. Why not put a small studio in his house and have the best of both worlds? Home comforts and top-quality recording equipment, and, blessing of all blessings, no commute.

Felder signed a solo deal with Warner Bros. and jumped into the deep end of making a record. He was going to work differently than he had as an Eagle. There'd probably be no touring in support of the album, and no constant demands of his time from the label. He'd produce the record, deliver it when it was ready, and take it one step at a time.

Airborne appeared in 1983, and it was a good, solid slice of mainstream '80s rock and roll. "Bad Girls," "Haywire," and "Never Surrender" (featuring Kenny Loggins) were all above-average, well-produced pop songs. But the album lacked the killer instinct—the song that would get radio buzzing and programmers interested. There was no "Hotel California," or indeed anything close to that modern classic. It wasn't that Felder could not have achieved more at the time, but he was clearly lacking the drive and obsessive commitment that filled every Eagles groove. He was tired, emotionally spent, and he needed a rest. Making records is what he and his friends did. But turning that music into commercial hit material? That's another level of commitment. Felder just didn't have that ambition, coming off the breakdown of America's most successful rock band.

"I didn't want to go back on the road [because] I had four little kids at home," he told the *Illinois Entertainer* in April 2013, "so I made that first studio record and started doing music for film and television, like that movie *Heavy Metal* and scoring movies of the week. That way I could be at home, still drive car pools, go to soccer games, and coach little league baseball. Then, when the band resumed in '94, it completely geared back up."

Fired Up

Felder went solo again in 2001, and again it wasn't his choice. In a complex legal move, Henley and Frey fired Felder from the Eagles. Felder sued them, claiming that Henley and Frey had acted unfairly in terminating him. "Despite each being a one-third owner of Eagles Ltd.," the suit noted, "Henley and Frey have consistently treated Felder as a subordinate, with complete disregard for his rights."

Around the same time the breakdown in relations with Don and Glenn began, Felder and his wife Susan were divorced after twenty-nine years of marriage. No judgments necessary. Never mind the fact that he had played the role of "single" rock star on the road for many years. Felder was genuinely distraught at the loss, however. When the bedrock of his home life discovered another world for herself, Felder rightly or wrongly felt a great sense of loss. To then lose his other family, the Eagles, was emotionally devastating.

Felder realized that bridges had been burned with the Eagles and set about a means of recovery. Every day, he would spend time jotting down thoughts and memories on a legal pad. Eventually he had pages and pages of journal and diary-style entries. His new girlfriend read some of the entries and encouraged Felder to assemble them together and see if it would make a book. He did, and he liked what he saw, feeling that his story—from poverty in Florida as a kid to millionaire rock star traveling the world in private jets on the strength of his skills with a guitar—was a classic of the American dream. He was right, and book publishers started a bidding war for his memoirs. Now he just had to write it.

In 2008, after some legal wrangling, *Heaven and Hell: My Life in the Eagles (1974–2001)* by Don Felder with Wendy Holden made the bookstores. It's a frank account of Felder's rock-and-roll journey and the Eagles' internal workings, and there are some generalized exposés of the band's notorious partying days. As for his own removal from the band, the book takes the view that he was slapped down for asking too many questions about the band's accounts and the division of funds. In the minor press war that ensued, Henley and Frey were quick to deny such claims and point the finger at Felder, who they said had made a power grab despite no longer being a creative force.

The book gave Felder some notoriety and reminded everyone that his story was, indeed, a marvelous example of rags-to-riches All-American success. It was also a great soap opera, and a compelling glimpse into the lifestyles of the rich and famous. The exposés were not so damaging that the band lost any favor with the public. In fact, the publicity probably served to boost ticket and CD and DVD sales—and Irving Azoff, most likely, found it all very amusing.

The book also brought Felder back into the mainstream. He toured with the memoir, played charity shows, and made some radio and TV appearances. And, as he did, and as he relived some of the experiences and emotions that he dug up for the book, he began to write songs. In a few years, he had enough for an album, and in 2012, he released *Road to Forever*, a belated follow-up to *Airborne*. The album debuted at #27 on the *Billboard* Heatseekers chart.

It was a very decent record, full of personal and honest songs and produced with the help of a select few music biz friends, including David Crosby, Stephen Stills, and Graham Nash, *American Idol*'s ace of bass Randy Jackson, Steve Lukather, and Tommy Shaw.

Felder was especially tickled to have one of his oldest friends, Stephen Stills, contribute backing vocals. "I think one of my earliest mates was Stephen Stills," he told Gibson.com's Anne Erickson in March 2014. "He and I had a band together when we were fourteen years old. He's always been a great singer, so to have Crosby, Stills, and Nash sing on my record, after our paths have crossed so many times over the years, was great. I've always loved those guys. Even though I've worked and played with all those guys, to have them all come in and sing on my record was a highlight for me."

Timothy B. Schmit, Parrothead

Nobody in the business was surprised that the always unassuming and very proper Timothy B. Schmit would take his own sweet time considering his options for the future. He'd been with the Eagles the shortest amount of time of everyone, and the Eagles machine had yet to consume his life, so he had plenty of current contacts in the recording industry. Initially, he kept himself interested and busy with session work and playing live as a sideman again. Schmit did some sessions for Bob Seger and Don Henley, toured with Warren Zevon and Jimmy Buffett, and, along with several other ex-Eagles, helped their old music-journalist pal Cameron Crowe with songs for the soundtrack to his breakthrough movie, *Fast Times at Ridgemont High*.

Schmit toured Europe with Toto in 1982 and followed that with three years with Jimmy Buffett and his Coral Reefer Band. He did more than play bass for Buffett, though. Schmit helped the tropical crooner with the nuttiest, most dedicated fans in the world with some marketing and branding. It was Timothy B. Schmit, of all people, who christened Buffett's die-hard fans "Parrotheads."

"I was driving to a gig in his car," he told VintageRock. com in 2012, "and it's one of those outdoor sheds where, if you come in later, you kind of drive through the people walking from the distant parking lot up to the show grounds. People started noticing that

Timothy B. Schmit's debut solo album from 1984, *Playin' It Cool*, harkened back to the classy jazz days of the 1930s.

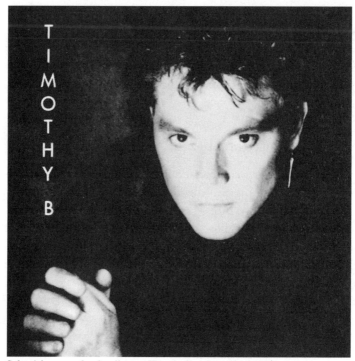

Schmit's second solo album, *Timothy B*, released in 1987.

there was a big car coming through, and they noticed it was Buffett. They all started going crazy—his audiences are really faithful and loyal and love to have a good time. I said, 'These are like your own personal Deadheads.' [And then] I said, 'No, they're Parrotheads. You've got your Parrotheads.' I guess he liked that and kept it."

Schmit did take time to work on a debut solo album, the oddly detached *Playing It Cool* from 1984. There's nothing especially wrong with it, but like Felder's debut it was competent rather than compelling. As the bass player in a band so dominated by Henley and Frey, he'd need to do a better job next time if he did indeed want to increase his own profile.

The follow-up, 1987's *Timothy B.*, was a definite improvement. Schmit had reconnected with his passion for rock and roll—something that had been lacking on the debut. This time, the result was punchier and more radio-friendly, and it contained at least one very strong song with hit potential, "Boys Night Out," which went Top 30. Eagles fans were delighted that same year to see Timothy B. and Randy Meisner onstage together with Richard Marx, performing a very special rendition of the old Eagles hit "Take It to the Limit" to wild applause.

Schmit's most recent album, *Expando*, looks back at his childhood days on the road with his musician father. Once the family had chosen to move around, they became quite expert in the trailer world, and their third such vehicle was a top-notch example called an Expando, so named because it "expanded" from eight feet to fifteen feet.

Expando, the album, was a return to Schmit's folk roots. His reputation in the business allowed him to recruit some distinguished guest artists for the album, including Dwight Yoakam, Keb' Mo', and, somewhat surprisingly, Kid Rock. With Schmit now nearer to seventy years of age than sixty, it would have been heartening for him to read that the BBC called *Expando* his "most satisfyingly complete solo offering yet."

Randy Meisner

Randy might have been exhausted by the Eagles' intense schedule and lifestyle, but he may also have immediately regretted jumping ship when he did. He retreated to Scottsbluff, Nebraska, where he purchased a farm and grew vegetables. He also worked on his lifelong hobby of collecting vintage cars, eventually accumulating fifteen antique models, including a Porsche, a Jaguar XJ-S, and '57 and '67 Corvettes.

Randy Meisner attempted to build a solo career on the back of his Eagles name, but the process was stymied by various factors, including the release of two solo albums called *Randy Meisner*—one in 1978 (top) and another in 1982 (bottom).

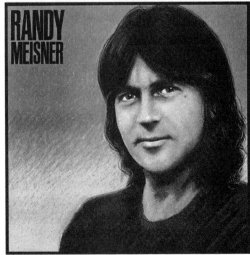

It was a conscious decision to remove himself from the pressures and craziness of the record industry. The problem was that Randy was no longer the easily pleased country boy he remembered. Nebraska was isolated, and he felt bored. "I

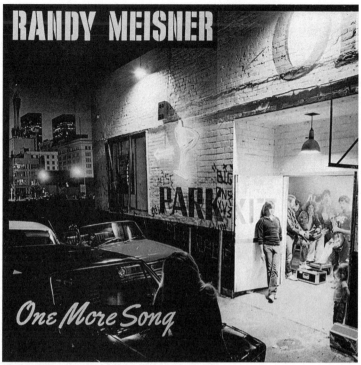

Meisner's second solo album, *One More Song*, was his most successful, thanks to the inclusion of two hit singles, "Deep Inside My Heart," with Kim Carnes, and "Hearts on Fire."

realized I'd changed so much," he told *People* magazine in January 1982, "and I missed the city. I thought I could get away, but music's in my blood."

Meisner came shooting out of the starting blocks with his debut solo album, but 1978's *Randy Meisner* did very little. Meisner was unsure of himself as a solo artist and quickly wished he were back in a band. "I really did want to do my own thing," he told RockHistoryBook.com, "and then I realized how much I really wanted to be in a group. All the pressure was on me as a solo artist then, every interview, every decision, and everything had to be made by me. Then I realized that I didn't want to do this anymore."

Feeling insecure, Meisner called on someone he trusted, and who he knew would provide him with some steel and support on his next album, *One More Song*. Don Henley provided backing vocals and encouragement, and his magic touch was in evidence once again. Meisner's duet with Kim Carnes, "Deep Inside My Heart," was a sizeable Top 30 hit, and the next single, the jaunty "Hearts on Fire," rose as high as #14 in 1981.

Meisner didn't work with Henley on his next record, another epony-mous album that probably confused fans and radio stations alike. It did very little, and Meisner retreated for several years. He tried teaming up with former Burrito Brother Rick Roberts in 1987 as the Meisner-Roberts Band, but while they had a promising sound, they failed to get organized enough to take things to the necessary level. Meisner could always do ses-sions, just to keep his hand in. A couple of years later, he was invited to be part of a reunion album featuring all five original members of Poco. *Legacy* was a terrific album, with a couple of hit records within its grooves, and the future looked promising. Sadly, the personnel assembled could never get together again.

Meisner remained very private for the next few years, making fans all the more delighted to see him onstage with the Eagles in 1998 for their induction into the Rock and Roll Hall of Fame.

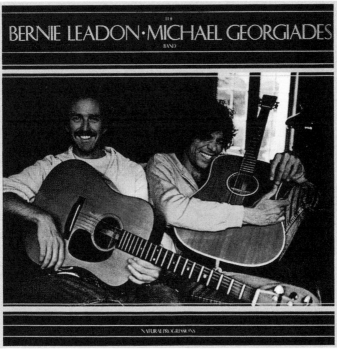

Bernie Leadon's post-Eagles career was quiet. He'd pick up recording sessions when he fancied it, join friends on band projects, and release the occasional studio project, like this 1977 album, *Natural Progressions*, with Michael Georgiades.

Bernie Leadon

Bernie Leadon had the most experience of life in rock and roll when the Eagles started, and he was the first to recognize the dangers of superstardom to physical and mental health. He quit the Eagles in 1975 and slipped off to Hawaii to recover.

Eventually, Leadon returned to music and based himself in the home of country music, Nashville, where he cherry-picked music projects. He did a few sessions and made the occasional album. And when he wasn't playing music, he was absorbed in his other passion: trains.

His first musical project was with an old friend, Michael Georgiades, on a 1977 album called *Natural Progressions*. Leadon spent some time playing with the Nitty Gritty Dirt Band, and then, in the early '90s, as part of a parody country band, Run C&W, that made a minor impact on the somewhat pompous country scene of the day.

Leadon's next solo album was *Mirror*, from 2004. He did a few interviews to support it but preferred to let the music do the talking. Little was heard of Bernie in the mainstream music world until 2013, when word had it that he was going back on the road with the Eagles. The rumors were true, and Leadon toured with the band and appeared during the opening acoustic segment, as well as the encores. Fans were delighted to see the original member back in the band.

33

No More Walks in the Wood

A s Don Henley matured as an artist and as a man, the core values he learned while growing up in Texas in the 1940s and 1950s have become increasingly motivating for him as an artist, as an Eagle, and as a social reformer.

It was probably a tough upbringing for any child in hot, dusty rural Texas in the 1940s. Don worked for his father in an auto-parts store, but those lessons about fan belts and spark plugs haven't really lasted. His father's greatest influence was teaching young Don about the land. Henley Sr. was a master gardener who made sure his son understood and appreciated the power and wonder of nature.

"He taught me, sometimes against my will, the magic of sun, dirt, and water," Henley told the *Worcester Telegram & Gazette* in November 2008. "He also taught me that my responsibilities didn't end at our property line. My mother was a schoolteacher, and she made sure that there were always books in the house. Those influences were the foundation of my environmentalism, although no such terminology existed at the time."

Literature Influence

Henley's parents also drummed into him the importance of an education. Don immersed himself in English literature at college. Aside from a passion for the usual Shakespeare and Thomas Hardy works, he was drawn to the writings of Emerson and Thoreau. They seemed relevant somehow, resonating with the hippie, back-to-the-land ethos of the late 1960s.

Henry David Thoreau's classic *Walden: Or, Life in the Woods* is an account of the disillusioned author looking for more from life than was available to him in his modern world and describes his attempts to get back to basics.

Walden, by Henry David Thoreau, pictured here, inspired Don Henley as a young English major, and he returned the favor by campaigning for the preservation of the Walden Woods in the 1990s.   *Benjamin D. Maxham*

Imagine a reality TV series pitting a man against nature, but with a philosophical twist. Thoreau was a counterculture pioneer. He saw his country changing rapidly during the industrial age, and not for the better. The Industrial Revolution had brought factories, sweatshops, workhouses, poverty, great riches—but only for a few—and frightening destruction of nature.

It was the writings of Thoreau and Emerson that most comforted Don as he faced the slow death of his father while first embarking on life as a musician. Dealing with his father's heart disease and impending death was traumatic, but Henley was helped by teachers at the University of North Texas, who encouraged him to study the works of the transcendental writers. He told *Preservation* magazine in 2004, "It helped me cope but also prompted me to think about our relationship to the world around us and guided me toward a lifelong interest in historic preservation and conservation."

When, in 1989, Henley read about some building projects threatening Walden Woods, he contacted the Thoreau scholars mentioned in the piece who were protesting the destruction. Henley then headed to Boston to discover exactly what was going on. What could he, a rock-and-roll musician, do to fight back? Publicity was the answer, and Henley formed the Walden Woods Project with the support of many other dedicated preservationists in 1990.

Schmit, Frey, and Henley

It was "stick to what you know" time, too, and what Henley knew about was music and awareness. His first move was to organize a benefit concert, for which he called on his friends, rounding up Sheryl Crow, Jimmy Buffett, Bonnie Raitt, Bob Seger, Timothy B. Schmit, and, of course, Glenn Frey.

First Buffett did a set, followed by Raitt and Seger, and then Henley took the stage to perform some of his solo hits, including "Heart of the Matter" and "The Boys of Summer." After closing with "All She Wants to Do Is Dance," Don then made a short speech before bringing out Frey for "Smuggler's Blues." The crowd went crazy as Henley, Frey, and Schmit launched into "Lyin' Eyes" and "Take It Easy."

Henley also put together a book of essays on the environment, *Heaven Is Under Our Feet*, with rock critic Dave Marsh. Contributors included Paula Abdul, Sting, Tom Cruise, Jack Nicholson, James Michener, Garry Trudeau, Jesse Jackson, Bette Midler, Kurt Vonnegut, E. L. Doctorow, and James Earl Jones, along with a foreword by former president Jimmy Carter. Henley was not afraid to use his connections when it mattered.

In 1993, *Common Thread: The Songs of the Eagles*, the Nashville tribute to the Eagles, raised in excess of three million dollars for the Walden Woods Project, enabling it to buy the threatened land from the developers. Today, the Walden Woods house the new Thoreau Institute. "We want to take Thoreau's teachings as the foundation of our work," Henley explains, at Walden.org, "but we intend to go much further than that. We want to teach environmental science and environmental philosophy."

Running on Empty

Never one to stand still, in 1993 Don cofounded the non-profit Caddo Lake Institute with his friend Dwight K. Shellman, an attorney. It all began when Henley, who was still living in California, heard about plans to build a canal in Caddo Lake, Texas—a move that would affect the ecology of the wetlands. It was personal to him. The lake was part of his life. His father loved the lake and fished there regularly.

By the end of 1993, Caddo Lake had been named a wetland of "international importance" under the 1971 Ramsar Treaty that was established to protect wetlands around the world. With that aim achieved, Shellman urged Henley to continue with the project and develop a scientific research center. They also worked on turning an old U.S. Army munitions plant on the lake over to the U.S. Fish and Wildlife Service. The lobbying and campaigning began all over again.

And there's still a great deal of work to be done. Alarming levels of mercury have been documented in the lake's food chain, including the highest level recorded in any snake on the planet. Much of the mercury has been traced to exhaust from nearby coal-burning plants.

Henley is keeping tabs on cutting-edge technology that could help with this kind of pollution. "Sound science may be our saving grace," he told the *Dallas Morning News* in April 2011. "But oftentimes in Washington—and certainly in Texas—politics trumps science. What Will Rogers said about land back in 1930 can be applied to water. They aren't making any more of it."

Recording Artists Coalition

A little closer to home, Henley teamed up with fellow musicians Sheryl Crow and Alanis Morissette to form the Recording Artists Coalition in 2000. In a few months, Henley had recruited rock and roll's biggest hitters: Billy Joel, Eric Clapton, and Bruce Springsteen.

The idea of the organization was to provide a unified group that could work against the powerful lobbying of major labels like Universal and Sony and the RIAA (the Recording Industry Association of America). California had a piece of music-biz legislation, "the seven-year rule," that made it clear that labor contracts in California were limited to seven years. However, many artists like Henley and Crow felt it was being abused by the conglomerates, who used a 1987 amendment to the law that allowed them to bypass the seven-year rule when demanding undelivered albums.

"This practice of singling out recording artists is discriminatory and it restricts the basic American philosophy of free-market competition," Henley told the California State Senate in September 2001. "A recording artist, like any other working person, should be given the ability to seek higher compensation and test his or her value in the open marketplace." Henley's RAC was also opposed to a "work for hire" clause in federal copyright law that allows record companies, if they choose, to keep an artist's recordings forever. In 2011, the Henley-founded RAC teamed up with the Grammys to present an annual award to artists who make a difference to their industry.

Digital Campaigner

More recently, Henley has turned his attention toward copyright protection and the Internet. Noting that record company revenues have fallen by at least half over the past decade, Henley concludes that the Internet and its free-for-all mentality is behind the crash. Disappointed that the younger generation appear to find it "cool" to find ways to not pay for music, Henley has been keen to stress that such action affects the whole music-business food chain—from caterers to makeup artists to instrument manufacturers to booking agents and so on.

"In the future," he told RGJ.com in June 2012, "there will be no artists—just 'content providers.' Empires like Google, AOL, Yahoo, and others have been built on distributing free content—other people's copyrighted, creative, or journalistic works—on the web, but these huge ISPs take no responsibility whatsoever. They're just neutral distributors, they say. But, to a great degree, they're really a 'fence' for stolen property. The Digital Millennium Copyright Act of 1998 needs to be rewritten. It's obsolete."

According to Henley, concert footage filmed at gigs and posted on YouTube and other such sites is also a danger to the industry. "That's illegal. It's a violation of U.S. Copyright Law, but people seem oblivious to that. They seem to think they are entitled to video or record whatever they want and post it on the web."

34

Common Ground

Gone Country

In 1991, Irving Azoff was the head of Giant Records. The company was in good shape, having just released a monster-selling charity single, "Voices That Care," and a huge album in the shape of the *New Jack City* movie soundtrack, and had signed some major names to its roster, notably Brian Wilson and Steely Dan.

In 1993, Azoff chose to open a Nashville division, and put record producer James Stroud in charge. Stroud was a former percussionist for the likes of the Pointer Sisters, Paul Simon, Gladys Knight, and Bob Seger, as well as the producer behind the triple-platinum "Misty Blue" by Dorothy Moore. In 1989, he discovered one of the biggest country acts of the '90s, Clint Black, and produced his breakthrough album, *Killin' Time.*

Azoff, ever the industry analyst, had been watching the dramatic increase in sales in country music and the power shift in country's home city, Nashville. As the '90s began, younger artists were making inroads, new producers were changing the formula, and the music was more popular than at any time in its history. The media called it "new country" when artists like Ricky Skaggs and Dwight Yoakam tired of the pop-influenced sound of the '70s and early '80s and went back to basics to discover a new sound that used new technology but had deep roots in the original sounds of the music.

Skaggs went back to Bill Monroe, founder of bluegrass, for his inspiration, but smacked it into overdrive with some hi-tech playing and production. Having brought traditional music to Emmylou Harris back in the early '80s, he was now revolutionized mainstream country with a hi-tech bluegrass-flavored sound that gave him twelve #1 hits as a major-label international superstar.

Johnny Rottten Likes Country

Country music wasn't feeling well when Dwight Yoakam headed to Nashville in the mid-'80s to introduce his brand of hardcore country music. In the late '70s and early '80s, country music was left staggering in an *Urban Cowboy* stupor, largely bland and pop-edged, with too many phased guitars and girlie background choirs. The record companies had told Yoakam he was too country, but then CBS told Johnny Cash the same thing. Outraged, Yoakam let rip at the Nashville establishment in the media. The rock press immediately took notice, and Yoakam was set as country's coolest maverick since Cash in the '60s.

It was on moving to Los Angeles in the early 1980s that Yoakam, a Buck Owens and Byrds fan in equal measure, found his true musical home. Playing the same clubs as the bands from L.A.'s burgeoning post-punk scene, Yoakam was so country he was rock. He even got the Johnny Rotten seal of approval. And then there was the debut album, *Guitars, Cadillacs, Etc., Etc.* If it was Garth Brooks that made country music popular again in 1990, it was Dwight who forged the trail, reminding music fans that country music in its purest form is as valid as rockabilly, blues, and rock and roll.

He also happened to be an Eagles supporter. "I mean, the Eagles proved to everyone watching that country music was a valid format for mainstream music fans," he told me in 1992. "They took country and played it in a way that spread the music around the world. That country music exploded in the 1990s has a direct connection to what the Eagles did in the 1970s."

Garth

Then, in 1989, an artist emerged who would single-handedly revolutionize Nashville, the music, the look, the business operations of country music. The hat-wearing, Oklahoma-raised Garth Brooks refused to be limited by country music's historically down-home, small-town mentality. Brooks had grown up watching MTV and listening to Dan Fogelberg, Billy Joel, and the Eagles. He loved the drama of KISS and the emotion of Don Henley and Elton John. But he also admired the deep humanity of his own country-music heroes, the two Georges, Strait and Jones.

Brooks' vocals, pop instincts, and country delivery combined to create a rocking but country sound that hadn't been heard on radio since the glory days of the early 1970s. He didn't sound exactly like the Eagles, but he captured the same sense of blending styles and warm, upbeat material that went straight to the heart. His 1991 album *Ropin' the Wind* went to the top of the *Billboard* chart—not the country chart but the overall chart. His next album, *The Chase*, sold faster than any country album in history, and Brooks' phenomenal sales had a domino effect on other country artists. People who liked Brooks would try out some other new Nashville product,

Country music came of age in the middle 1990s. Garth Brooks mixed country rock and pop and took the Nashville music global, selling out concerts around the world, including huge shows in the U.K. and Ireland.

Photo by Nubar Alexanian/ Woodfin Camp/ The LIFE Images Collection/ Getty Images

and they tended to like it. Suddenly, the poor cousins of the American record business were grabbing sales and attention from the big boys in L.A. and New York.

As far as Brooks was concerned, the Nashville he embraced was closer to the Eagles and Dan Fogelberg of the 1970s than it was to country music from the '60s, '70s, and '80s. And it seemed the American—and later world-wide—audience agreed with him. For anyone not interested in the current vogue for house music and hip-hop, radio was a barren place; pop was too dance-oriented, and rock and roll had been taken over by those loud and aggressive screamers out of Seattle, as Nirvana, Pearl Jam, and Soundgarden spewed their grunge across the United States. Simple, lilting, good-natured rock and roll was only found on "oldies" and classic-rock stations. New material that captured the easygoing rock-and-roll days of the past was not coming from L.A., New York, or London; Nashville was the new center for melodic soft rock with a country twist.

Numerous Nashville bands attempted to duplicate the Eagles' vocal magic, but none succeed exactly—a compliment to just how good musically the Eagles actually were. "If the Eagles were around now, if they released a record like 'Desperado' to radio today, it would be to country radio," Garth Brooks told me in 1991. "Rock and roll has changed, and so has country music. The kinds of sounds that were radio hits in the early '70s like James Taylor and the Eagles would now be labeled country music."

Country music had changed, and was now offering less twang, more production, less hokey lyrics, more story-telling authenticity. And pop music that relied on melody and lyrics was now being produced in small studios on Nashville's Music Row.

Garth Brooks' great rival in 1989 and 1990 was a Texas hat-wearing singer/songwriter called Clint Black. Black was country through and through, and a gifted songwriter, but he got his start singing '70s singer/songwriter classics by the likes of James Taylor, Fogelberg, America, and the Eagles in lounges and clubs in Houston. "Country music and rock and roll used to be kind of different animals, but now, most of the artists on country music grew up on both," he told me in 1990. "I listened to classic country and to James Taylor and Jackson Browne and the Eagles so our sound has some of everything. And I think that the fans, like us, also grew up with the singer/songwriters and rock and roll, so they have moved and changed as well."

Booom!

Baby boomers flocked to country music, and Nashville responded with its own version of MTV, a twenty-four-hour country music video channel called CMT, or Country Music Television. Sitting next to the Grand Ole Opry, home of traditional country music, the CMT studios were run by a hip young crowd. TVs in the complex were tuned to VH1 and MTV, while the country-music videos offered for broadcast were becoming slicker and more contemporary by the day. As CMT Head of Programs Tracy Storey explained at the time, the channel was responding to a new, younger audience that had grown up on country and rock and roll. CMT was selling itself as music for people who liked the Eagles but couldn't find that style of music on the radio or TV. Country was the new home for country-rock—for melodic music that told a story.

Don Henley is nothing if not an astute social observer, and he had seen the change in country music for himself. Despite never associating himself with the country label before, he understood the music better than most and responded positively to a duet request from country singer Trisha Yearwood (then a new face on the block, now an award-winning superstar married to Brooks). He slipped his world-weary vocals into "Walk Away Joe" like he was a CMT regular, blending beautifully with Yearwood's Ronstadt-like singing and helping make the song a crossover hit. Indeed, so successful was the pairing and the single that Yearwood and Henley performed it live at the 1992 Country Music Association Awards show, broadcast live around the world from Nashville. Yearwood couldn't believe her luck; she referred to herself as the coolest girl on the planet, since here she was, a country girl who grew up on the Eagles, playing the biggest show in the Nashville calendar with *the* Don Henley.

Soon after that, James Stroud and Irving Azoff hatched the idea of an Eagles tribute album. If the country music stars of the '90s would keep name-checking the '70s L.A. band in interviews, maybe there was some mileage in combining the two. There was little—make that no—chance of the Eagles re-forming to make a country-music album for Azoff, but what if Nashville's new stars all picked their favorite Eagles track for a compilation album? Azoff won Henley's blessing for the project by promising a portion of the royalties to the Walden Woods Project, founded in 1990 by Henley to help preserve the forest near Henry David Thoreau's Walden Pond retreat.

Giants of Country

Giant Records assembled a stellar lineup of country's major stars, including Vince Gill, Travis Tritt, Little Texas, Lorrie Morgan, Clint Black, Billy Dean, John Anderson, Alan Jackson, Suzy Bogguss, Diamond Rio, Trisha Yearwood, and Tanya Tucker. Producer James Stroud then asked his artists what Eagles songs they wanted to perform, assembled a list, and figured out who would cut what track.

"It was a pretty easy task," he told me in 2011, "because everyone involved was such a huge Eagles fan they were all willing to fit in with our needs and make the project work. They all wanted to do different songs, fortunately. Travis Tritt told me he was doing 'Take It Easy'—'It's my song,' he said. But it was pretty easy; nobody held out for a particular song or anything like that. It was one of the coolest records I've ever been involved with. In fact I think we should do a *Common Thread 2*—it's not like the Eagles don't have plenty of great material!"

Trisha Yearwood comes as close as anyone to matching the vocal heights of the Eagles at their prime with her version of "New Kid in Town." Clint Black is note-perfect on "Desperado," Alan Jackson masterfully redneck on "Tequila Sunrise," while Tanya Tucker—a '70s contemporary of the Eagles—blows everyone away with her rendition of "Already Gone." "Hell, it's hard to mess up a song like that," she told me in 2008. "Those guys knew how to write songs, and as a singer that's all you ask for. That Eagles project was one of the coolest things I have done. Singers love good songs and the Eagles wrote some of the best of all time."

Travis Tritt's raspy and sincere version of the Eagles' first single, "Take It Easy," sets the album up. It's a strong, rocking version, but it does indeed prove right those who claimed the Eagles would fit perfectly on country radio. The song fits Tritt's contemporary country vocals well, and the instrumentation is fuller and rockier than on the Eagles original but close enough to be respectful.

In the early 1990s, Tritt was one of the most popular and charismatic characters in country music. His soulful fusion of Southern rock and country brought millions of rock fans to the genre, and Tritt rode his popularity and subsequent power in the industry for his own benefit. He wanted to see the Eagles back together, as did millions of country and rock-and-roll fans. Stories of bad blood and feuds between members only made the thought of a reunion more appealing.

Never one to hold back, Tritt told Azoff that if he was going to make a video to promote his version of "Take It Easy," he had one small request: he wanted the Eagles in the video. In fact, he had come up with an amusing concept: while he plays the song, Don Henley and Glenn Frey should be trading blows behind him. It was a funny idea, and one that was discussed. It wasn't going to happen, of course, but Tritt's desire to have the L.A. legends in the video clip was taken seriously. Azoff set about making it a reality and soon had Henley and Frey on board. And with that done, the others followed easily. Time had been a healer, and while expectations were kept low of them all actually being in the same place at the same time again, everyone was secretly hopeful that this day out at a video shoot could lead to something more—something far more significant—for the Eagles.

Come the day of the shoot, Tritt was a bag of nerves, especially since Henley showed up forty-five minutes after the rest of the band, putting a huge question mark over the reunion. But show up he did. Tritt had his backing band in place for the video, but before they got down to filming Tritt's promo video, the Eagles, as musicians tend to do, started jamming and noodling around on a song. They played "Rocky Mountain Way" like the past fourteen years had never happened.

It was a magical moment for everyone there, and the Eagles seemed to be enjoying themselves—even Henley. As he told *The Morning Call* in September 1994, "We played together; they had some instruments set up, and we played 'Rocky Mountain Way,' 'Take It Easy,' and some blues. And we kind of liked it."

Cash Cow

James Stroud told me in 2011 that seeing the Eagles back together again was a very emotional moment for Travis and for him. "I looked across the room and saw Irving in tears. I asked him if he was OK and he said he was just thinking about how much money he was going to make from the reunion!"

Could Henley's famous quote that the Eagles would get back together when Hell freezes over be defrosting? Certainly, those around the band and those involved in *Common Thread* had hopes that something new from the Eagles could come to fruition.

The fact that the album was an instant smash hit on release didn't go unnoticed in the Eagles camp, and nor by Irving Azoff, either. The record sold a remarkable two million copies in just two months and boosted sales of the Eagles' back catalogue by 20 percent. Two Eagles albums went back into the Top 15 of *Billboard*'s compilation chart. Azoff, thinking about a potential Eagles tour, told the *L.A. Times* in January 1994 that he was confident that they could play any venue, such was their renewed popularity. The *Common Thread* album, he added, "has impressed upon them that they're still a vibrant, important force on the marketplace. Everybody's on speaking terms and I do think they're awed and a little bit shocked by this success. But there's nothing officially in discussion right now. It wouldn't surprise me if they did get back together, and it wouldn't surprise me if they didn't."

Azoff—still a band insider and confidante, even if he wasn't officially their manager—chose to make the reunion a priority. With the ice thawing, he felt the time was right to test how warm the reunion waters really were. He chatted to the band members, talked up the idea of a reunion, outlined the potential rewards, set up different scenarios, and generally sold the notion, as subtly or directly as the situation required. He even came up with something concrete to make the reunion a reality: how about they film a one-off reunion special for MTV?

It was an intriguing idea.

35

Hell Freezes Over

Reunion Talk

T hose tears of joy that Nashville producer James Stroud spotted on Irving Azoff's cheeks quickly turned into a subtle but cleverly orchestrated plan to get the Eagles back together. Of course, Azoff wanted it for business purposes—that was his job, after all. But more than anything, he wanted it to happen as a fan. Azoff was as emotionally and spiritually invested in the Eagles as any of the members. He had lived and breathed and eaten Eagles music and career plans since the early 1970s. He was still pulling strings and opening doors and fighting a few battles when the Eagles became solo acts. Whether up front or behind the scenes, he was deeply involved in Eagle business.

The test came when they appeared in the same room for the video shoot and stayed. Not only did they get through the shoot, the band even played music together—the true common thread that sewed them all together. Now, Azoff had a plan. He knew he had to convince two Eagles—Henley and Frey—to forgive and forget, at least temporarily, and see if there was any real mileage in a reunion.

Persuasion

Azoff knew the pair's idiosyncrasies well. He'd been working with them for two decades, after all, and he knew how to cajole, persuade, and set up excitement for the reunion. Plenty of cups of coffee, dinners, drinks, and chat ensued and the trio finally sat down with Irving Azoff to make a decision.

The fact that Henley and Frey had shown up for the Travis Tritt video shoot and that they were even prepared to discuss the possibility of being stuck with each other again essentially meant that the reunion was always going to get the green light. Neither Henley nor Frey was the kind of man to be seduced and tempted by management. They both had a soft spot for the idea. It was really a matter of how the whole reunion would be handled.

But was the magic still there? Did Henley and Frey even care any more? The answer was yes, and they even began to write new material again. Only two months after the video shoot, during lunch with their management, Henley and Frey agreed to formally reunite.

Unplugged

The first stop was to film an MTV special on a soundstage in Burbank, Hollywood. Naturally, the band was nervous. It had been a long time; the music culture had evolved and fragmented. Would they still have the same chemistry? Could they in fact still play at the same high standard as they had in their prime? And let's never forget that part of what made the Eagles so listenable, so widely accepted, was their impeccable musicianship.

The only criticism of the band's playing had been that it was overly perfect, too clean-cut for rock and roll. Nobody knocked these guys for their technical ability, but life had not been kind. Walsh, in particular, was concerned as to whether he still had the dexterity of old after years of abusing his system. "We were rusty," he told MTV. "We were eager to get our chops back, and to show that we weren't has-beens."

Rehearsals were long and thorough. The Eagles didn't take chances on any live performance, let alone something as historic as this reunion set. Musically, and personality-wise, things slotted back into place. "There was a bond, a great familiarity with the old stuff, so it came back to us fairly quickly," Henley told the *Cleveland Plain Dealer* in July 1994. "The first few days we were a little rusty, but it's all about repetition—doing it over and over."

The playing, the vocal subtleties from Henley and Frey, the band harmonies, and Walsh's wild-card energy were all still intact. And, of course, they still had those glorious freewheeling songs that sounded even better with the addition of nostalgia for the lost '70s of freedom, peace, and long, hot summer days with no car payments and mortgages.

If anyone doubted the band's musical status, the acoustic version of "Hotel California" filmed at the Warners Soundstage was simplicity as perfection. With just acoustic guitars, Felder and Walsh let the song breathe, the flamenco flourish taking it back to its beginnings as what Henley called a Mexican bolero, while the latter's voice sounded better, if anything, than it had during those strained, substance-addled sessions for their last studio album, *The Long Run.*

Un-Frozen

And then it was time to tour. The Eagles' 1994 *Hell Freezes Over* tour started on May 27, on home ground, at the Irvine Meadows Amphitheater in Irvine, California, for a cool six nights straight in the Laguna Hills.

Tickets weren't cheap—most were around the $100 mark—but the band sold 255,000 of them in a matter of hours of the dates going on sale. The band would spend most of the next two years trekking the globe,

Titled in reference to a famous Henley quote about the possibility of a reunion— "when Hell freezes over"—this album matches tracks filmed for an MTV concert special with four new studio tracks. According to *Rolling Stone*, "the result is a tasteful, somewhat insular compilation of songs by former Eagles, rather than a fresh statement by a newly reunified band."

performing some of their most beloved tunes, including "Take It Easy," "Tequila Sunrise," "Lyin' Eyes," and, of course, "Hotel California."

But this was a very different concert for anyone that had seen the group in the 1970s. Back then, the band was a tight unit, playing songs from the most recent album plus greatest hits and perhaps the odd surprise track. Now they had new material, and solo career highlights to include, too. For the first time ever, it was the Eagles playing "Dirty Laundry" and "The Boys of Summer" and "Smuggler's Blues." Perhaps it was to be expected, but this was undoubtedly a challenge to both audience and band.

Frey set the tone of the night well with trademark humor. "For the record, we never broke up, we just took a fourteen-year vacation," he said, grinning confidently at the audience.

Glenn Frey

As the set wore on, it was noticeable that all the new songs held up well. "Get Over It" rocked as hard as protest venom should, while the band went New Age on "Learn to Be Still." Frey, always the upbeat rocker, then took things back to 1972 with the country-tinged crowd-pleaser "The Girl from Yesterday." Reviewers were kind, fans adoring, and the tour kicked into gear, traveling the world for the next two years, except for a short intermission when Frey's stomach issues flared up and he needed hospital treatment.

This was a new-look, new-feel Eagles. The good old bad old days of "third encore" binges and excess were over. Seventies lothario Don Henley had got himself married; groupies were out, personal trainers were in. Throw out the vodka, fill the fridge with juice and vitamin water. It was a healthy, positive experience for a band enjoying their second go round.

The Eagles then issued a live album, *Hell Freezes Over*, that went straight to the top of the *Billboard* chart, going on to sell over six million copies in the United States alone. The Eagles were back. Even the singles performed admirably, given the wildly different musical and radio landscape the band was now placed in, with "Get Over It" and "Love Will Keep Us Alive" both making the *Billboard* Top 40.

36

Hall of Fame

Recognition and Reunion

T
he Rock and Roll Hall of Fame has an unusual place in the rock landscape. It tends to be scorned by those ignored and adored by many that have been inducted and honored. Led by industry notables like *Rolling Stone* magazine editor and publisher Jann S. Wenner and record-company men Seymour Stein and Bob Krasnow, the foundation started its job of inducting rock music's great and good in 1986. And it was all started by a man who had played a key role in the Eagles story himself: Atlantic Records founder and chairman Ahmet Ertegün.

California Dreaming

The Hall of Fame opened its doors to the Eagles in the band's first year of eligibility, 1997. The subtext was California the night that the Eagles were inducted, on January 12, 1998. The swanky Waldorf Astoria hotel in New York saw the Eagles' FM cousins, Fleetwood Mac, inducted, as well as the Mamas & the Papas, a group whose hit song "California Dreamin'" might well have summed up all of Fleetwood Mac and the Eagles' early aspirations.

"It represents a time of great success and a time of great excess," said Wenner, the vice chairman of the Rock and Roll Hall of Fame Foundation. Then there was Santana, a different strain of California, coming from San Francisco, but whose Latin fusions had also made the West Coast sound a global phenomenon.

Buffett Service

Singer/songwriter and king of good-time tropical beach music Jimmy Buffett was tasked with inducting the Eagles into the Hall of Fame and introduced the band with typical joie de vivre. Buffett had kick-started his own career in the late 1970s, and when his career-changing and subsequent trademark song "Margaritaville" debuted, he promoted it with a string of slots opening for the Eagles in the United States.

A grinning Buffett said, "The Eagles are going into the Rock and Roll Hall of Fame as one of the signature bands that began in the '70s and are still alive and kicking ass as we head for the millennium. They've laughed, frolicked, cried, fought, but most of all they have beaten the odds and are as popular today as they were in that incredible summer back in 1972. And here I am, still opening for this goddamn band! Now it's the Eagles' turn."

As rock-and-roll bands last longer and progress from decade to decade, band members come and go, leaving the Hall of Fame to deal with a question that's still to be properly resolved. Is the induction honoring the original lineup or the current incarnation? Should everyone associated with the band's lineups be included in the ceremony? Debates rage on, thus controversy ensues and will likely continue.

Ironically, for a band that had been through supposedly as acrimonious a split as the Eagles, the evening proved a simple, open-arms affair. Previously, the reunited band had veered away from inviting Meisner or Leadon onstage for any impromptu shows or appearances. After all, the Eagles were nothing if not a smooth, well-oiled, and painstakingly choreographed concert machine. Calling up an old pal from the audience, or bringing them out for an encore, was not the Eagles' style. But to the surprise of many in the media, the Hall reversed this policy by including all seven living Eagles in the induction as the band were honored by the industry and their peers.

Seven Up

And then there were seven, as the five 1998 Eagles plus originals Leadon and Meisner surrounded Buffett, hugged their old touring partner, and prepared for their acceptance speeches. It was then the turn of the individual Eagles to take to the microphone to issue their words of thanks and acknowledgment for the honor of being inducted into the Hall of Fame. Interestingly, their different styles and approaches onstage perfectly reflected the various personalities within the extended family of Eagles.

Henley, ever the intellectual, was significantly the first Eagle to speak and took the opportunity more seriously than most. He looked professorial as he questioned fame and what it means to the artist and to the public, suggesting that perhaps the Hall of Fame should be the "Hall of Accomplishment" instead. It was a comment on celebrity and Henley's desire for music to be taken seriously and for it to be discussed and analyzed in certain forums. "I've had a lot of mixed emotions about the name 'Hall of Fame,'" he said. "It's the fame part that bothers me a little, here in the waning hours of the twentieth century. In what we call Western culture, in this age of media, friends, fame is just not what it used to be."

It was a contradictory performance, at once dispassionate thanks to the intellectualizing of the Hall's role and purpose and yet disarming, since his nervy and seemingly under-rehearsed speech was most unlike Henley's usual style. He then got back on track, remembering to thank those who had helped the band along the way, starting with Irving Azoff, "without whom we wouldn't be here today." At this point, the far more relaxed and jovial-looking Frey interjected with a comment of his own: "Well, we might still have been here, but we wouldn't have made as much money." Henley relaxed immediately at this injection of levity and humor and responded with his own quite pertinent quip: "Right. As I've said before, he may be Satan, but he's our Satan!"

Walsh, dressed in a suit with a brick pattern that made him resemble a wall if he stood too still, made a point of thanking the behind-the-scenes crew who worked hard to make the Eagles shows as seamless as everyone knows them to be. "I'd also like to thank all the guys that drive this equipment around—that drive the trucks, set it up, fix it, and put it back in the truck, so we can do what we do. God bless the road crew. Thank you!"

Timothy B. Schmit—typically polite and courteous—was clear to acknowledge that he wasn't part of the early days and paid a warm tribute to Randy Meisner. "On a brief personal note," he said, "I'd like to say that I was not in the trenches with this particular band, and so I'd like to thank my predecessor, Randy Meisner, for being there and paving the way for my being here tonight. With him beside me and the rest of these guys, I'm very honored. Thank you very much."

In turn, Meisner genuinely thanked Schmit and summed up the warmth of the "reunion" with the words, "It's just great playing with the guys again."

Indictment

The always independently minded Leadon initiated his speech with a joke about being "indicted" rather than inducted. "Really proud to have lived long enough to be indicted," he said. "I'd like to thank everybody on the grand jury who voted for me." He was then gracious enough to look back at the beginnings of the band and acknowledge the part played by John

Boylan in bringing the four original musicians together in the first place, to play with Linda Ronstadt. Don Felder praised the songs of Henley and Frey before thanking his wife Susan for her support over his twenty-six years with the Eagles.

Finally, Frey, in great spirits on the night, took the microphone and appeared to genuinely want to clear up rumors and misconceptions about rifts and dislikes within the group.

"We got along fine!" he explained. "We just disagreed a lot! Tell me one worthwhile relationship that has not had peaks and valleys? That's really what we're talking about here. You cannot play music with people for very long if you don't genuinely like them. I guarantee you that over the nine years that the Eagles were together during the '70s, over the three years that we were together during our reunion, the best of times ranked in the 95 percentile, the worst of times ranked in the very small percentile—that obviously everybody but the seven of us has dwelled on for a long, long time. Get over it!"

And then, in true Hall of Fame tradition, the seven-piece Eagles took their positions. Henley sat jacketless on drums while Frey kicked off the song that started it all, "Take It Easy." Leadon marked his comeback with characteristic Fender twang and the seven Eagles played like they'd been rehearsing for years. Meisner looked as happy as the proverbial kid in a candy store, and the magic continued into an immaculate rendition of "Hotel California." Then, suddenly, it was over—this wasn't a real concert, after all. The house lights came on, and Jann Wenner thanked everyone for coming before reminding them to head home.

At the end of 1999, the Eagles were honored by the Recording Industry Association of America when *The Eagles—Their Greatest Hits 1971–1975*, released in 1976, was named the top-selling album of the century. "I think it's just an amazing award," Felder told CNN's *Showbiz Today*. "It's kind of a testament to the songwriting of these two guys over here, Don Henley and Glenn Frey. The songs on that record really kind of withstood the test of time."

The Eagles played a special New Year's show at the Staples Center in Los Angeles on December 31, 1999. The concert would be the last for Felder, however, as yet another new-look Eagles would emerge in the new millennium.

37

Heaven and Hell

Lawsuits

Don Felder was fired from the Eagles in February 2001. It was an unusual move, and one that caught him unawares. Hurt and angry, he fired back with a lawsuit, claiming wrongful dismissal and asking for a mere $50 million in compensation. He was angered that since he was not an employee, he could not simply be terminated. The suit also claimed that despite "each being a one-third owner of Eagles Ltd., Henley and Frey have consistently treated Felder as a subordinate, with complete disregard for his rights."

The Eagles in turn maintained that they had good reason for firing Felder, and that the termination was because of his actions, including his disrupting band activities. Follow the money, they say, and what the troubles boiled down to was that Felder, having been part of the Eagles Ltd. company, felt it unfair that, after 1994, Henley and Frey were getting a bigger piece of the pie than before. He also argued that he was being shut out of the decision-making process and not given proper financial facts and figures.

Whatever the arguments—and arguments were hardly news anymore in the Eagles universe—the band announced in the April of 2001 that session guitarist Steuart Smith would be replacing Felder in the band.

Tell All

Nothing much was heard from either camp about the dismissal and subsequent lawsuits until several years later, in 2007, when more litigation arose once the remaining Eagles learned that Felder was about to publish his memoirs, *Heaven and Hell: My Life in the Eagles (1974–2001)*. Publication was delayed in the courts but the book did finally appear in stores in 2008.

Felder resurfaced with a series of promotional appearances, telling his life story and reminiscing about his years with the Eagles. Critics saw this as a chance for Felder to get one over on Frey and Henley. The Eagles had always been very closed and guarded in many ways, particularly when it came to their personal lives and the wild days of the mid-1970s. Felder exposed details of some of the "third encore" parties and wrote openly about drug use. Some saw it as a "revenge" book.

Felder disagreed, telling Michael Roberts of *Denver Westword* in 2008, "I really didn't intend it to come off that way. As a matter of fact, I deliberately tried very hard not to make it a revenge book. I just tried to tell the story of my life, and to give as unbiased and balanced a view as I could of what it was like during the period with the Eagles. Kind of a Polaroid snapshot of a lot of the things that were going on. I wasn't out to hang anybody's head from the highest pole in town. That wasn't the intent."

All the Best

With no new Eagles recordings to promote, the band's record company decided to offer up another compilation album, *The Very Best of the Eagles*—a collection of tracks that spanned the debut album to 1979's *The Long Run*.

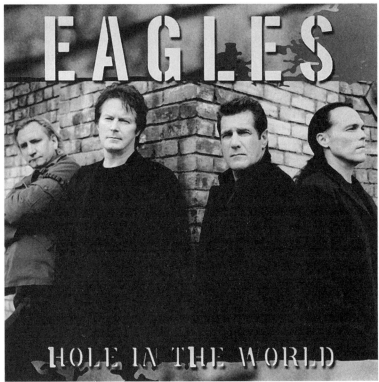

Don Henley and Glenn Frey responded to the 9/11 terror attacks with this 2003 Eagles single, "Hole in the World," which also shows up on the *Very Best Of* collection.

It did include one new song, "Hole in the World," Henley's reaction to the terrible events in New York on September 11, 2001. The album appeared in stores in 2003 as a two-disc set. It entered the *Billboard* charts at #3 and went on to sell over three million copies.

Farewell

The Eagles continued to tour, with Steuart Smith ably taking Felder's parts onstage, and the strangely named Farewell Tour kicked off in the summer of 2003. When it was announced in February, *Billboard* presumed it was a tentative announcement of the band packing it in: "For what may be the beginning of the end, the Eagles have confirmed several dates for their upcoming Farewell 1 tour. Although no explanation for the trek's moniker has been announced, seven shows scattered from May through July have, with tickets already available to members of the veteran Southern California rock band's new official fan club."

Perhaps it was intended as an attention-grabber and a seat-seller. With seats selling in typically brisk fashion, the tour was another success, with the show in Melbourne, Australia, recorded for posterity and released as a live CD/DVD set entitled *Farewell 1 Tour—Live from Melbourne.* Whatever the reasons behind the name of the tour, any thoughts of retirement faded once Frey had his say in the set's liner notes. "The longer this goes on, the better these songs sound. There is a 'sort of' honesty in calling the tour Farewell 1, with its implication that Farewell 2 will follow soon." Henley had a new song on the last album, so now Frey chipped in with a new one from his pen, "No More Cloudy Days," while Joe Walsh contributed a confessional ode to alcoholism, "One Day at a Time."

With solo careers—and the ego wars that ensued—now behind them, and with the Felder situation in the past, the early 2000s were a good period for the Eagles on a personal level. Henley and Frey rekindled their friendship and, artists being artists, thoughts once again had been turning to the notion of making another new record. "We're gonna attempt to write a new album," Henley told *What's On in London* magazine in the summer of 2001. "The general mood of the band is so good and so positive right now that I think we might just pull it off."

38

Long and Winding Road

Do It Yourself

t was the resolving of deep-seated 1970s-rooted resentments and personality clashes that fanned the flames of a new Eagles album. In Eagles-land, things do move slowly; it's a giant machine, after all. Just to tour a new album took them around two years—and that's with very few breaks during the road trek.

But in the early 2000s, with harmony restored and Henley and Frey running the show without interruption or dissent, the two Eagle leaders began to seriously contemplate recording new songs again. The record business had changed since the last time they made an album, and Henley had been heavily involved in analyzing the power shifts that had occurred since the 1990s. Record labels were no longer vast banks of cash that handed out candy to young artists, let them record in expensive studio for months on end, and then take back their investment dollars from album profits. Labels had shrunk; technology put creation back in the hands of the artists. Who needed Criteria Studios or the Record Plant when you could record on a laptop and send files over the Internet?

Home Grown

The plan was to slowly but surely write and record material while the Eagles convoy careened around the globe and then, when the work was complete and there was a solid window available for promotion and sales, the album could be let loose on the public. So the band, with Azoff's encouragement, formed their own record company, thus ensuring greater control and a larger share of the profits.

"The Eagles don't have a record deal," Frey told the *Herald Sun* in October 2001. "We're going to make a new record with our own money, our way, and we're going to put it out ourselves. Call me kooky, but that's what I want to do."

The only downside to paying for all the recording costs is the up-front dollar investment. In the case of some of the richest men in rock, this was a non-issue, but the control they gained was a massive incentive to enjoy the new album and make it as far removed from the last studio record as humanly possible.

Mostly it was just personal, as Henley told *USA Today* in October of 2007. "We needed to do this album for our own personal fulfillment," he said. "People tell us, 'You've got enough money and fame. Why do this album?' Being musicians is not a hobby. It's a calling. There's a life-affirming aspect to creating music. There's more to it than getting songs on the radio and touring. It keeps us young and vital and off the shrink's couch."

Music City

Before *Long Road Out of Eden* was released, however, the Eagles tested the waters with a new single—or at least a new recording of a very old and very good J. D. Souther song, "How Long." It was a classic Eagles tune and a live favorite that had mystifyingly been left unrecorded all those years.

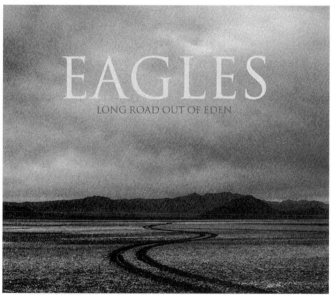

Initially, *Long Road Out of Eden* was available in North America only via the Eagles' own website, Wal-Mart, and Sam's Club.

The band debuted the single in Nashville. Ever since Henley's duet with country star Trisha Yearwood in the '90s and their involvement in their Eagles tribute album, there had been a reevaluation of where Eagles music fit on the genre landscape. Radio stations had merged and consolidated over the years, and airplay was harder than ever to find for any act outside the Top 20. Rock and roll had numerous sub-categories, and then there was oldies radio, but the Eagles wanted to be relevant.

Henley and Frey were too edgy—too rock and roll—for country music in the early 1970s. Long hair was scorned, and literate, clever songwriters were distrusted in what was still a very traditional, conservative town. But by 2007, Nashville was a completely different environment. Rock and roll lived and breathed there. CMT was owned by Viacom, which also owned MTV, and country was finally hip and cool.

Henley and Frey both made regular statements about how they, the Eagles, were really a country band in the 2007 marketplace. "We have a very strong following in the country music audience," Frey told *CMT Insider* in 2007, "and it's not because we're a country band, but I think it's because we have respect for country music, American music, the popular song. Sometimes we rock a little more than country. What I like to say is we're kind of country-tinged. The first country band that I thought we influenced was Alabama. In the '80s, when Alabama broke through, they had a lot of songs where the choruses were always three-part harmony and there was a whole lot of singing going on."

Indeed, the Eagles had been a massive influence on a genre of music that lives or dies on the strength of its songwriting. And so Nashville was delighted to welcome the Eagles to its prestigious Country Music Association Awards show, where the affable Vince Gill was clearly tickled to be able to introduce his personal heroes the Eagles to the stage. "For thirty-five years or more, these guys have been writing songs like this entire room wished they could write. They've been making records like we wished we could make and playing music like we wished we could play. These guys for thirty-five years have been the blueprint of what country-rock is all about. We are honored to have them on the CMA stage, ladies and gentlemen, the Eagles . . ."

Having witnessed several superstar events at the CMA Awards shows over several years, many in the media were shocked at the audience and industry reaction. This was different—this reaction was one of respect and awe, a truly remarkable welcome for any band to walk onstage to.

Brothers in Arms

And they looked like a band. Elder statesmen, perhaps, but still gloriously cool in their sharp black suits. As they say on sports commentaries, the crowd—a mix of the general public plus celebs and musicians—went wild. Everyone stood in respect for the Eagles. It was one of the loudest, most sincere standing ovations in CMA history.

The record itself presented a unified front, despite having been recorded over a seven-year period. Now, Henley and Frey were finally happy with it. "We ultimately concluded that what people like about the Eagles is our singing," Frey told *USA Today* in October 2007. "So the criteria became: Can we sing this? Does it sound like the Eagles? It didn't matter if it was rock, a ballad, a cappella, country or a Mexican song. As long as it's a good song with our voices and Joe Walsh's guitar, we'd be all right."

The band's old-time folk meets country influence was upfront in the mix and in the running order, with the opening harmony-laden "No More Walks in the Wood" taking its cue from the Henley's Walden-inspired environmentalism but presenting it in a classic old-school Eagles vein. "How Long" absolutely sounds like a Troubadour song, for those nostalgia buffs and Eagles historians, while Frey's wish for Walsh to bring his magic is confirmed on the guitarist's snappy "Guilty of the Crime."

Frey's vocals belie his years, which is probably down to his dramatic change in lifestyle. His vocal work on "No More Cloudy Days" is impeccable. And, somehow, Henley manages to balance his desire for social comment with good catchy material—something he mastered at the end of his solo career. "Business as Usual" is pure Henley.

The Eagles were back and happy with their achievement. And there would probably be more, too, with Henley admitting to CBS News, "It's addictive. And you wanna keep doing it."

Rolling Stone was impressed by the album, with reviewer David Fricke drawing comparison between the ten-minute title track and the band's past glories, noting, "There is a potent restraint to 'Long Road Out of Eden,' in the bleak, hollow mix of acoustic guitar and electric piano in the verses and the overcast sigh of the harmonies."

But that was only part of the story. The Eagles grabbed almost as many headlines for their new business model and distribution deal as they did for the new music.

Walmart

Owning the album themselves this time around, the Eagles were able to skip the tried-and-tested record-company business model and do something different. Having conceived, recorded, mastered, and packaged *Long Road Out of Eden* in-house, the band met with Walmart to investigate the best way of offering the album exclusively to the retail giant. It was an idea that had previously been attempted with great success by country superstar Garth Brooks, whose records had flown out of the stores. The Internet may be big, Henley reasoned, but he understood very well that people still like to buy CDs and DVDs, especially if the price is right.

Part of the deal meant that the record would be sold exclusively by Walmart for one year. It wasn't a decision Henley took lightly. "I've never been a fan of big-box retailers," he admitted to *USA Today*. "My daddy was a small businessman." But his overall belief was that record companies are hardly paragons of business virtue either, and that it's better to be on the inside fighting unfair practices than on the outside. Frey took a simpler approach. "I felt like they gave us the best chance to sell the most records," he explained, in the same interview.

The deal worked, and the recording industry took notice. The new Eagles album debuted at #1 and sold almost four million copies in America. It was the top-selling album in the United States that year, and was also a smash around the globe, debuting at #1 in the album charts of Norway, the United Kingdom, Australia, New Zealand, and the Netherlands. Sales would eventually put it at #1 in ten more countries. And aside from sheer volume and popularity, the Eagles were welcomed back by their peers when they won two Grammy Awards for "How Long" and "I Dreamed There Was No War."

What Henley would do next was anyone's guess, but he was upbeat and positive when talking to *Catholic Online* in 2008: "These past 37 years have been amazing and wonderful beyond my wildest dreams, and I am as thankful as I can be. But I'm tired of packing and unpacking. I'm tired of airplanes and hotel rooms. I'm ready for a quieter, simpler life. Of course, I've been saying that for 30 years."

39

History of the Eagles

Bernie Is Back

Henley and Frey had been kicking around ideas for an Eagles documentary movie since the turn of the century. But it would be quite an undertaking, and would need to be done, in typical Eagles fashion, with care and attention to detail. It was also vital to find the right production team to handle such a personal project. The Eagles, since the early days, had shied away from too much publicity. Inherently cautious of the press, the band had a reputation for being closed and uncooperative. But Henley and Frey also recognized that in order for any such movie to be successful, artistically and financially, it had to be a warts and all production.

Taxi Driver

Henley and Frey weren't overly impressed with directors from the music and rock-and-roll documentary school. Frey asked his management to send him copies of Oscar-winning documentaries from the past few years. "The work of Alex Gibney was very impressive," he told *Arts Beat* in February 2013. "I went to New York and we had a meeting, and the only thing we had to agree on was that we were going to tell the truth. We were going to let him and Alison Ellwood make the movie. We said, 'Absolutely, talk to everybody. Let's unearth as much stuff as we can and tell the story'."

Alex Gibney had won his Academy Award for *Taxi to the Dark Side*, a movie far removed from any rock-and-roll story. The film looked at torture and abuse in contravention of the Geneva Convention by the American government in the wake of 9/11. It focuses on the 2002 abduction, torture, and death of a taxi driver at the Bagram air base. Gibney had also been previously nominated for his exposé of U.S. corporation fraudsters, *Enron: The Smartest Guys in the Room*.

Archives

Gibney brought in Alison Ellwood to direct the film, and it was she who was tasked with compiling footage from the archives and gathering as many interviewees as she could. The filmmakers interviewed all of the principals and many of their cohorts, from producers to photographers to songwriting collaborators J. D. Souther and Jack Tempchin—gifted storytellers with surprisingly clear memories and a sense of perspective about the hard times. Also featured are new and exclusive interviews with Jackson Browne, Linda Ronstadt, Kenny Rogers, Irving Azoff, and many other seminal artists and contemporaries who have been closely involved with the Eagles.

Talking Heads

The film is surprisingly conventional in its style, given that Frey and Henley kept clear of music documentary producers and directors. The "talking heads" format is clear and direct, and the cutaway footage is truly compelling, but the format does become strained after a while. Credit to the band, however, for allowing their critics to have their say on camera, including David Geffen and former bandmate Don Felder, whose emotional interview is one of the most touching of the piece.

Felder told the *Hollywood Reporter* in March 2013 that he had a few reservations about the finished product. On a lighthearted note, however, he said he enjoyed reminiscing over the changing band hairstyles, recalling that Henley's "fro" led to the nickname of "furry basketball." He was surprised, though, at how the film sidestepped the segregation between the members in the mid-'70s. "Everybody rode in their own cars, everybody had their own hotel room, their own bodyguard, their own dressing room backstage. When you got on the private plane, you had your own private lounge where you could close the door."

Despite the lawsuits and the resulting book, Felder clearly has fond memories of his time with the Eagles—he was with the band from 1974 until 2001, after all—and his comments and demeanor suggest he would be in favor of some kind of reconciliation, if not a full-scale reunion. "It's like going through a marriage and then having it fall apart," he said to the *Hollywood Reporter.* "You think, if only I had not said that, or if we could've gone to counseling, or whatever, things could have been different. But

Excitement builds for a History of the Eagles concert in 2013.
Courtesy of ABetterMachine.com

unfortunately, it is what it is, and any sort of attempt or possibility of us getting back onstage together is completely up to Don and Glenn."

Living History

The obvious companion piece to such a comprehensive, career-spanning project was a tour that would reflect the legacy aspect of the film. The Eagles discussed the possibility of a major tour, realizing that such an undertaking could well be the last they ever do.

"This could very well be our last, major tour," Henley told the *Milwaukee Journal Sentinel.* "Covering the entire globe will take us about two years. . . . So, by the time we get through this tour, it'll be 2015, and we'll all be in our late sixties. It's been an incredible experience for all of us, but it may be time to say adios and bow out gracefully." Of course, Mick Jagger said something similar twenty years ago.

The tour was assembled with one or two surprises. Once word was out that the show would reflect the documentary and tell the story of the band as much as having them just perform the Eagles catalogue of hits and deep cuts, fans lobbied to see Felder, Meisner, and Leadon back where they belonged. Felder—referred to by Frey and Henley as "Mr. Felder" throughout the whole documentary film—was never going to be invited; the bad blood flows too fast and thick between the parties. Meisner's ill health ruled him out, too, but then there was Leadon. He had been the first to run but was also a fan and critic favorite whose stock in the music-biz credibility stakes had only risen through the years of Gram Parsons worship as the Americana genre took hold worldwide.

Weekends with Bernie

Eagles concerts in the 2000s were always of the highest musical standards, but there was also an intangible sense that the shows had become overly rehearsed—predictable, even. The fact that the History tour lent itself to a different concept—a themed evening of the story behind the songs and the band itself—would revitalize the Eagles' live performance. This would be a very different show, and one that the Eagles themselves would visibly delight in.

When the music press reported that Leadon had been invited back for the tour, interest in the band soared even higher. Leadon had been out of the limelight for some time, but his reputation in music circles had risen, thanks in part to the development of the Americana genre and rediscovery of the founding fathers (like Leadon) by acts like the Jayhawks, the Decemberists, and the Avett Brothers, who were all heavily influenced by the originators of the rock-meets-country sound. The band announced the tour on the Eagles website, saying, "The Eagles—Glenn Frey, Don Henley, Joe Walsh, and Timothy B. Schmit—will perform classics spanning their career including 'Hotel California,' 'New Kid in Town,' 'Take It to the Limit,' 'One of These Nights,' 'Lyin' Eyes,' 'Rocky Mountain Way,' 'Best of My Love,' and 'Take It Easy.' Hits from band members' solo catalogs will also be featured during the evening."

Rumors started—possibly based more wishful thinking than anything else—that past Eagles were to be welcomed back into the fold for one last happy family tour. The kids wanted to see the parents reconcile and move back in together, but that was never realistic, certainly with regard to Felder's involvement. Leadon and Meisner were a different matter. Finally, after the whispers got too loud, Henley admitted in an interview with the *Milwaukee Journal Sentinel* on July 4, 2013, that Leadon would be part of the tour. "Bernie Leadon is definitely on this tour. Randy Meisner, if he were healthy and willing, might have been included, too, but his current health will not permit. We are all wishing him well."

The band began rehearsing with Leadon, who hadn't figured musically since the 1998 reunion at the Rock and Roll Hall of Fame induction. It was an easy process, as Henley explained to MSN's Mark Brown in July 2013. "It took a couple of weeks to sort out harmonies, guitar parts, volume levels, etc., but once it all came together it was like he never left. Bernie is a very accomplished musician and he's an important part of the band's history. It's also good to have another harmony voice in the stack. We're all getting along just fine, thank you."

Around the same time, Meisner was taken so ill after a serious choking accident that old friend Rusty Young was minded to post a note on the Poco website, Poconut.org. "Some of you may have heard that Randy Meisner is in a California hospital and you're concerned," he wrote. "I just talked to his wife Lana and want to give you guys the latest. Randy was at home when something he was eating obstructed his breathing and he lost consciousness. Lana rushed him to the emergency room where he got immediate care. Things are going to be a little rough for Randy for a while, but his doctors are optimistic he'll recover from this incident. If you can, say a little prayer or just send love Randy's way. Rusty."

A month so later, Young reported that Meisner was home and improving.

No Photos Aloud

All of the venues the Eagles performed at displayed signage consistent with Don Henley's longstanding campaign for copyright protection for artists and content creators. The camera policy stated, "In order to maximize your enjoyment, as well as enjoyment of those around you, please turn off your cell phones & other electronic devices during the concert. Please do not text or film during the concert." And then, in capital letters, "DO NOT VIDEO WITH SMART PHONES."

And then it's showtime.

The Eagles engine room takes center stage. Frey and Henley sit on stools together with acoustic guitars, recreating their mellow early days in Los Angeles, when they first joined forces and the Laurel Canyon folk set played guitars and sang the songs that created a rock-and roll revolution. Frey and Henley sing "Saturday Night" and then bring out Bernie Leadon, with Henley saying, "This is a glimpse of what it was like late in the summer of '71. Glenn and I were out on the road with Linda Ronstadt and told her we were going to put a band together. She suggested a guitar player named Bernie Leadon."

Leadon plays to an appreciative audience, performing his classic "Train Leaves Here This Morning" and sticking around for more early-days magic.

It's a brilliant beginning to a legacy concert. Talking to the *L.A. Times* in January 2014, Henley admitted that this was his favorite part of the show. "I like the opening segment of the show where we recreate the simple rehearsal shack atmosphere of 1971, sitting around with just acoustic guitars, playing the early tunes. During that segment we play a song that Bernie co-wrote with the late Gene Clark, who was a member of the Byrds, and I am always reminded of what a skilled musician Bernie is."

Glenn Frey then introduces bassist Timothy B. Schmit, adding that Poco were one of his favorite bands, before the Eagles perform an immaculate "Peaceful Easy Feeling." Joe Walsh makes his entrance on "Witchy Woman," and with that the gang's back together. The Eagles move easily into rock-and-roll mode through the main part of the concert, backed up by a bank of HD TV screens that work as nostalgic video backdrops to the material.

After scorching through Walsh's "Life in the Fast Lane," the group bid their farewells, saving "Hotel California" for the encore, of course. After that, they launch into "Take It Easy," "Rocky Mountain Way," and "Desperado," before really leaving the stadium for their hotel suites.

40

Don Henley Must Die

Eagles Love, Eagles Hate

With the benefit of always-reliable, trusty old hindsight, you could say that the band's long-running dislike and disdain for the press arose from Glenn Frey's macho response to his own musical insecurity in the band's formative years. Perhaps because some movers and shakers in the so-called country-rock fraternity—Gram Parsons among them—accused the group of blandness and banality, Frey and Henley felt apprehensive when first thrust by Geffen onto the U.S. stage.

The incident at Madison Square Garden, where the Eagles wore "SONG POWER" T-shirts while Frey dissed the locally beloved New York Dolls, kicked off a decade-long standoff between the band and the media. Henley and Frey turned down interview requests with the predominantly East Coast–based media and slipped into a kind of rock-star paranoia, convinced that the Springsteen- and Clash-loving rock-and-roll writers of the day regarded the country-rock superstars as lightweight and insignificant.

Dirty Laundry

Writing in *Newsday* in 1972, the sharp-tongued rock critic Robert Christgau admitted that he hated the Eagles. He clarified that he used the word *hate* to "convey an anguish that is very intense, yet difficult to pinpoint." While listening to the Eagles' music gave him pleasure, he said, it also made him feel "alienated from things I used to love. As the culmination of rock's country strain, the group is also the culmination of the counterculture reaction that strain epitomizes."

This may not have been an easy criticism for the targeted artists to take, but Christgau was writing about something more than the Eagles. They typified something about America that the writer was uneasy with. When it came to the actual group, he was also quite complimentary, calling them "the tightest and most accomplished rock band to emerge since Neil Young's

Crazy Horse." He asserted that the members' history with other acts did not lead to "the usual compilation of disgruntled sidemen doing battle with their own well-deserved anonymity. The difference is partly chemistry—the Eagles are an organic group, not a mixture of musicians—but mostly raw talent. These guys can execute. Not only do they all sing and compose, which is nothing new—they're good at it."

It was *Rolling Stone* magazine that disturbed Henley & co. the most. In the beginning, the magazine wasn't even part of the New York media bloc, being that it was based in San Francisco until its move in 1977. But despite the magazine delivering several kind words about the band's first two records, the Eagles' antipathy grew over time.

Rolling Stone, via the pen of Bud Scoppa, had jumped all over the band's debut album, calling their first 45 release "simply the best sounding rock single to come out so far this year. The first time through, you could tell it had everything: danceable rhythm, catchy, winding melody, intelligent, affirmative lyrics, and a progressively powerful arrangement mixing electric guitar and banjo, and a crisp vocal, with vibrant four-part harmony at just the right moments for maximum dramatic effect." Hardly the words of a media outlet determined to bury the band in question.

The follow-up record, the ambitious *Desperado* album, also found favor with the august *Rolling Stone*. The band also received much critical love from David Rensin of the *Phonograph Record* publication in June 1973. "The back cover photo may depict the Eagles as dead losers, but with DESPERADO it is clear that nothing is further from the truth," he wrote. "DESPERADO is a fine and better-than-expected second step for the Eagles, who with this album, I'm sure, are reaffirming the faith I placed in them from the beginning."

Both *Rolling Stone* and the influential New York–based trade publication *Billboard* loved the band's 1975 *One of These Nights* record. "A major reason I like *One of These Nights* more than its forerunners is its relative lack of conceptual pretension," *Rolling Stone*'s Stephen Holden wrote in 1975. "The best songs portray L.A. culture fairly straightforwardly, using occult eroticism ('One of These Nights,' 'Too Many Hands,' and 'Visions') and sexual duplicity and malaise ('Hollywood Waltz,' 'Lyin' Eyes,' 'After the Thrill Is Gone') as metaphors for the city's transient, hedonistic ambience." *Billboard* called said record "an absolutely stunning album and the ultimate distillation of the Eagles style, satin-smooth vocal harmonies blending effortlessly into tight and exciting guitar jam."

Maybe by focusing on the rare criticisms within generally positive critiques, Henley and Frey did indeed develop a mistrust for the press. Marc Eliot, in his comprehensive 1998 book on the band, *To the Limit*, quotes Henley as saying, "We'd been abused by the press, so we developed a 'fuck you' attitude toward them."

In 1977, Henley took umbrage with a mildly mixed *Rolling Stone* review of *Hotel California*, and in retaliation, instead of talking to the magazine, he granted an overblown interview to rival publication *Crawdaddy*. It was a controversial move at the time. The perceptive and straight-to-the-point writer and interviewer, Barbara Charone, listened as Henley laid out his complaints about the press, and critics in particular. He stated, for example, that explaining the lyrics of his songs would ruin the poetry, and that the press "seem to emphasize the songs that were hits rather than the ones that weren't. They seem to think that you can write a catchy tune that's a hit that means something. I think our songs have more to do with the streets that Bruce Springsteen's."

It was a lofty comparison that failed to win over even the more neutral rock critics of the day, especially at a moment in pop history when Springsteen was seriously being touted as the next coming—a bona-fide fusion of Dylan and the Beatles. Looking back, Henley probably had a good point, but as in all things public, timing is everything.

In March 1978, Frey told the *L.A. Times* how his band felt dissed by *Rolling Stone*. "With the exception of Cameron Crowe's cover story on us, I don't think the magazine has been particularly insightful as far as it comes to the Eagles. When *Hotel California* came out, they didn't even give us the lead review. It was just treated like 'Oh, another album from the Eagles, ho-hum.'"

In retrospect, of course, Henley's satirical lyrics have been revered and acclaimed as marvelous social comment and satire, but at the time, the band were too close to their own image of excess and greed to be seen as both aggressor and victim in the out-of-control "me" culture of the 1970s.

In the 1970s, however, the English major and erudite wordsmith Don Henley took to writing letters to publications whenever concerned or unhappy at his band's reception. It served only to make the Eagles a bigger target for journalists and writers, whether for musical and cultural criticism and comment or for light-hearted fun-poking in less serious parts of their publication. *Rolling Stone* magazine's gossip/news section, "Random Notes," included a story in 1978 about a radio station defeating the Eagles in a charity softball game. Henley didn't much care for the writer Charles M. Young's point of view and wrote a letter to the reporter. So began a minor skirmish between band and magazine that culminated in a softball grudge match (for charity, it must be added) between the rock-and-rollers and the scribes.

Young, a university-educated journalist, had joined the esteemed *Rolling Stone* magazine in 1976 as an associate editor. His specialty was the new sound around town: the gobbing, spitting, and snarling punk rock that was erupting from basements and bars all over New York. Young painted wonderful word-pictures of the tremendously influential CBGB scene that so dramatically changed mainstream rock and roll in America in the mid-1970s. He was in the middle of the scene, championing bands like the Ramones and Patti Smith and getting the magazine's first punk cover with a Sex Pistols story.

Making fun of his family roots (his father was a minister), the writer became "The Rev. Charles M. Young" and loved poking fun at rock and roll and all its pretentions via the "Random Notes" gossip section. A keen member of the *Rolling Stone* softball team, he sniggered when he heard that a radio station team had beaten the Eagles at a softball charity challenge.

Young recalled the incident to *Rolling Stone* in August 2012: "I got a letter from Henley insulting me and then I insulted him back in the column. And Henley for his whole life has been an inveterate writer of letters. If someone displeases him, he can send out these little masterpieces of venom. Glenn Frey is equally smart, which is to say very smart." Young hadn't intended to start a feud with the band; he just wanted to "write a funny Random Note. And then they responded with this letter going after me and then I went back after them in the column and they were kind of the biggest band of the world and we were fighting over softball."

And so the idea of a softball match between the two rock-and-roll titans emerged. This was never going to be some causal grudge match in a local ballpark. First off, the *Rolling Stone* staff flew to Dedeaux Field at UCLA for the game. Then started the negotiations for what was at stake. *Rolling Stone* offered up a simple trade: if the band won, they'd agree to grant the magazine an interview. If the writers won, then the somewhat less-well-paid losers would treat the Eagles to hot dogs in New York.

Henley and Frey upped the stakes, of course, and after a few round of one-upmanship the deal was very simple: the losers would simply give $5,000 to UNICEF. Plus, if the musicians won, they'd get to write about their victory in *Rolling Stone*.

With the escalation of stakes came an escalation in tension and intent. Right before the game, word circulated that the Eagles were going to wear metal cleats as opposed to the far safer rubber-soled shoes players usually wore for such matchups. *Rolling Stone* complained, and Henley and crew backed down, telling the *L.A. Times*, "We wear metal cleats in all our games. [Jann] Wenner [publisher and owner of the magazine] must think Frey and I are psychotic and out to get their guys . . . so we're stuck with these peace cleats."

With the game being hosted in L.A., and with that extra deal of media attention, several celebrities made an appearance. Daryl Hall and Chevy Chase were there, and visibly rooting for their musician friends were Joni Mitchell, Donald Fagen, and Stephen Bishop. Instead of the expected pre-match tune, the Eagles had the stadium announcer cue up what he called out to the crowd as the national anthem, but which actually turned out to be "Life in the Fast Lane." A little bit of humor before the war, perhaps.

Charles M. Young, Ben Fong-Torres, Cameron Crowe, and Joe Klein lined up against the Eagles. The pickers won easily by 15–8 in a game that failed to turn brutal or ugly. An impressive Henley pitched throughout the easy victory—and very well too, it must be said—but it was big-hitting Timothy B. Schmit who stole the glory for the musicians. It was all over by mid-afternoon, and both teams wound up the tension-filled day with an amicable dinner in a Hollywood restaurant. Indeed, Young, the originator of the softball war, won over the Eagles with his admittance that the writers had been obvious losers on the day. Respect was earned, and Young spent much of this next year inside the Eagles camp for a major *Rolling Stone* piece on their next album, *The Long Run*.

Anarchy in the U.K.

If the Eagles exhibited an innate tendency to annoy and irritate some in the media with a large measure of paranoia and disdain, so many in the press and the general population began to dismiss and even pour scorn on Henley, Frey, and the boys. The duo's penchant for letter-writing to air grievances hardly warmed the media to them, but much of the negativity stemmed from their easygoing, mellow style at a time when rock and roll was becoming increasingly aggressive. The vast numbers of records they sold hardly helped. They had become the rock music equivalent of the Dallas Cowboys or Manchester United, with the concomitant jealousies that massive and continued success brings to any top dog.

While the Eagles climbed to the top and ruled the FM radio waves with lush, perfectly played, and immaculately presented commercial productions, the likes of Stiv Bators and Johnny Ramone and Johnny Rotten were telling kids via the so-called punk explosion that talent was unnecessary. Punk hit the streets of London and New York in 1976 and smashed into the mainstream the following year. Punk, its exponents proclaimed, was an attitude and a way of life more than it was about musical proficiency and tradition.

That sense of cultural anarchy gave punk its identity. As Charles M. Young wrote in *Rolling Stone*, "A punk vocalist is basically cathartic, and it was very much a rebellion against the cult of the Guitar Hero, as though they were saying, 'We could do it ourselves. These musicians that we hear on FM radio aren't God and you don't have to be a virtuoso to play really powerful, effecting rock & roll guitar.'"

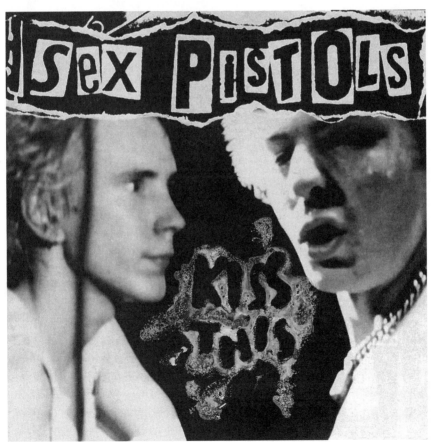

The angry and raucous music that punk bands like the Sex Pistols introduced in 1976 and 1977 was a far cry from the Eagles' more peaceful sound.

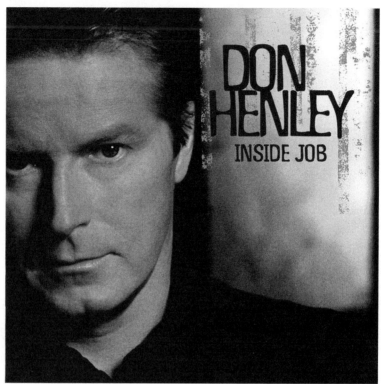

Henley's fourth solo album, *Inside Job*, appeared in stores in 2000.

Working as an embedded journalist and reporting extensively on the *Long Run* period would show the initially dismissive Young that there was far more to the Eagles than proficiency and a desire to have hit records. But punk and the subsequent new-wave movement were knee-jerk in nature. The always-vocal Johnny Rotten of the Sex Pistols slammed the old guard but was quietly a serious fan of Pink Floyd—one of the biggest "dinosaur" bands of them all.

For the Eagles and many of their peers, criticism and negativity from the next generation of media commentators was the order of the day. And the Eagles, such was the volume of their success, got it harder than most. This was particularly confusing and galling for Henley and Frey, since only a handful of years previously they had appeared from Los Angeles as hip young gunslingers—the outlaws, the country-rock mavericks.

When old-school rock-and-rollers like Neil Young and Pete Townshend became aware of the cultural shift, they made concerted efforts to win friends with the new wave of reporter and critic, and indeed adjusted their music accordingly. The Eagles, however, took a different approach. They remained steadfast in their musical style (more or less), and opted to complain or snipe back at the media.

When you have the biggest-selling album of all time—*Their Greatest Hits 1971–1975*—under your belts, you're always going to be seen as a target. Envy is a powerful motivator for hate and dislike. Even the movie industry got in on the act when *The Big Lebowski*'s Dude character slammed the band and set them up once again as easy targets of scorn and mockery.

Nixon vs. Henley

Slowly, the Eagles changed their tack on criticism—a move exemplified by Henley's remarkable reaction to a spiteful attack from a fellow musician, Mojo Nixon.

Alongside sidekick Skid Roper, Nixon made a career in the 1980s with humor-based music and a media profile that was spiky, irreverent, and wildly outspoken. Their act was wholeheartedly left of center, resulting in tracks like "Stuffin' Martha's Muffin," "Elvis Is Everywhere," and the catchy "Debbie Gibson Is Pregnant with My Two-Headed Love Child," before the emphatic "Don Henley Must Die" rose to #20 in the charts in 1990.

There was a time when Henley would have fought back with as much might as he and Irving Azoff could muster, but this time around, perhaps more mellow and clearly more media savvy, he took a different approach.

Mojo Nixon was booked to play a small bar in Austin, the Hole in the Wall, which is across from the University of Texas in a very hip part of town. The club only held a hundred or so people, but on the evening in question, word began to circulate that Henley was going to show up at the gig. And it made sense. This particular bar was close to a friend's house in Austin, and Henley had been seen drinking there on many occasions. And so the rumors were correct, as Mojo recalled to the *Denver Westword* in April 2012.

"So we're playing, and sure as shit, the motherfucker shows up," he said. "For once in my life, I was flabbergasted. I was like 'homminahom-minahomminahommina.' So finally I said, 'Hey, you wanna fistfight? You wanna steak?' He said, 'Hey, I wanna sing the song. Especially the part about not wanting to get together with Glenn Frey.' 'Cause you know, it's 'Don Henley must die. Don't let him get together with Glenn Frey.' This is before everybody had camera phones and cell phones, so no pictures. There's no evidence. He was belting it out: 'Don Henley must die! Don't let him get together with Glenn Frey!' It was fuckin' funny."

Henley won over the crowd and the satirical musician. Ahead of a show in Reno in June 2012, Henley talked to RGJ.com about the episode: "He went after a lot of artists who were successful at that time—Phil Collins, Sting, and others. We didn't meet his 'standards.' That was his shtick. But after I showed up at the club in Austin and sang the song onstage with him, he seemed to find some respect for me. He said that I had 'balls as big as church bells.'"

Artists on the Eagles

The Eagles—and Glenn Frey and Don Henley in particular—may have been harshly and probably unfairly treated in the media over the past four decades, but their peers have resolutely stood behind them. Witness this collection of pro-Eagles quotes from a selection of artists, each taken from interviews with the author over the past twenty-five years.

Garth Brooks

"When I was growing up and listening to music, for me it was George Strait and George Jones, but also people like Dan Fogelberg and Billy Joel and the Eagles. The Eagles were making country music mainstream in the '70s, not a million miles from what Nashville is still trying to do today."

Brady Seals

"You cannot match Don Henley as a performer, a singer, or a songwriter. When I was in a country band, Little Texas, the Eagles were the benchmark—the standard we all aspired to. The best, simple as that."

Clint Black

"Well, I started out playing in bars and lounges, me and my guitar, so you know, you need great songs to sing. So I used to do Eagles songs, because those tunes really hold up with just an acoustic guitar because they are great songs."

Stevie Nicks

"Don Henley will always be very special to me and I hope we'll always work together. The Eagles were a landmark group when Fleetwood Mac was first out. The songs, the harmonies, the musical perfection. I don't think they ever really got the credit they deserved."

David Crosby

"The Eagles were very different to what we were doing with Stills and Nash, but they came from the same place—that L.A. environment of the late 1960s which created so much incredible music. They were always very controlled, perfect on stage whereas we were more improvised. Great songs."

Jackson Browne

"They were great guys, and those Troubadour days were important for everyone. Obviously the Eagles took things to another level, mostly I think because Glenn and Don were talented and dedicated."

Al Perkins

"It was the songs. The Burritos, the Dillards, Poco—great bands, but the Eagles just had the songs that everybody could love."

Byron Berline

"They never got the respect they deserved, probably because when you get to be really successful and huge, people look to knock you down. But we all knew how good they were."

Tom Petty

"The Byrds and the Eagles, man, they showed that folk and country music could be mixed up with rock and roll and it would work. The Eagles were incredible musicians, great harmonies and, you know the songs that we all loved in the 1970s."

Bonnie Raitt

"That circle of artists that hung out at the Troubadour in 1969/1970 was just incredible. Some were just really talented and successful like the Eagles, others never really surfaced on the same level but it was a great talent pool. Incredible really."

Dwight Yoakam

"I mean, the Eagles proved to everyone watching that country music was a valid format for mainstream music fans. They took country and played it in a way that spread the music around the world. That country music exploded in the 1990 has a direct connection to what the Eagles did in the 1970s."

Ricky Skaggs

"Man, those harmonies, those songs. Great musicians and consummate professionals, those guys brought a new audience to a country music sound. They were absolutely pioneers in the growth of country music in the 1980s, and there's not a country act in Nashville that doesn't owe them some gratitude for what they achieved globally and what they gave us with their music."

Norman Blake

"I come from a traditional bluegrass and folk background, but when they had Bernie Leadon in there plus those harmonies they played a kind of music that attracted a new audience, and I think brought new fans to country and folk-style music."

Shania Twain

"Simply one of the best groups, especially vocally, of all time, in my opinion. And when I was getting started, they were absolutely a role model in how to blend different styles of music and make it your own. Inspirational."

41

An Eagles A-Z

Anaheim to *Zachariah*

T his outwardly straightforward tale of a group of hopeful musicians forming a band and setting the world alight is crammed with fascinating facts, nerdy trivia, and bizarre connections that make for a fascinating A–Z of all things Eagles.

A

Anaheim. Anaheim, California, is where Disneyland hosted the celebrated Linda Ronstadt concerts in July 1971 that featured all four original Eagles onstage together for the very first time.

Azoff, Irving. He was the new breed of manager and record-company executive who turned the Eagles from a group into a corporation, a band into a brand.

B

Back. Playing drums over several decades has caused serious damage to Don Henley's back, and over the past twenty years the singing drummer has become much more of a singer who occasionally gets behind the drum kit.

Boylan, John. Linda Ronstadt's boyfriend and manager, and the producer of her sensational albums *Linda Ronstadt* and *Don't Cry Now*. It was Boylan who brought Meisner, Henley, Frey, and Leadon together.

Brandon & Leah. This pop duo is made up of Bruce Jenner's son Brandon (yes, of *Kardashians* TV-show fame) and Leah Jenner, formerly Leah Felder, daughter of Don.

Browne, Jackson. Almost a child prodigy, Browne wrote the Eagles' first single, "Take It Easy," with help from Frey. Frey knew it was a good song; he'd heard Browne working on it for hour after hour from his downstairs apartment in L.A.'s Echo Park.

C

"Chug All Night." This was the song Frey demoed for David Geffen in 1971. Frey later said he didn't like the song and advised a fan in 1994 not to listen to it again.

Criteria Studios. Famed Miami recording studios the Eagles first used for *On the Border.*

Crow, Sheryl. Crow was a professional backing singer before breaking into stardom in her own right. One of her clients was Henley, and she recorded and sang with Don on the *End of the Innocence* album and tour. Years later, as a superstar herself, she sang on Henley's "The Garden of Allah."

D

Desperado. The band's second album, *Desperado* was a Wild West gunfighter concept LP. And it was recorded in London. A commercial disappointment in 1973, the record is now revered as a classic country-rock album.

Detroit. Home of Motown, hunting ground of Bob Seger, birthplace of J. D. Souther and Glenn Frey.

Dillards, the. A high-energy, cutting-edge bluegrass band much beloved by Henley in his formative years. Doug Dillard was a "character," and a top musician, as his Troubadour antics in the late 1960s and early '70s prove.

Diltz, Henry. Acclaimed photographer, artist, and musician whose shots of the Laurel Canyon/Troubadour crowd from Neil Young to the Eagles to David Crosby and Joni Mitchell are legendary. He was responsible for the cowboy photo shoot for *Desperado.*

Dude, the. The Jeff Bridges character in *The Big Lebowski*, responsible for the infamous quote "I had a rough night, and I hate the fucking Eagles, man."

E

eBay. Joe Walsh is known to be a heavy user of the site, which he uses to pick up radio equipment. Rumor has it he was late onstage one night because he had been frantically involved in winning an eBay bid backstage!

Ertegün, Ahmet. The record business legend who persuaded David Geffen to take on his own record company when Ertegün declined to sign Jackson Browne to Atlantic.

F

Fleetwood Mac. Contemporaries of the Eagles, they similarly came to encompass the Southern California rock-and-roll sound and lifestyle.

Flying Burrito Brothers, the. The seminal country-rock band formed by Gram Parsons and Chris Hillman that bridged the gap between the Byrds and the Eagles with a hippie mix of country and rock and roll. Bernie Leadon joined the band after their first album.

Four Speeds, the. This band, formed in Linden, Texas, in 1963, would later become the Speeds, then Felicity, then Shiloh. Their lead singer and drummer was Don Henley.

G

Grammys, the. The Eagles have six. "Lyin' Eyes" won Best Pop Vocal Performance by a Duo, Group or Chorus in 1975; "Hotel California" was Record of the Year in 1977; "New Kid in Town" won Best Arrangement for Voices, also in 1977; "Heartache Tonight" picked up Best Rock Vocal Performance by a Duo or Group in 1979; in 2008 the comeback Eagles won Best Country Performance by a Duo or Group with Vocal for "How Long"; and "I Dreamed There Was No War" was awarded Best Pop Instrumental Performance in 2009.

Guest star. The charismatic Joe Walsh made several appearances in TV shows over the years, including top-rated series like *The Drew Carey Show*, *MAD TV*, and *Duckman*.

H

Heaven and Hell: My Life in the Eagles (1974–2001). Don Felder's warts-and-all account of life with the most successful band in America.

Heavy Metal. This 1981 movie featured Felder's "Takin' a Ride" as its theme song.

Hillman, Chris. Another key figure in the folk-rock and country-rock story in California. Early on, he was friends with Bernie Leadon in San Diego, before later becoming a Byrd and a Burrito Brother. He still plays occasionally with Bernie Leadon and ex-Shiloh pedal-steel player Al Perkins.

I

Inhale. Glenn Frey was voted his high school's "most likely to . . ."

J

Jethro Tull. British progressive-rock (prog-rock) band led by the eccentric flute playing of Ian Anderson. The Eagles opened several U.S. Jethro Tull dates in 1972.

Johns, Glyn. One of rock's greatest record producers, Johns had a love/hate relationship with the Eagles. He loved their country vocals but hated their rock ambition. As producer of the Who, he just didn't see the Eagles as a rock band. Johns produced two and a half albums for the Eagles in his home base of London, England.

Jones, Davy. Like Henley, Jones is a 1970s South Beach celebrity tennis player—and sometime Henley opponent. He was also one of the Monkees in the 1960s, and performed songs on the same *Ed Sullivan Show* that introduced the Beatles to America—and the future Eagles—in 1964.

K

King, Carole. A key part of the Laurel Canyon/Troubadour singer/songwriter set. Eagles producer Bill Szymczyk cut his engineering teeth on some of her song demos in New York.

L

L.A. Kings, the. Hockey star Gene Carr was a pal of Glenn Frey's in the 1970s, with Frey often wearing Carr's #12 shirt for concerts.

Lead-on. Bernie Leadon sings lead on these Eagles songs: "Train Leaves Here This Morning," "Earlybird," "Twenty-One," "Bitter Creek," and "My Man."

Led Zeppelin. Another huge early-1970s band who rivaled the Eagles and the Who for rock-and-roll shenanigans and outrageous behavior.

M

Maserati. As mentioned in Joe Walsh's "Life's Been Good," the Maserati ("my Maserati does 185/I lost my license now I don't drive") is an Italian super-speed, super-luxury car. The Maserati Walsh refers to looked fast and was marketed as such but would have struggled to actually hit 185 miles per hour.

Miami Vice. One of Frey's better solo moments was appearing in *Miami Vice*, in an episode called "Smuggler's Blues," which was inspired by his song of the same name.

N

Nicks, Stevie. The glamorous Fleetwood Mac chanteuse was involved in romantic dalliances with Don Henley, Joe Walsh, and J. D. Souther.

O

One of These Nights. Glenn Frey's favorite Eagles album.

P

Pro-Am Golf. Both Felder and Frey are keen golfers and regulars on the Pro-Am circuit.

Q

Queen, Homecoming. Frey's wife Cindy was given this accolade in 1984 at Millikan High School in Long Beach, California.

R

"Ramblin' Gamblin' Man." This 1968 track from Detroit's Bob Seger features a young Glenn Frey on guitar and vocals.

Run C&W. Bernie Leadon was part of a '90s Nashville parody act called Run C&W.

S

Smith, Steuart. The guitarist who replaced Don Felder in 2000. He also played on Henley's *Inside Job* and has been with the Eagles ever since.

Sunset Grill. The inspiration behind the song of the same name, this restaurant served Henley's favorite hamburgers, smothered in Velveeta cheese.

T

Troubadour, the. A home-from-home for L.A.'s singer/songwriter folkies in the Eagles' early days.

U

Universal Pictures. The company behind Irving Azoff's 1978 movie *FM*, the soundtrack to which includes the Eagles cut "Life in the Fast Lane" and the Joe Walsh hit "Life's Been Good."

V

"Victim of Love." Don Felder's other writing contribution to the *Hotel California* album, besides the title track.

W

WB6ACU. Guitarist Joe Walsh is a lifelong radio ham. WB6ACU is his call sign.

X

"X" Eagle. Former member Bernie Leadon teamed up with the 2013 Eagles for their world tour.

Y

Yearwood, Trisha. The country singer who dared ask Henley to duet with her on "Walkaway Joe." He said yes, and the song helped ease the Eagles back into country music.

Z

Zachariah. Don Johnson stars in this hippie western in which Joe Walsh and the James Gang play live in the desert.

42

Timeline

The Eagles, Year by Year

When a band like the Eagles exists, in one form or another, for five decades, the comings and goings of members, the order of events, and even the years of significant album releases can become murky. This section gives a quick overview of the band's story, while also highlighting a few oddities since they started their journey in 1972.

1946

- Randy Herman Meisner is born on March 8.

1947

- Donald Hugh "Don" Henley is born on July 22.
- Bernard Mathew "Bernie" Leadon III is born on July 19.
- Donald William "Don" Felder is born on September 21.
- Joseph Fidler "Joe" Walsh is born on November 20.

1948

- Glenn Lewis Frey is born on November 6.

1967

- Leadon lands in Los Angeles to play guitar with Hearts & Flowers.

1968

- Leadon plays distinctive, twangy guitar on the influential country-rock album *The Fantastic Expedition of Dillard & Clark*.

- Henley begins to write the song "Desperado."
- Meisner joins a new band, Pogo, soon to change their name to Poco.

1969

- Frey from Detroit and J. D. Souther from Amarillo, Texas, form a duo called Longbranch Pennywhistle.

1970

- Henley arrives in Los Angeles with his band Shiloh, ready to work with producer Kenny Rogers.
- Frey and Henley are both in the audience at the Troubadour club when new British artist Elton John makes his debut performance.

1971

- David Geffen opens his own label, Asylum Records. "Take It Easy" writer Jackson Browne is the label's first act.
- Linda Ronstadt's backing band at Disneyland in July features Frey, Henley, Leadon, and Meisner, performing together for the first—but not last—time.
- David Geffen signs the Eagles to Asylum and then sends them to Aspen, Colorado, to rehearse.

1972

- The Eagles travel to London to record with legendary producer Glyn Johns.
- The band's debut album, *Eagles*, is released in June.
- The Eagles go on the road in America, opening for rock bands like Jethro Tull, Procol Harum, and Yes.
- "Take It Easy" is the group's first single. It reaches #12 on the *Billboard* chart.

1973

- The Eagles record again in winter in London with Glyn Johns.
- Henley and Frey write together for the first time.
- The Wild West concept album *Desperado* is released in April.

1974

- After recording sessions become too fractured, the Eagles replace Glyn Johns with Bill Szymczyk, who produces the rest of the *On the Border* album.
- Hotshot guitar player Don Felder plays on "Good Day in Hell." Frey asks him to join the band.
- *On the Border* is released.
- The Eagles play to an audience of 300,000 at the California Jam festival in Ontario, California, in April.

1975

- "Best of My Love" is the Eagles' first #1.
- Leadon pours a can of beer over Frey and leaves the Eagles.
- Joe Walsh replaces Leadon on guitar.

1976

- The Eagles release their first compilation album, *Their Greatest Hits 1971–1975.*
- The band's next original album, *Hotel California*, is released in December.

1977

- After the *Hotel California* tour finishes, Meisner quits the band for a quieter life back home in Nebraska.
- Timothy B. Schmit, who had earlier replaced Meisner in Poco, now replaces him in the Eagles.
- "New Kid in Town" goes to the top of the *Billboard* singles chart.
- Frey, J. D. Souther, and Walsh are guests at Jimmy Buffett's second wedding in Colorado.
- The band start recording their next album, *The Long Run.*

1979

- The Eagles release their new album *The Long Run* in September.
- "Heartache Tonight" goes to #1 in November.

1980

- In July, Felder and Frey come to blows at a show in Long Beach, California.
- The Eagles break up.
- Joe Walsh runs for president.

1981

- Felder contributes two songs to the soundtrack of the movie *Heavy Metal.*

1982

- Henley releases a solo album, *I Can't Stand Still,* containing the hit single "Dirty Laundry."
- Frey releases his first solo album, *No Fun Aloud.*

1984

- Henley releases the chart-topping *Building the Perfect Beast,* which establishes him as a serious solo artist.

1985

- Frey makes his acting debut in an episode of *Miami Vice.* The episode also features his single "Smuggler's Blues."

1987

- Schmit achieves a Top 40 hit with "Boys Night Out."

1991

- The hit movie *Thelma & Louise* features music by Frey.

1993

- An all-star country-music tribute album, *Common Thread: The Songs of the Eagles,* is produced in Nashville. The album features a Travis Tritt version of "Take It Easy." Tritt wants the Eagles in his promo video. He gets his wish.

- Frey's TV series, *South of Sunset*, lasts just one episode before CBS cancels it.
- The Eagles perform live at Warner Bros.' Burbank Studios for an MTV special that will be broadcast the next year.

1994

- *Hell Freezes Over* is the Eagles' first album since *The Long Run.*
- The Eagles' sellout reunion tour is briefly interrupted in September due to a serious recurrence of Frey's diverticulitis.
- Walsh sobers up.

1996

- Frey appears in the blockbuster Tom Cruise/Renée Zellweger movie *Jerry Maguire.*

1998

- The Eagles are inducted into the Rock and Roll Hall of Fame by Jimmy Buffett. Leadon and Meisner join the others onstage for two songs, "Take It Easy" and "Hotel California."
- Henley's environmental project, the Thoreau Institute, opens in Walden Woods in Lincoln, Massachusetts. At the opening ceremony, Henley is joined by the Eagles, Jimmy Buffett, and President Bill Clinton.

1999

- *Their Greatest Hits 1971–1975* has now sold more than twenty-six million copies, making it the top-selling album of the twentieth century.
- Felder plays his last show as an Eagle in December.

2000

- The Songwriters Hall of Fame inducts Henley and Frey at the Sheraton Hotel, New York.

2001

- Felder is fired from the Eagles and promptly files a lawsuit against Henley and Frey.
- The group resumes touring, with the lineup now Frey, Henley, Walsh, Schmit, plus Steuart Smith.

2003

- The Eagles release an updated hits album, *The Very Best of the Eagles*, featuring the new single "Hole in the World."
- Henley, Walsh, and Schmit work on Warren Zevon's last record, *The Wind.*
- *The Very Best of the Eagles* is certified double-platinum in December.

2004

- The Eagles' 2004 Farewell 1 world tour covers the U.S.A., Canada, Hong Kong, Singapore, Thailand, Japan, and Australia.

2005

- The Eagles continue their Farewell 1 Tour and release *Farewell 1 Tour— Live from Melbourne.*
- *Billboard* magazine says the Eagles have the second-highest-grossing tour of the year.

2006

- They may not speak, but Felder and Frey have golf in common. They are both listed on *Golf Digest*'s list of music's top 100 golfers. Felder is at #38 with a 10.2 handicap, with Frey down at #49 with a 12.6.

2007

- *Long Road Out of Eden* is released. It's the band's first new album since 1979.
- "How Long," written by J. D. Souther, is released to radio.
- Don Henley is honored as MusiCares Person of the Year.

2008

- The Eagles win the Grammy Award for Best Country Performance by a Duo or Group with Vocal for "How Long."
- The Eagles get the front cover of *Rolling Stone* magazine.
- The *Long Road Out of Eden* tour begins in the U.K. at the O2 in London. The tour runs till November 19, 2011, when it closes down in Las Vegas.

2013

- In February 2013, the Eagles release *History of the Eagles*, a career-spanning film documentary. It debuts at Sundance and is then broadcast by Showtime.
- The massive *History of the Eagles* tour begins July 6 in Louisville, Kentucky. Bernie Leadon is invited back for the tour, as is Randy Meisner, but he's not well enough to consider the offer.

2014

- The Eagles kicked off 2014 in style with a special "History of the Eagles" five-night run at the re-opening of the historic L.A. Forum in Inglewood, California. The band toured most of the year, and in August they announced a string of dates in Australia for the early part of 2015.
- In October, the *History of the Eagles* documentary was made available for streaming on Netflix.

Selected Discography
Tracks That Matter

his discography lists the most significant albums and singles by the Eagles as a group and as solo acts, as well as important country-rock albums that were part of the Eagles' orbit in the late 1960s and early 1970s. The chart position of each single indicates the highest ranking achieved on the *Billboard* Hot 100 chart in the U.S.A.

EAGLES DISCOGRAPHY

Eagles Albums

Eagles

Asylum Records

Produced by: Glyn Johns

Released: June 1972

Track listing: Take It Easy/Witchy Woman/Chug All Night/Most of Us Are Sad/Nightingale/Train Leaves Here This Morning/Take the Devil/Earlybird/Peaceful Easy Feeling/Tryin'

Desperado

Asylum Records

Produced by: Glyn Johns

Released: April 1973

Track listing: Doolin-Dalton/Twenty-One/Out of Control/Tequila Sunrise/Desperado/Certain Kind of Fool/Doolin-Dalton (Instrumental)/Outlaw Man/Saturday Night/Bitter Creek/Doolin-Dalton-Desperado (Reprise)

On the Border

Asylum Records

Produced by: Glyn Johns and Bill Szymczyk

Released: March 1974

Track listing: Already Gone/You Never Cry Like a Lover/Midnight Flyer/My Man/On the Border/James Dean/Ol' 55/Is It True/Good Day in Hell/Best of My Love

One of These Nights

Asylum Records

Produced by: Bill Szymczyk

Released: June 1975

Track listing: One of These Nights/Too Many Hands/Hollywood Waltz/Journey of the Sorcerer/Lyin' Eyes/ Take It to the Limit/Visions/After the Thrill Is Gone/I Wish You Peace

Their Greatest Hits 1971–1975

Asylum Records

Produced by: Glyn Johns and Bill Szymczyk

Released: February 1976

Track listing: Take It Easy/Witchy Woman/Lyin' Eyes/Already Gone/Desperado/One of These Nights/Tequila Sunrise/Take It to the Limit/Peaceful Easy Feeling/Best of My Love

Hotel California

Asylum Records

Produced by: Bill Szymczyk

Released: December 1976

Track listing: Hotel California/New Kid in Town/Life in the Fast Lane/Wasted Time/Wasted Time (Reprise)/Victim of Love/Pretty Maids All in a Row/Try and Love Again/The Last Resort

The Long Run

Asylum Records

Produced by: Bill Szymczyk

Released: September 1979

Track listing: The Long Run/I Can't Tell You Why/In the City/The Disco Strangler/King of Hollywood/Heartache Tonight/Those Shoes/Teenage Jail/The Greeks Don't Want No Freaks/The Sad Café

Eagles Live

Asylum Records

Produced by: Bill Szymczyk

Recorded: at the L.A. Forum, October 20–22, 1976; Santa Monica Civic Auditorium, July 27–29, 1980; and Long Beach Arena, July 31, 1980

Released: November 1980

Track listing: Hotel California/Heartache Tonight/I Can't Tell You Why/The Long Run/New Kid in Town/Life's Been Good/Seven Bridges Road/Wasted Time/Take It to the Limit/Doolin-Dalton (Reprise II)/Desperado/Saturday Night/All Night Long/Life in the Fast Lane/Take It Easy

Greatest Hits Volume 2

Asylum Records

Produced by: Glyn Johns and Bill Szymczyk

Released: October 1982

Track listing: Hotel California/Heartache Tonight/Seven Bridges Road/Victim of Love/The Sad Café/Life in the Fast Lane/I Can't Tell You Why/New Kid in Town/The Long Run/After the Thrill Is Gone

Hell Freezes Over

Geffen Records

Produced by: the Eagles, Elliot Scheiner, and Rob Jacobs

Released: November 1994

Track listing: Get Over It/Love Will Keep Us Alive/The Girl from Yesterday/ Learn to Be Still/Tequila Sunrise/Hotel California/Wasted Time/Pretty Maids All in a Row/I Can't Tell You Why/New York Minute/The Last Resort/ Take It Easy/In the City/Life in the Fast Lane/Desperado

Selected Works 1972–1999

Elektra

Produced by: the Eagles, Elliot Scheiner, Jay Oliver, and Mike Harlow

Live tracks recorded: December 31, 1999, at the Staples Center, Los Angeles, California

Released: November 2000

Disc 1: *The Early Days:* Take It Easy/Hollywood Waltz/Already Gone/Doolin-Dalton/Midnight Flyer/Tequila Sunrise/Witchy Woman/Train Leaves Here This Morning/Outlaw Man/Peaceful Easy Feeling/James Dean/Saturday Night/On the Border

Disc 2: *The Ballads:* Wasted Time (Reprise)/Wasted Time/I Can't Tell You Why/Lyin' Eyes/Pretty Maids All in a Row/Desperado/Try and Love Again/ Best of My Love/New Kid in Town/Love Will Keep Us Alive/The Sad Café/ Take It to the Limit/After the Thrill Is Gone

Disc 3: *The Fast Lane:* One of These Nights Intro/One of These Nights/The Disco Strangler/Heartache Tonight/Hotel California/Born to Boogie/In the City/Get Over It/King of Hollywood/Too Many Hands/Life in the Fast Lane/ The Long Run/Long Run Leftovers/The Last Resort/Random Victims Part 3

Disc 4: *The Millennium Concert:* Hotel California/Victim of Love/Peaceful Easy Feeling/Please Come Home for Christmas/Ol' 55/Take It to the Limit/ Those Shoes/Funky New Year/Dirty Laundry/Funk #49/All She Wants to Do Is Dance/Best of My Love

The Very Best of the Eagles

Warner Strategic Marketing

Produced by: the Eagles, Glyn Johns, Bill Szymczyk, Elliot Scheiner, and Rob Jacobs

Released: October 2003

Track listing: Take It Easy/Witchy Woman/Peaceful Easy Feeling/Desperado/ Tequila Sunrise/Doolin-Dalton/Already Gone/Best of My Love/James Dean/ Ol' 55/Midnight Flyer/On the Border/Lyin' Eyes/One of These Nights/ Take It to the Limit/After the Thrill Is Gone/Hotel California/Life in the Fast Lane/Wasted Time/Victim of Love/The Last Resort/New Kid in Town/ Please Come Home for Christmas/Heartache Tonight/The Sad Café/I Can't Tell You Why/The Long Run/In the City/Those Shoes/Seven Bridges Road

Note: *The first run of the series included a limited-edition bonus DVD including "Hole in the World Video," "Making the Video," and "Backstage Pass to Farewell 1."*

Eagles (Box Set)

Warner Music Group

Produced by: the Eagles, Glyn Johns, Bill Szymczyk, Elliot Scheiner, Jay Oliver, and Mike Harlow

Released: March 2005

Includes: the albums *Eagles, Desperado, On the Border, One of These Nights, Hotel California, The Long Run,* and *Eagles Live,* plus the singles "Please Come Home for Christmas," "Funky New Year (live)," "Love Will Keep Us Alive," "Get Over It," and "Hole in the World"

Long Road Out of Eden

Eagles Recording Company/Lost Highway

Produced by: the Eagles, Steuart Smith, Richard F. W. Davis, Scott Crago, and Bill Szymczyk

Released: October 2007

Track listing: No More Walks in the Wood/How Long/Busy Being Fabulous/ What Do I Do with My Heart/Guilty of the Crime/I Don't Want to Hear Any More/Waiting in the Weeds/No More Cloudy Days/Fast Company/Do Something/You Are Not Alone/Long Road Out of Eden/I Dreamed There Was No War/Somebody/Frail Grasp on the Big Picture/Last Good Time in Town/I Love to Watch a Woman Dance/Business as Usual/Center of the Universe/It's Your World Now

Eagles Singles

Take It Easy/Get You in the Mood

Asylum

May 1, 1972

Chart Position: 12

Witchy Woman/Earlybird

Asylum

August 1, 1972

Chart Position: 9

Peaceful Easy Feeling/Tryin'

Asylum

December 1, 1972

Chart Position: 22

Tequila Sunrise/Twenty-One

Asylum

April 17, 1973

Chart Position: 64

Outlaw Man/Certain Kind of Fool

Asylum

August 6, 1973

Chart Position: 59

Already Gone/Is It True

Asylum

April 19, 1974

Chart Position: 32

James Dean/Good Day in Hell

Asylum

August 14, 1974

Chart Position: 77

Best of My Love/Ol' 55

Asylum

November 5, 1974

Chart Position: 1

One of These Nights/Visions

Asylum

May 19, 1975

Chart Position: 1

Lyin' Eyes/Too Many Hands

Asylum

September 7, 1975

Chart Position: 2

Take It to the Limit/After the Thrill Is Gone

Asylum

November 15, 1975

Chart Position: 4

New Kid in Town/Victim of Love

Asylum

December 7, 1976

Chart Position: 1

Hotel California/Pretty Maids All in a Row

Asylum

February 22, 1977

Chart Position: 1

Life in the Fast Lane/The Last Resort

Asylum

May 3, 1977

Chart Position: 11

Please Come Home for Christmas/Funky New Year

Asylum

November 27, 1978

Chart Position: 18

Heartache Tonight/Teenage Jail

Asylum

September 18, 1979

Chart Position: 1

The Long Run/Disco Strangler

Asylum

November 29, 1979

Chart Position: 8

I Can't Tell You Why/The Greeks Don't Want No Freaks

Asylum

February 4, 1980

Chart Position: 8

Seven Bridges Road/The Long Run

Asylum

December 15, 1980

Chart Position: 21

Get Over It (studio)/Get Over It (live)

Geffen

October 18, 1994

Chart Position: 31

Love Will Keep Us Alive/New York Minute (live)/Help Me Through the Night (live)

Geffen

November 1994

Hole in the World

Eagles Recording Company II

July 15, 2003

Chart Position: 69

How Long

Lost Highway

August 20, 2007

Chart Position: 101

Busy Being Fabulous

Lost Highway

January 2008

DON HENLEY DISCOGRAPHY

Don Henley Albums

I Can't Stand Still

Asylum

Produced by: Don Henley, Danny Kortchmar, and Greg Ladanyi

Released: August 1982

Track listing: I Can't Stand Still/You Better Hang Up/Long Way Home/ Nobody's Business/Talking to the Moon/Dirty Laundry/Johnny Can't Read/ Them and Us/La Eile/Lilah/The Unclouded Day

Building the Perfect Beast

Geffen

Produced by: Don Henley, Danny Kortchmar, and Greg Ladanyi

Henley's debut studio album, *I Can't Stand Still*, includes his biggest hit, "Dirty Laundry," which reached #3 on the *Billboard* Hot 100 in 1983.

Released: November 1984

Track listing: The Boys of Summer/You Can't Make Love/Man with a Mission/ You're Not Drinking Enough/Not Enough Love in the World/Building the Perfect Beast/All She Wants to Do Is Dance/A Month of Sundays/Sunset Grill/Drivin' with Your Eyes Closed/Land of the Living

The End of the Innocence

Geffen

Produced by: Don Henley and Danny Kortchmar

Released: June 1989

Track listing: The End of the Innocence/How Bad Do You Want It?/I Will Not Go Quietly/The Last Worthless Evening/New York Minute/Shangri-La/ Little Tin God/Gimme What You Got/If Dirt Were Dollars/The Heart of the Matter

The End of the Innocence sold over six million copies in the U.S. alone; one song, "I Will Not Go Quietly," features none other than labelmate Axl Rose on background vocals.

Don Henley Singles

Johnny Can't Read/Long Way Home

Asylum

1982

Chart Position: 42

Dirty Laundry/Lilah

Asylum

1982

Chart Position: 3

I Can't Stand Still/Them and Us

Asylum

1982

Chart Position: 48

The Boys of Summer/A Month of Sundays

Geffen

1984

Chart Position: 5

All She Wants to Do Is Dance

Geffen

1985

Chart Position: 9

Not Enough Love in the World

Geffen

1985

Chart Position: 34

Sunset Grill

Geffen

1985

Chart Position: 22

The End of the Innocence

Geffen

1989

Chart Position: 8

The Last Worthless Evening

Geffen

1989

Chart Position: 21

The Heart of the Matter

Geffen

1990

Chart Position: 21

How Bad Do You Want It?

Geffen

1989

Chart Position: 48

New York Minute

Geffen

1989

Chart Position: 48

Taking You Home

Geffen

2000

Chart Position: 58

GLENN FREY DISCOGRAPHY

Glenn Frey Albums

No Fun Aloud

Asylum

Produced by: Glenn Frey, Allan Blazek, and Jim Ed Norman

Released: May 1982

Track listing: I Found Somebody/The One You Love/Partytown/I Volunteer/ I've Been Born Again/Sea Cruise/That Girl/All Those Lies/She Can't Let Go/Don't Give Up

The Allnighter

MCA

Produced by: Glenn Frey and Allan Blazek

Released: June 1984

Track listing: The Allnighter/Sexy Girl/I Got Love/Somebody Else/Lover's Moon/Smuggler's Blues/Let's Go Home/Better in the U.S.A./Living in Darkness/New Love

Soul Searchin'

MCA

Produced by: Elliot Scheiner and Glenn Frey

Released: August 1988

Track listing: Livin' Right/Some Kind of Blue/True Love/Can't Put Out This Fire/I Did It for Your Love/Let's Pretend We're Still in Love/Working Man/ Soul Searchin'/Two Hearts/It's Your Life

Frey's 1992 solo offering, *Strange Weather*, included the excellent "Part of Me, Part of You," as featured on the *Thelma & Louise* movie soundtrack.

Strange Weather

MCA

Produced by: Elliot Scheiner and Glenn Frey

Released: June 1992

Track listing: Silent Spring/Long Hot Summer/Strange Weather/Aqua Tranquillo/Love in the 21st Century/He Took Advantage/River of Dreams/ I've Got Mine/Rising Sun/Brave New World/Delicious/A Walk in the Dark/ Before the Ship Goes Down/Big Life/Part of Me, Part of You/Ain't It Love

After Hours

Universal

Produced by: Glenn Frey, Richard F. W. Davis, and Michael Thompson

Released: May 2012

Track listing: For Sentimental Reasons/My Buddy/Route 66/The Shadow of Your Smile/Here's to Life/It's Too Soon to Know/Caroline, No/The Look of Love/I'm Getting Old Before My Time/Same Girl/After Hours

Glenn Frey Singles

I Found Somebody/She Can't Let Go
Asylum

1982

Chart Position: 31

The One You Love
Asylum

1982

Chart Position: 15

All Those Lies
Asylum

1982

Chart Position: 41

Sexy Girl
MCA

1984

Chart Position: 20

The Allnighter
MCA

1984

Chart Position: 54

The Heat Is On/Shoot Out

MCA

1984

Chart Position: 2

Smuggler's Blues

MCA

1985

Chart Position: 12

You Belong to the City

MCA

1985

Chart Position: 2

True Love

MCA

1988

Chart Position: 13

Soul Searchin'/It's Cold in Here

MCA

1988

Livin' Right

MCA

1988

Chart Position: 90

Part of Me, Part of You

MCA

1991

Chart Position: 55

I've Got Mine

MCA

1992

Chart Position: 91

River of Dreams

MCA

1992

DON FELDER DISCOGRAPHY

Don Felder Albums

Airborne

Asylum

Produced by: Don Felder

Released: November 1983

Track listing: Bad Girls/Winners/Haywire/Who Tonight/Never Surrender/Asphalt Jungle/Night Owl/Still Alive

Road to Forever

Top 10 Inc.

Produced by: Don Felder and Robin DiMaggio

Released: October 2012

Track listing: Fall from the Grace of Love/Girls in Black/Wash Away/I Believe in You/You Don't Have Me/Money/Someday/Heal Me/Over You/Road to Forever/Life's Lullaby

Don Felder Singles

Heavy Metal/All of You

Full Moon

1981

Chart Position: 48

RANDY MEISNER DISCOGRAPHY

Randy Meisner Albums

Randy Meisner

Elektra

Produced by: Alan Brackett

Released: June 1978

Track listing: Bad Man/Daughter of the Sky/It Hurts to Be in Love/Save the Last Dance for Me/Take It to the Limit/Lonesome Cowgirl/Too Many Lovers/If You Wanna Be Happy/Really Want You Here Tonight/Every Other Day/Heartsong

One More Song

Epic

Produced by: Val Garay

Released: October 1980

Track listing: Hearts on Fire/Gotta Get Away/Come On Back to Me/Deep Inside My Heart/I Need You Bad/One More Song/Trouble Ahead/White Shoes/Anyway Bye Bye

Randy Meisner Singles

I Really Want You Here Tonight/Heartsong

Asylum

1978

Deep Inside My Heart

Epic

1980

Chart Position: 22

Hearts on Fire

Epic

1980

Chart Position: 14

Never Been in Love

Epic

1982

Chart Position: 28

BERNIE LEADON DISCOGRAPHY

Bernie Leadon Albums

Natural Progressions (with Michael Georgiades)

Asylum

Produced by: Glyn Johns

Released: January 1977

Track listing: Callin' for Your Love/How Can You Live Without Love?/ Breath/Rotation/You're the Singer/Tropical Winter/As Time Goes On/ The Sparrow/At Love Again/Glass Off

Mirror

Really Small

Produced by: Ethan Johns

Released: September 2003

Track listing: Vile and Profane Man/Volcano/Center of the Universe/What Do I Own/Backup Plan/Everybody Want/Sears and Roebuck Catalog/Rich Life/Hey, Now Now/God Ain't Done with Me Yet

TIMOTHY B. SCHMIT DISCOGRAPHY

Timothy B. Schmit Albums

Playin' It Cool

Asylum

Produced by: Timothy B. Schmit and Josh Leo

Released: October 1984

Track listing: Playin' It Cool/Lonely Girl/So Much in Love/Something's Wrong/Voices/Wrong Number/Take a Good Look Around/Tell Me What You Dream/Gimme the Money

Timothy B

MCA

Produced by: Dick Rudolph

Released: September 1987

Track listing: Boys Night Out/Don't Give Up/Hold Me in Your Heart/ Everybody Needs a Lover/Into the Night/A Better Day Is Coming/Jazz Street/I Guess We'll Go On Living/Down Here People Dance Forever

Tell Me the Truth

MCA

Produced by: David Cole, Bruce Gaitsch, Don Henley, Danny Kortchmar, John Boylan, and Timothy B. Schmit

Released: July 1990

Track listing: Tell Me the Truth/Was It Just the Moonlight/Something Sad/ Down by the River/In Roxy's Eyes/Let Me Go/Perfect Stranger/All I Want to Do/Tonight/For the Children

Schmit's *Expando* was a self-produced, home-recorded album of all-original material released on Lost Highway Records in 2009.

Expando

Lost Highway

Produced by: Timothy B. Schmit

Released: October 2009

Track listing: One More Mile/Parachute/Friday Night/Ella Jean/White Boy from Sacramento/Compassion/Downtime/Melancholy/I Don't Mind/Secular Praise/A Good Day

Timothy B. Schmit Singles

So Much in Love/She's My Baby

Asylum

1982

Chart Position: 59

Boys Night Out
MCA
1987
Chart Position: 25

Don't Give Up
MCA
1987

JOE WALSH DISCOGRAPHY

Joe Walsh Albums

Barnstorm
Dunhill
Produced by: Bill Szymczyk
Released: September 1972
Track listing: Here We Go/Midnight Visitor/One and One/Giant Bohemoth/ Mother Says/Birdcall Morning/Home/I'll Tell the World/Turn to Stone/ Comin' Down

The Smoker You Drink, The Player You Get
Dunhill
Produced by: Joe Walsh and Bill Szymczyk
Released: June 1973
Track listing: Rocky Mountain Way/Book Ends/Wolf/Midnight Moodies/ Happy Ways/Meadows/Dreams/Days Gone By/(Day Dream) Prayer

So What
Dunhill
Produced by: Joe Walsh and John Stronach
Released: December 1974

Barnstorm was Walsh's first solo project after quitting the James Gang. It was experimental and folksy, and he even used synthesizers as he broke with his hard-rock image.

Track listing: Welcome to the Club/Falling Down/Pavane/Time Out/All Night/Laundry Mat Blues/Turn to Stone/Help Me Through the Night/County Fair/Song for Emma

But Seriously Folks

Asylum

Produced by: Bill Szymczyk

Released: May 1978

Track listing: Over and Over/Second Hand Store/Indian Summer/At the Station/Tomorrow/Inner Tube/Theme from Boat Weirdos/Life's Been Good

There Goes the Neighborhood

Asylum

Produced by: Joe Walsh

Released: May 1981

Track listing: Things/Made Your Mind Up/Down on the Farm/Rivers (of the Hidden Funk)/A Life of Illusion/Bones/Rockets/You Never Know

Analog Man

Fantasy

Produced by: Jeff Lynne and Joe Walsh

Released: June 2012

Track listing: Analog Man/Wrecking Ball/Lucky That Way/Spanish Dancer/Band Played On/Family/One Day at a Time/Hi-Roller Baby/Funk 50/India/Fishbone/But I Try

Joe Walsh Singles

Rocky Mountain Way

Dunhill

1973

Chart Position: 23

Life's Been Good

Asylum

1978

Chart Position: 12

All Night Long

Asylum

1980

Chart Position: 19

A Life of Illusion

Asylum

1981

Chart Position: 34

KEY COUNTRY-ROCK ALBUMS FROM 1967–1973

Influences and peers, therefore excluding the Eagles

The Byrds: *Sweetheart of the Rodeo*

Gram Parsons: *Grievous Angel*

Dillard & Clark: *The Fantastic Expedition of Dillard & Clark*

Poco: *Pickin' Up the Pieces*

Rick Nelson: *Live at the Troubadour*

The Nitty Gritty Dirt Band: *Will the Circle Be Unbroken*

Linda Ronstadt: *Linda Ronstadt*

Stephen Stills & Manassas: *Manassas*

Bob Dylan: *Nashville Skyline*

The Flying Burrito Brothers: *The Gilded Palace of Sin*

Gene Clarke: *White Light*

Michael Nesmith & the First National Band: *Magnetic South*

Buffalo Springfield: *Last Time Around*

Steve Young: *Rock Salt & Nails*

The Nitty Gritty Dirt Band: *Uncle Charlie & His Dog Teddy*

Rick Nelson: *In Concert at the Troubadour*

John Hartford: *Aereo-Plain*

The Flying Burrito Brothers: *Burrito Deluxe*

Michael Nesmith: *Magnetic South*

New Riders of the Purple Sage: *New Riders of the Purple Sage*

Commander Cody & His Lost Planet Airmen: *Lost in the Ozone*

The Flying Burrito Brothers: *The Flying Burrito Brothers*

Pure Prairie League: *Pure Prairie League*

Michael Nesmith: *Pretty Much Your Standard Ranch Stash*

Ian Matthews: *Valley Hi*

New Riders of the Purple Sage: *The Adventures of Panama Red*

INDIVIDUAL EAGLES' CONTRIBUTIONS TO ESSENTIAL COUNTRY-ROCK ALBUMS: 1967–1974

Randy Meisner

Poco: *Pickin' Up the Pieces*

Rick Nelson: *Garden Party*

Linda Ronstadt: *Linda Ronstadt*

Bernie Leadon

Dillard & Clark: *The Fantastic Expedition of Dillard & Clark*

The Nitty Gritty Dirt Band: *Rare Junk*

Dillard & Clark: *Through the Morning, Through the Night*

The Flying Burrito Brothers: *Burrito Deluxe*

The Flying Burrito Brothers: *The Flying Burrito Brothers*

Don Felder

Pure Prairie League: *Two Lane Highway*

J. D. Souther: *You're Only Lonely*

Glenn Frey

Longbranch Pennywhistle: *Longbranch Pennywhistle*

Linda Ronstadt: *Linda Ronstadt*

J. D. Souther: *John David Souther*

Jackson Browne: *For Everyman*

Linda Ronstadt: *Don't Cry Now*

Linda Ronstadt: *Heart Like a Wheel*

Dan Fogelberg: *Souvenirs*

Don Henley

Linda Ronstadt: *Linda Ronstadt*

Rick Roberts: *Windmills*

Jackson Browne: *Late for the Sky*

Linda Ronstadt: *Heart Like a Wheel*

Souther-Hillman-Furay Band: *Trouble in Paradise*

J. D. Souther: *Black Rose*

Selected Bibliography

Books

Bego, Mark. *Linda Ronstadt: It's So Easy*. Austin, TX: Eakin Press, 1990.

Crosby, David, and Carl Gottlieb. *Long Time Gone: The Autobiography of David Crosby*. New York: Doubleday, 1988.

Doggett, Peter. *Are You Ready for the Country: Elvis, Dylan, Parsons and the Roots of Country Rock*. New York: Penguin, 2003.

Einarson, John. *Desperados: The Roots of Country Rock*. New York: Cooper Square Press, 2001.

Eliot, Marc. *To the Limit: The Untold Story of the Eagles*. Boston: Da Capo Press, 2005.

Felder, Don. *Heaven and Hell: My Life in the Eagles (1974–2001)*. Hoboken, NJ: Wiley, 2006.

Fong-Torres, Ben. *Eagles: Taking It to the Limit*. Philadelphia: Running Press, 2011

Frame, Pete. *Complete Rock Family Trees*. London: Omnibus, 1993.

Hoskyns, Barney. *Hotel California: The True-Life Adventures of Crosby, Stills, Nash, Young, Mitchell, Taylor, Browne, Ronstadt, Geffen, the Eagles, and Their Many Friends*. Hoboken, NJ: Wiley, 2006.

Ronstadt, Linda. *Simple Dreams: A Musical Memoir*. New York: Simon & Schuster, 2013.

Smith, Joe. *Off the Record: An Oral History of Popular Music*. New York: Warner Books, 1988.

Vaughan, Andrew. *The Eagles: An American Band*. New York: Sterling, 2010.

Vaughan, Andrew. *John Hartford: Pilot of a Steam Powered Aereo-Plain*. Nashville, TN: Stuffworks, 2013.

Vaughan, Andrew. *Who's Who in New Country Music*. New York: St. Martin's Press, 1990.

Articles

Ames, Denise. "One-on One with Jack Tempchin." *The Tolucan Times,* November 2, 2013.

Bradley, Lloyd. "Glenn Frey: Life After the Eagles." *The Independent,* July 2, 1992.

Charone, Barbara. "The Eagles: One of These Nightmares, *Crawdaddy!* April 1977.

Christgau, Robert. "Trying to Understand the Eagles." *Newsday,* June 1972.

Crowe, Cameron. "Conversations with Don Henley and Glenn Frey." *Eagles: The Very Best Of* (liner notes), August 2003.

Crowe, Cameron. "The Eagles: Chips off the Old Buffalo." *Rolling Stone,* September 25, 1975.

Crowe, Cameron, "Flying High, Fueled by Tequila." *Zoo World,* September 13, 1973.

Di Perna, Alan. "Interview: Joe Walsh Discusses His Career, Gear and New Album, 'Analog Man.'" *Guitar World,* June 5, 2012.

Erickson, Anne. "Guitar Talk with Don Felder." Gibson.com, March 28, 2013.

Gundersen, Edna. "The Eagles Raise Their Voices in Harmony After 28 years." *USA Today,* October 30, 2007.

Hilburn, Robert. "The Eagles—A Long Run Is Over." *L.A. Times,* May 23, 1982.

Levy, Piet. "Don Henley Hints at End of an Era for the Eagles." *Milwaukee Journal Sentinel,* July 4, 2013.

Meijers, Constant. "Up to Date with Don Henley, Joe Walsh, Glenn Frey and Randy Meisner." *ZigZag,* December 1976.

Rensin, David. "The Eagles: *Desperado.*" *Phonograph Record,* June 1973.

Scoppa, Bud. "Don Felder Gives 'History of the Eagles' a Mixed Review." *Hollywood Reporter,* March 9, 2013.

Sheff, David. "Bassist-Composer Randy Meisner Courageously Bailed Out of the Eagles So That He Could Rock His Own Boat." *People,* January 12, 1981.

Thrills, Adrian. "How the Eagles Tore Each Other to Shreds: Fights, Drugs and Girls—The '70s Rockers Never Did Take It Easy." *Daily Mail,* May 2, 2013.

Yarborough, Chuck. "Eagles' Don Henley on the DVD 'The History of the Eagles,' His Own Influences, the Reunion, His Drum Style and His Education as a Songwriter." *Cleveland Plain Dealer,* July 3, 2013.

Websites

ABetterMachine.com
angelfire.com/rock3/deliverin/MEISNER/randyconcerts.htm
EaglesBand.com
Eaglesfans.com
EaglesOnlineCentral.com
facebook.com/NebraskaRocks
Gibson.com
Lawomantours.com
NME.com
RockandRollCollection.com
RollingStone.com
UltimateClassicRock.com

Index

Page numbers in italics refer to images.

THE FAQ SERIES

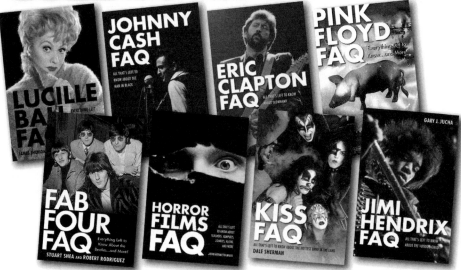

HAL•LEONARD®
PERFORMING ARTS
PUBLISHING GROUP

FAQ.halleonardbooks.com